xiv

xx   P.108

xix   9.109   P.161

P.4   P.110   P.168

P.5   P.111   P.174

P.7   P.111   P.208

P.8   P.112

       P.112

25   P.119

.46   P.119

P.53   P.120

P.64   P.124

P.77   P.128

P.72

P.73   P

       77

       P.69

       P.62

       P.90 ?

       P.91 ?

       P.91.5 inchi
                      (relation) !

       P.92

       P.93

       P.146

       P.101

       P.102

       P.105

       P.106

D0058778

THE MINDFUL BRAIN

THE MINDFUL BRAIN

DANIEL J. SIEGEL

THE MINDFUL BRAIN

*Reflection and Attunement in
the Cultivation of Well-Being*

W. W. NORTON & COMPANY
New York • London

All illustrations are the property of the author, unless noted otherwise. To contact the author, please visit mindsightinstitute.com. "The Mindful Brain" is a trademark of Mind Your Brain, Inc.

Copyright © 2007 by Mind Your Brain, Inc.

All rights reserved
Printed in the United States of America
First Edition

For information about permission to reproduce
selections from this book, write to
Permissions, W. W. Norton & Company, Inc.,
500 Fifth Avenue, New York, NY 10110

Composition and book design by MidAtlantic Books & Journals
Manufacturing by Quebecor World, Fairfield Graphics
Production Manager: Leeann Graham

Library of Congress Cataloging-in-Publication Data

Siegel, Daniel J., 1957-
    The mindful brain : reflection and attunement in the cultivation of well-being /
Daniel J. Siegel. — 1st ed.
        p. cm.
    Includes bibliographical references and index.
    ISBN-13: 978-0-393-70470-9 (hardcover)
    ISBN-10: 0-393-70470-X (hardcover)
    1. Psychophysiology. 2. Awareness.   I. Title.
    [DNLM: 1. Psychophysiology. 2. Brain--physiology. 3. Mind-Body Relations (Meta-
physics) 4. Mind-Body and Relaxation   Techniques.   WL 103 S5712m 2007]

QP360.S485   2007
612.8--dc22   2006030093

ISBN 13: 978-0-393-70470-9
ISBN 10: 0-393-70470-X

W. W. Norton & Company, Inc., 500 Fifth Avenue, New York, N.Y. 10110
www.wwnorton.com

W. W. Norton & Company Ltd., Castle House, 75/76 Wells St., London W1T 3QT

12 13 14 15 16 17 18 19 20

TO CAROLINE

CONTENTS

CONTENTS

ACKNOWLEDGMENTS

ACKNOWLEDGMENTS

Words cannot fully express the gratitude I feel toward the many people along this journey to explore the mind and understand mindfulness. My colleagues at the UCLA Mindful Awareness Research Center, including Sue Smalley, Lidia Zylowska, Sigi Hale, Shea Cunningham, Deborah Ackerman, David Creswell, Jonas Kaplan, Nancy Lynn Horton, Diana Winston, and others, have been a great source of inspiration and learning. Peter Whybrow, our director at the Semel Institute for Neuroscience and Human Behavior, has been of great support in bringing mindfulness into that academic setting. At the Foundation for Psychocultural Research (FPR)/UCLA Center for Culture, Brain, and Development, I am fortunate to be a part of a team of scholars dedicated to crossing the usual boundaries separating disciplines and am thankful to Robert Lemelson of the FPR and to my co-principal investigators there, Patricia Greenfield, Mirella Dapretto, Alan Fiske, and John Schuman, for our ongoing collaboration. Marco Iacoboni has also been a fabulous colleague with whom I have been able to share clinical ideas about the mirror neuron system and collaborate on educational programs for therapists in this emerging area.

At the Mindsight Institute, Erica Ellis has been extremely helpful in administering our educational program and working closely with me on finalizing the references and copyedited text. Those fellow therapists who study interpersonal neurobiology with me at the Institute are a continual source of intellectual stimulation and challenge, and they have been an important sounding board in helping to translate these intricate ideas about the mindful brain into an accessible and hopefully useful form for others. I am especially thankful for the collaboration of the members of GAINS, the Global Association for Interpersonal Neurobiology Studies.

I appreciate the ongoing professional collaboration with Allan Schore and Lou Cozolino, and I thank Lou for his permission to use the wonderful drawings of the brain from his excellent book, *The Neuroscience of Human Relationships* (2006). Maws & Company created the artwork for Figures 4.1, 4.2, 4.3, 6.1, and 14.1, and I am grateful for how clearly those drawings are able to express my ideas about mindful awareness.

A vital source of inspiration are my patients, whose courage to face the direct experience of memory and emotion, of trying to find a way beneath the restrictive personal identities that have enslaved them for so long, continues to give meaning to my professional life in these many years of practice.

As this exploration of mindfulness has unfolded, Rich Simon organized a meeting at his annual Networker Symposium gathering in which he brought together Diane Ackerman, Jon Kabat-Zinn, John O'Donohue, and me. It was love at first insight, and the varied relationships among each of us has continued to grow in marvelous ways. Our Mind and Moment meeting in February, 2006 was a pinnacle of my educational journey, and I am profoundly grateful to Diane, Jon, and "O'John" for our time together.

In learning about mindfulness, Jon Kabat-Zinn encouraged me to dive deeply into direct experience and guided me to the Mind and Life Institute's gathering of scientists to sense first-hand a week of silence. I'm grateful for his suggestions and appreciative of Adam Engle, chair of the Mind and Life Institute, and to Joseph Goldstein and Sharon Salzberg and the other faculty of the Insight Meditation Society who hosted that transformative event.

In the writing of the book itself, it has been extremely helpful to have the insightful comments from a number of individuals who read earlier drafts and gave important feedback on the voice of the book itself. These individuals include Diane Ackerman, Erica Ellis, Bonnie Mark Goldstein, Daniel Goleman, Susan Kaiser-Greenland, Jack Kornfield, Lynn Kutler, Rich Simon, Marion Solomon, and Caroline Welch.

Rich Simon not only read this and other manuscripts of mine, but he has served as a comrade-in-arms in facing the challenging task of writing a first-person account for a professional audience while at the same time exploring the science of the mind with rigor and clarity. He is both a social feng shui master, as the experience of his now thirty years of running the Psychotherapy Networker reveals, as well as a brilliant editor with vision for the larger issues between and beyond the lines of the text. I thank him for his vital support.

I was very fortunate to be able to rely on a number of individuals' expertise on mindfulness and on the brain to check on various details of the science and explorations in the book. Jack Kornfield and Dan Goleman made helpful clarifications and I thank them for their thoughtful comments on the text. Ellen Langer was a pleasure to engage with in examining ideas about mindful learning and mindful awareness. I am grateful for her insights and her willingness to take the time to go over a wide array of issues in our discussions. Richard Davidson was also of great support in reviewing certain aspects of brain research as they relate to his important contributions in the emerging field of contemplative neuroscience. His wisdom and kindness are greatly appreciated.

I am also deeply appreciative of David Creswell, Susan Kaiser-Greenland, Sara Lazar, and Lidia Zylowska for sharing their unpublished research data with me to include in this text. Their generosity has enabled this theoretical synthesis and conceptual integration about the relational nature of the mindful brain to offer cutting-edge knowledge in this exciting field.

I'd also like to thank Andrea Costella and Deborah Malmud for shepherding this unusual project with professional perseverance. This book is not a typical text in that it synthesizes deep personal experience with scientific analysis. I am grateful that they supported the project and helped it come to life. Deborah Malmud has also been a pleasure to work with in my capacity as the Series Editor for the Norton Series on Interpersonal Neurobiology, and I am grateful for her clear thinking about how to bring this emerging interdisciplinary view into the academic, professional, and public worlds.

Finally, I would like to thank my wife and children for their never-ending support of my whacky ways and my passion for this work. I feel deeply grateful to watch the reflective emergence of my two adolescents who continually challenge me to be fully present in our lives. I have been fortunate to be able to explore these evolving ideas regularly with my wife who has taught me so much about mindfulness. Her insights have been extremely helpful in trying to make the mindful brain come alive on these pages.

PREFACE

Welcome to a journey into the heart of our lives. Being mindfully aware, attending to the richness of our here-and-now experiences, creates scientifically recognized enhancements in our physiology, our mental functions, and our interpersonal relationships. Being fully present in our awareness opens our lives to new possibilities of well-being.

Almost all cultures have practices that help people develop awareness of the moment. Each of the major religions of the world utilizes some method to enable individuals to focus their attention, from meditation to prayer, yoga to tai'chi. Each of these traditions may have its own particular approach, but they share a common desire to intentionally focus awareness in a way that transforms people's lives. Mindful awareness is a universal goal across human cultures. Although mindfulness is often seen as a form of attentional skill that focuses one's mind on the present, this book takes a deep look at this type of awareness through the perspective of mindfulness as a form of healthy relationship with oneself.

In my own field of studying interpersonal relationships within families, we use the concept of "attunement" to examine how one person, a parent, for example, focuses attention on the internal world of another, such as a child. This focus on the mind of another person harnesses neural circuitry that enables two people to "feel felt" by each other. This state is crucial if people in relationships are to feel vibrant and alive, understood, and at peace. Research has shown that such attuned relationships promote resilience and longevity. Our understanding of mindfulness can build on these studies of interpersonal attunement and the self-regulatory functions of focused attention in suggesting that mindful awareness is a form of intrapersonal attunement. In other words, being mindful is a way of becoming your own best friend.

We will explore how attunement may lead the brain to grow in ways that promote balanced self-regulation via the process of *neural integration*, which enables flexibility and self-understanding. This way of feeling felt, of feeling connected in the world, may help us understand how becoming attuned to oneself may promote these physical and psychological dimensions of well-being with mindful awareness.

Turning to the brain can help us see the commonality of mechanisms between these two forms of intra- and interpersonal attunement. By examining the neural dimension of functioning and its possible correlation with mindful awareness, we may be able to expand our understanding of why and how mindfulness creates the documented improvements in immune function, an inner sense of well-being, and an increase in our capacity for rewarding interpersonal relationships.

I am not a member of any particular mindful awareness tradition, nor have I had formal training in mindfulness per se before taking on this project, so this book will be a fresh look, without presenting only one specific form of mindfulness. This will be an exploration of the overall concept of mindfulness. Mindfulness can be cultivated through many means from experiences within attuned relationships, to approaches in education that emphasize reflection, to formal meditation.

THE NEED

We are in desperate need of a new way of being—in ourselves, in our schools, and in our society. Our modern culture has evolved in recent times to create a troubled world with individuals suffering from alienation, schools failing to inspire and to connect with students, in short, society without a moral compass to help clarify how we can move forward in our global community.

I have seen my own children grow up in a world where human beings are ever more distant from the human interactions that our brains have evolved to require—yet are no longer part of our inherent educational and social systems. The human connections that help shape our neural connections are sorely missing in modern life. We are not only losing our opportunities to attune to each other, but the hectic lives many of us live leave little time for attuning to ourselves.

As a physician, psychiatrist, psychotherapist, and educator, I have been saddened and dismayed to find so absent from our work as clinicians a firm grounding in the healthy mind itself. After asking over 65,000 mental health professionals face-to-face in lecture halls around the world if they had ever had a course on the mind, or on mental *health*, 95% replied "no." What then have we been practicing? Isn't it time for us to become aware of the mind itself, not just to highlight symptoms of illness?

Cultivating an experiential understanding of the mind is a direct focus of mindful awareness: We come not only to know our own minds, but to embrace our inner worlds and the minds of others with kindness and compassion.

It is my deepest hope that by helping each other attune to our minds we can move ourselves and our culture beyond the many automatic reflexes that have led our human community down such destructive paths. The human potential for compassion and empathy is huge. Realizing that potential may be challenging in these troubled times, but perhaps it may be as direct as attuning to ourselves, one mind, one relationship, one moment at a time.

THE APPROACH

Mindfulness is a very important, empowering, and personal internal experience, so this book will of necessity blend personal ways of knowing along with external visions from science about the nature of the mind. This is both the challenge and the thrill of the writing, and I have set out to integrate the subjective essence of mindful awareness while providing objective analyses of direct sensory experience and research findings along with practical ways that these experiences, ideas, and research findings can be applied.

Being clear about these different ways of knowing is extremely important as we go forward: subjective experience, science, and professional applications are three separate entities in the body of knowledge that we will need to maintain as distinct dimensions of reality for this integrative effort to be valid and useful. Premature blending of these three elements can lead to erroneous conclusions about subjectivity, misinterpretations of science, and misapplications of these ideas to clinical practice and education. By presenting these ideas, experiences, and research findings first, we will then be ready to "cleanly" apply their synthesis to the important work of helping others learn, grow, and alleviate suffering. If we mix them too soon for the sake of getting to "the practical," we run the risk of confusing the ways we have come to build our vision of the mind and moment.

To achieve this goal of clarity in ways of knowing, the book is divided into four parts. An introductory section offers an overview of mindful awareness and examines why turning to the brain is helpful in illuminating the nature of the mind itself. In the second section we will explore direct experiences and see the immediacy of the moment that retrospective analysis from others can only hint at from a distance. The purpose of these experiential chapters is to explore the essence of mindfulness and what may get in its way, and keep us from being present in our own lives. We will explore how this form of being aware can be achieved through intentional training that disentangles the mind from automatic intrusions.

In the third section we explore various facets of the mindful brain that emerge from these experiential immersions and from the insights of the scientific and professional literature. We will integrate the lessons learned from direct experience with a review of existing research on the brain and the nature of the mind. This synthesis will attempt to weave the subjective and objective dimensions of understanding our lives.

In the fourth section we will reflect further on the implications and applications of these mindful brain perspectives on education, clinical work, and the discipline of psychotherapy itself. These applications will build on what came before as we link subjectivity and science with practical applications in daily life. This section will offer some initial ideas about how to integrate these concepts about internal attunement into practical, everyday usage of mindful awareness in our professional and personal endeavors.

INTERPERSONAL NEUROBIOLOGY

Understanding the deep nature of how our relationships help shape our lives and our brains has been a passion driving my professional life. Since the early 1990s, I have been involved in trying to create an interdisciplinary view of the mind and mental health (Siegel, 1999). The perspective of interpersonal neurobiology embraces a wide array of ways of knowing, from the broad spectrum of scientific disciplines to the expressive arts and contemplative practice. We will be applying the basic principles of this approach to our exploration of mindful awareness.

Interpersonal neurobiology relies on a process of integrating knowledge from a variety of disciplines to find the common features that are shared by these independent fields of knowledge. Much like the fable of the blind men and the elephant, each discipline examines a necessarily focused and limited area of the elephant, of reality, in order to know that dimension deeply and in detail. But to see the whole picture, to get a feeling for the whole elephant, it is vital that we try to bring different fields together. While each blind man may not agree with the perspective of the other, each has important contributions to make in creating a sense of the whole.

And so we will be using this integrative approach to bring together various ways of knowing in order to understand mindfulness in perhaps a broader way than any single perspective might permit. At the foundation we will be trying to combine first person knowing with scientific points of view. Beyond this important subjective/objective marriage, we will combine insights from neuroscience with those of attachment research. This approach will enable us to consider how the fundamental process of attunement might be at work in the brain in states of interpersonal resonance and the proposed form of intrapersonal attunement of mindfulness.

Turning to the brain and attachment studies is not meant to favor these two fields over any others, but rather to use them as a starting point. A variety of fields will come into play as we examine the research on memory, narrative, wisdom, emotion, perception, attention, and learning along with explorations that go deeply into internal subjective experience.

I love science and am thrilled to learn from empirical explorations into the deep nature of ourselves and our world. But I am also a clinician, steeped in the world of subjective experience. Our internal world is real, though it may not be quantifiable in ways that science often requires for careful analysis. In the end, our subjective lives are not reducible to our neural functioning. This internal world, this subjective stuff of the mind, is at the heart of what enables us to sense each other's pain, to embrace each other at times of distress, to revel in each other's joy, to create meaning in the stories of our lives, to find connection in each other's eyes.

My own personal and professional interest in mindfulness emerged recently in an unexpected way. After writing a text exploring how the brain and relationships interact to shape our development, I was invited to offer lectures at my daughter's preschool about parenting and the brain. After creating some workshops for parents, the preschool director, Mary Hartzell, and I wrote a book in which we placed "mindfulness" as our first grounding principle. As educators we knew that being considerate and aware, being mindful, was the essential state of mind of a parent (or teacher or clinician) to promote well-being in children.

After our book was published, numerous people asked how we came to teach parents to meditate. This was a great question since neither Mary nor I is trained to meditate nor did we think that we were "teaching meditation" to parents. Mindfulness, in our view, was just the idea of being aware, of being conscientious, with kindness and care. What we actually taught them was how to be reflective and aware of their children, and themselves, with curiosity, openness, acceptance, and love.

I am continually learning from my patients and from my students, whether they are parents or high school students, therapists or scientists. These questions about mindfulness and parenting inspired me to examine the existing research in the growing field of mindfulness-based clinical interventions. What struck me in learning about this area was that the outcome measures for its clinical applications appeared to overlap with the outcome measures of my own field of research in attachment: the study of the relationship between parents and children.

This overlap of the ways in which well-being and resilience were promoted by secure attachment and by mindful awareness practice was fascinating. This similarity also dovetailed with the functions of a certain integrative region of the brain, the middle aspects of the prefrontal cortex. I became intrigued by this convergence and was eager to learn more about the fascinating field of mindfulness. The outcome of this journey to explore these ideas, experientially and conceptually, is this book on the mindful brain.

This book is for people interested in knowing more about the mind and how to develop it more fully, in themselves and in others. These ideas may be especially useful for those who help others get along and grow, from teachers and clinicians to mediators and community leaders. Each of the people in the broad spectrum of these life roles is crucial in helping foster well-being in our human society.

With this exciting view of integrating ideas among the worlds of relationships, brain, and mind, I dove into direct experience within the depths of the mind. I invite you to come along with me as we explore the nature of mindful awareness that unfolded, moment by moment, in this mind-opening journey of discovery.

THE MINDFUL BRAIN

PART I

MIND, BRAIN, AND AWARENESS

MIND, BRAIN, AND AWARENESS

Chapter One

A MINDFUL AWARENESS

Being aware of the fullness of our experience awakens us to the inner world of our mind and immerses us completely in our lives. This is a book about how the way we pay attention in the present moment can directly improve the functioning of body and brain, subjective mental life with its feelings and thoughts, and interpersonal relationships.

The essential proposal is that this ancient and useful form of awareness harnesses the social circuitry of the brain to enable us to develop an attuned relationship within our own minds. To explore this idea, we will be turning to the research on our social lives, examining the particular regions of the brain, including the mirror neuron system and related circuits, that participate in attunement and may be active when we resonate with our own intentional states.

The term *mindful brain* is used in this approach to embrace the notion that our awareness, our mindful "paying attention or taking care," is intimately related to the dance between our mind and our brain. Being "mindful" has a range of definitions, from the common everyday notion of "bearing in mind or inclined to be aware" to the specific educational, clinical, and scientific definitions of the term we will explore. It is with this broad general common-usage definition that I will present a review of the new developments in science that have emerged regarding the more

specific forms of mindfulness and one's own subjective experience of the moment at the heart of one's life.

FINDING THE MIND IN OUR EVERYDAY LIVES

Since the mid – 1980s there has been growing attention to
"mindfulness" in the Western world. This focus has been on a
number of dimensions of daily life, from our personal lives to the
experience of children in schools and patients in therapy. The
busy lives people lead in the technologically driven culture that
consumes our attention often produce a multitasking frenzy of activity that leaves people constantly *doing*, with no space to breathe
and just *be*. The adaptations to such a way of life often leaves
youth accustomed to high levels of stimulus-bound attention, flitting from one activity to another, with little time for self-reflection or interpersonal connection of the direct, face-to-face sort
that the brain needs for proper development. Little today in our
hectic lives provides for opportunities to attune with one another.

In our personal lives, many of us have found this societal whirl-
wind deeply dissatisfying. We can adjust, responding to the drive
to do, but often we cannot thrive in such a frenetic world. On this
personal level people in modern cultures are often eager to learn
about a new way of being that can help them flourish. Mindfulness in its most general conception offers a way of being aware
that can serve as a gateway toward a more vital mode of being in
the world: We become attuned to ourselves.

In a review, Paul Grossman (in press) has stated that the "collo-
quial use of mindfulness often connotes being heedful or taking
care within a clearly evaluative context: A parent tells a child, mind
your manners, or 'mind your language,' implying to take care to
behave in a culturally prescribed manner. 'Mindful of the poor
road conditions, he drove slowly,' 'What is man, that thou art
mindful of him?' (Psalms, viii. 4), 'I promise to be mindful of your
admonitions,' or 'always mindful of family responsibilities.' All

these formulations reflect an emphasis on carefully paying attention so as to not reap the consequences of heedless behaviors."

DEFINING THE MIND

Good definition of mind

I have found a useful definition of the mind, supported by scientists from various disciplines, to be "a process that regulates the flow of energy and information."

Our human mind is both embodied—it involves a flow of energy and information that occurs within the body, including the brain—and relational, the dimension of the mind that involves the flow of energy and information occurring between people—from the writer to the reader, for example. Right now this flow from me as I type these words to you as you read them is shaping our minds—yours and mine. Even as I am imagining who you might be and your possible response, I am changing the flow of energy and information in my brain and body as a whole. As you absorb these words your mind is embodying this flow of energy and information as well.

BEING MINDFUL

senses

definition

Mindfulness in its most general sense is about waking up from a life on automatic, and being sensitive to novelty in our everyday experiences. With mindful awareness the flow of energy and information that is our mind enters our conscious attention and we can both appreciate its contents and also come to regulate its flow in a new way. Mindful awareness, as we will see, actually involves more than just simply being aware: It involves being aware of aspects of the mind itself. Instead of being on automatic and mindless, mindfulness helps us awaken, and by reflecting on the mind we are enabled to make choices and thus change becomes possible.

How we focus attention helps directly shape the mind. When we develop a certain form of attention to our here-and-now experiences and to the nature of our mind itself, we create the special form of awareness, mindfulness, which is the subject of this book.

SOME BENEFITS

Studies have shown that specific applications of mindful awareness improve the capacity to regulate emotion, to combat emotional dysfunction, to improve patterns of thinking, and to reduce negative mindsets.

Research on some dimensions of mindful awareness practices reveals that they greatly enhance the body's functioning: Healing, immune response, stress reactivity, and a general sense of physical well-being are improved with mindfulness (Davidson, Kabat-Zinn, Schumacher, Rosenkranz, Muller et al., 2003). Our relationships with others are also improved perhaps because the ability to perceive the nonverbal emotional signals from others may be enhanced and our ability to sense the internal worlds of others may be augmented (see Appendix III, Relationships and Mindfulness). In these ways we come to compassionately experience others' feelings and empathize with them as we understand another person's point of view.

We can see the power of mindful awareness to achieve these many and diverse beneficial changes in our lives when we consider that this form of awareness may directly shape the activity and growth of the parts of the brain responsible for our relationships, our emotional life, and our physiological response to stress.

MINDFULNESS IN LEARNING AND EDUCATION

In addition to such personal and health advantages of mindfulness, the concept of "mindful learning" has been proposed by

Ellen Langer (1989, 1997, 2000), an approach which has been shown to make learning more effective, enjoyable, and stimulating. The essence of this approach is to offer learning material in a conditional format rather than as a series of absolute truths. The learner in this way is required to keep an "open mind" about the contexts in which this new information may be useful. Involving the learner in the active process of education also is created by having students consider that their own attitude will shape the direction of the learning. In these ways, this form of mindfulness can be seen to involve the learner's active participation in the learning process itself. Langer suggests that the point of conditional learning is to leave us in a healthy state of uncertainty, which will result in our actively noticing new things.

Educator Robert J. Sternberg considered this educational mindfulness as something akin to a cognitive style (2000). Research on mindful learning (Langer, 1989) suggests that it consists of openness to novelty; alertness to distinction; sensitivity to different contexts; implicit, if not explicit, awareness of multiple perspectives; and orientation to the present. Taking these dimensions of mindfulness into account within the educational setting may permit students to deepen and broaden the nature of learning throughout their lifelong careers as learners. Teachers can use terms such as "may," "might be," or "sometimes" instead of "is" to promote conditional uncertainty. (See Chapter 12 for more on the role of mindfulness in education.)

Langer herself (1989) has suggested that we be careful about seeing her concept of mindfulness as having the same meaning as the historical and modern use of that term in contemplative practices. For the time being, we will use the qualifier, "mindful learning" to refer to Langer's important conceptualizations regarding how the mind seems to disentangle itself from premature conclusions, categorizations and routinized ways of perceiving and thinking. When we are certain, Langer says, "we don't feel the need to pay attention. Given that the world around us is always in flux, our certainty is an illusion" (Langer, August 2006, personal communication). Ultimately, this form of mindfulness is a flexible state of mind in which we actively notice new things, are sensitive to context, and engage in the present.

I could find no formal studies published that compare mindful learning with its goal-directed educational component to the more ancient contemplative form of what we will call "reflective mindfulness." This reflective form of mindfulness, what we will also refer to as "mindful awareness" or just "mindfulness" in this text, has now begun to be intensively studied, with new findings that will be discussed in the chapters ahead.

Finding similarities and differences between these two uses of the term *mindfulness* may help us elucidate the deeper nature of each version. Interestingly, research in both forms has revealed that, though achieved through differing means, they are independently associated with positive outcomes in people's lives, such as an enhanced sense of pleasure, internal awareness, and physiological health. In this book we will be exploring the possible neural mechanisms shared in common by these two important and on the surface distinct dimensions of how we shape our minds in the moment.

MINDFUL AWARENESS

Direct experience in the present moment has been described as a fundamental part of Buddhist, Christian, Hindu, Islamic, Jewish, and Taoist teaching (Armstrong, 1993; Goleman, 1988). In these religious traditions, from mystical Christianity with centering prayer (Fitzpatrick-Hopler, 2006; Keating, 2005) to Buddhist mindfulness meditation (Kornfield, 1993; Nhat Hahn, 1991; Wallace, 2006), one sees the use of the idea of being aware of the present moment in a different light from the cognitive aspect of mindfulness.

Many forms of prayer in different traditions require that the individual pause and participate in an intentional process of connecting with a state of mind or entity outside the day-to-day way of being. Prayer and religious affiliation in general have been demonstrated to be associated with increased longevity and well-being (Pargament, 1997). The common overlap of group belonging and prayer makes it hard to tease apart the internal from the interpersonal process, but in fact we may find that this is just the point: pausing to become mindful may indeed involve an internal sense of belonging.

The clinical application of the practice of mindfulness meditation derived from the Buddhist tradition has served as a focus of intensive study on the possible neural correlates of mindful awareness. Here we see the use of the term *mindfulness* in a way that numerous investigators have been trying to clearly define (Baer, Smith, Hopkins, Krietemeyer, & Toney, 2006; Bishop, Lau, Shapiro, Carlson, Anderson, Carmody et al., 2004). These studies, across a range of clinical situations, from medical illness with chronic pain to psychiatric populations with disturbances of mood or anxiety, have shown that effective application of secular mindfulness meditation skills can be taught outside of any particular religious practice or group membership.

In many ways, scholars see the nearly 2500-year-old practice of Buddhism as a form of study of the nature of mind (Germer, Siegel, & Fulton, 2005; Lutz, Dunne, & Davidson, in press; Epstein, 1995; Waldon, 2006) rather than a theistic tradition. "Reading early Buddhist texts will convince the clinician that the Buddha was essentially a psychologist" (Germer, 2005, p. 13). It is possible to practice Buddhist-derived meditation, and ascribe to aspects of the psychological view of the mind from this perspective, for example, and maintain one's beliefs and membership in other religious traditions. In contemplative mindful practice one focuses the mind in specific ways to develop a more rigorous form of present-moment awareness that can directly alleviate suffering in one's life.

Jon Kabat-Zinn has devoted his professional life to bringing mindfulness into the mainstream of modern medicine. In Kabat-Zinn's view, "An operational working definition of mindfulness is: the awareness that emerges through paying attention on purpose, in the present moment, and nonjudgmentally to the unfolding of experience moment by moment" (Kabat-Zinn, 2003, pp. 145–146). This nonjudgmental view in many ways can be interpreted to mean something like "not grasping onto judgments," as the mind seems to continually come up with reactions that assess and react. Being able to note those judgments and disengage from them may be what nonjudgmental behavior feels like in practice. "On purpose" implies that this state is created with the intention of focusing on the present moment. The InnerKids program, designed to teach young children to learn basic mindfulness skills, defines mindfulness as "Being aware of what's happening as it's happening" (Kaiser-Greenland, 2006a).

Kabat-Zinn (2003) went on to note that the Buddhist origins of this view of mindfulness and the natural laws of the mind reveal

> a coherent phenomenological description of the nature of the mind, emotion, and suffering and its potential release, based on highly refined practices aimed at systematically training and cultivating various aspects of mind and heart via the faculty of mindful attention (the words for mind and heart are the same in Asian languages; thus "mindfulness" includes an affectionate, compassionate quality within the attending, a sense of openhearted, friendly presence and interest). And mindfulness, it should also be noted, being about attention, is also of necessity universal. There is nothing particularly Buddhist about it. We are all mindful to one degree or another, moment by moment. It is an inherent human capacity. The contribution of the Buddhist tradition has been in part to emphasize simple and effective ways to cultivate and refine this capacity and bring it to all aspects of life. (pp. 145–146)

Ultimately the practices that develop mindful ways of being enable the individual to perceive the deeper nature of how the mind functions. There are many ways of cultivating mindful awareness, each of which develops an awareness of the faculties of the mind, such as how we think, feel, and attend to stimuli. Mindfulness meditation, as one example, is thought to be especially important for training attention and letting go of a strict identification with the activities of the mind as being the full identity of the individual. One form of cultivation of the mind's awareness of itself is derived from the traditional Buddhist approach of Vipassana, or insight meditation (Kornfield, 1993), which we shall be exploring in depth in Part II.

Mindful awareness practices (MAPs) as we call them at the Mindful Awareness Research Center at UCLA (http://www.marc.ucla.edu, see Appendix I), can be found in a wide variety of human activities. Historically, various practices have been developed over thousands of years in the forms of mindfulness meditation, yoga, tai chi chuan, and qui quong. In each of these activities, the practitioner is focusing the mind in a very specific way on moment-to-moment experience.

In almost all contemplative practices, for example, there is an initial use of the breath as a focal point in which to center the mind's attention. Because of this commonality of breath use across cultural practices, we will be discussing the possible significance of breath awareness for the overall processes of the mindful brain.

Modern applications of the general concept of mindfulness have built on both traditional skills of meditation and have also developed unique nonmeditative approaches to this human process of being mindful. A useful fundamental view is that mindfulness can be seen to consist of the important dimensions of the self-regulation of attention and a certain orientation to experience, as Bishop and colleagues have proposed (Bishop et al., 2004): (1) "the self-regulation of attention so that it is maintained on immediate experience, thereby allowing for increased recognition of mental events in the present moment"; and (2) "a particular orientation toward one's experiences in the present moment, an orientation that is characterized by curiosity, openness, and acceptance" (p. 232). In the Dialectical Behavior Therapy approach, mindfulness has been described as "(1) observing, noticing, bringing awareness, (2) describing, labeling, noting, and (3) participating, all of which are done (1) nonjudgmentally with acceptance, (2) in the present moment, and (3) effectively" (Dimidjian & Linehan, 2003, p. 166). Shapiro, Carlson, Astin, & Freedman (2006) have described the mechanisms of mindfulness as consisting of intention, attention, and an attitude that each contribute to a process of viewing in a new way they term "re-perceiving." These and other authors acknowledge that mindfulness also may result in common outcomes, such as patience, nonreactivity, self-compassion, and wisdom. In Acceptance and Commitment Therapy, mindfulness "can be understood as a collection of related processes that function to undermine the dominance of verbal networks, especially involving temporal and evaluative relations. These processes include acceptance, defusion, contact with the present moment, and the transcendent sense of self" (Fletcher & Hayes, 2006, p. 315).

A synthetic study of numerous existing questionnaires regarding mindfulness (Baer, Smith, Hopkins, Krietemeyer, & Toney, 2006) reveals five factors that seemed to cluster from independently created surveys: (1) nonreactivity to inner experience (e.g., perceiving feelings and emotions without having to react to them); (2) observing/noticing/attending to sensations, perceptions, thoughts, feelings (e.g., remaining present with sensations and feelings even when they are unpleasant or painful); (3) acting with awareness/(not on) automatic pilot, concentration/nondistraction (e.g., breaking or spilling things because of carelessness, not paying attention, or thinking of something else; (4) describing/ labeling with words (e.g., easily putting beliefs, opinions, and expectations into words); (5) nonjudgmental of experience (e.g., criticizing oneself for having irrational or appropriate emotions).

Except for observation, these were found to be the most statistically useful and reliable constructs in considering an operational definition of mindfulness. They seemed to reveal four relatively in-dependent facets of mindfulness. Observation was found present more robustly in those subjects, who were college students, who meditated regularly. Observation was considered a learnable skill; future research needs to clarify it as an independent factor. For now we will discuss the five factors that Baer and colleagues (2006) de-lineated as we explore the nature of mindfulness and the brain.

At this point in the scientific endeavor to operationalize a clear definition for mindful awareness, the most parsimonious approach will be to build on the cumulative wisdom of the breadth of prac-titioners and researchers in the field. This will be our framework for exploring the ways in which this form of mindful awareness may involve the social neural circuitry of the brain as mindfulness is promoted by a form of internal attunement.

Reflection on the nature of one's own mental processes is a form of "metacognition," thinking about thinking in the broadest sense; when we have meta-awareness this indicates awareness of aware-ness. Whether we are engaging in yoga or centering prayer, sitting and sensing our breathing in the morning, or doing tai chi at night, each MAP develops this capacity to be aware of awareness.

Awareness of awareness is one aspect of what we can consider a form of reflection. In this way, mindful awareness involves re-flection on the inner nature of life, on the events of the mind that are emerging, moment by moment.

LIFE ON AUTOMATIC PILOT: MINDLESSNESS AND MINDFULNESS

The difference between jogging "mindlessly" versus jogging "mindfully" is that in the latter we are aware, each moment, of what we are doing as we are doing it. If we jog and daydream about what we will be doing that night, or what happened yes-terday, then we are not engaged in mindful jogging. There is noth-ing wrong with daydreaming and letting the mind wander: In fact,

[margin note: meta =]

as we'll see, mindful practice can intentionally focus awareness on *whatever* arises, as it arises. If we intend to enable our minds to daydream and are aware of our awareness of our imagination, then that would be a mindful reverie, though perhaps not a mindful jog because we would be unaware of our feet and the path in front of us.

Notice here that we can often perform behaviors, such as jogging down a trail, and be lost in thinking about something other than the physical activity. We have neural circuits that carry out this automatic behavior all the time, enabling us to do several things at once, like jog and daydream simultaneously. Yet fortunately, we don't usually trip and fall or crash the car on the highway.

For some people, this "living on automatic" is a routine way of life. If our attention is on something other than what we are doing for most of our lives we can come to feel empty and numb. As automatic thinking dominates our subjective sense of the world, life becomes repetitive and dull. Instead of experience having an emergent feeling of fresh discovery, as a child sensing the world for the first time, we come to feel dead inside, "dead before we die." Living on automatic also places us at risk of mindlessly reacting to situations without reflecting on various options of response. The result can often be knee-jerk reactions that in turn initiate similar mindless reflexes in others. A cascade of reinforcing mindlessness can create a world of thoughtless interactions, cruelty, and destruction.

Being mindful opens the doors not only to being aware of the moment in a fuller way, but by bringing the individual closer to a deep sense of his or her own inner world, it offers the opportunity to enhance compassion and empathy. Mindfulness is not "self-indulgent," it is actually a set of skills that enhances the capacity for caring relationships with others.

Mindfulness heightens the capacity to become filled by the senses of the moment and attuned to our own state of being.

As we also become aware of our awareness, we can sharpen our focus on the present, enabling us to feel our feet as we travel the path of our lives. We engage with ourselves and with others, making a more authentic connection, with more reflection and consideration. Life becomes more enriched as we are aware of the extraordinary experience of being, of being alive, of living in this moment.

COAL AND KIND AWARENESS

In addition to this reflective awareness of awareness in the present moment, mindfulness has the following qualities that I describe for my patients and students: We approach our here-and-now experience with curiosity, openness, acceptance, and love (COAL). (See Appendix II for additional terms.)

Imagine this situation. Let's say one stubs one's toe badly and feels the intensity of the pain. Okay, one might say, I am "mindful" of that pain. Now if one said inside one's head, "What an idiot I was for stubbing my toe!" the mental suffering experienced will be greater than only the pain emanating from one's toe. In that eventuality, one is aware of the pain, but one is not filled with the COAL mindset. In this case, one's brain actually creates more suffering by amplifying the intensity of the pain with self-blame for having the accident. This is all the difference between intensifying the distress versus coming to feel the pain without suffering.

The essayist, naturalist, and poet Diane Ackerman told the story at our Mind and Moment gathering of poets, practitioners, and psychotherapists about a time when she had an accident in Japan and nearly died (see Appendix I for an explanation of this and other conferences and organizations on mindfulness). She had been climbing down a cliff to study some rare birds on a small island and fell, breaking several ribs and painfully struggling to breathe. Her description of the event (Ackerman, Kabat-Zinn, O'Donohue,

& Siegel, 2006) revealed how she approached the moment-to-moment encounter with curiosity, openness, acceptance, and love. This mindset enabled her to learn from the event, to gather the internal strength she needed to hold on, literally, and to not only survive in spite of the accident, but to thrive because of it.

This distinction between awareness with COAL and just paying attention with preconceived ideas that imprison the mind, ("I shouldn't have hit my foot, I'm so clumsy" "Why did I fall off this cliff? What is wrong with me!") is the difference that makes all the difference. This is the difference between being aware, and being mindfully aware.

Cultivating mindful awareness requires that we become aware of awareness *and* that we be able to notice when those "top-down" preconceptions of shoulds and ought-to's are choking us from living mindfully, of being kind to ourselves. The term *top-down* refers to the way that our memories, beliefs, and emotions shape our "bottom-up" direct sensation of experience. Kindness to ourselves is what gives us the strength and resolve to break out of that top-down prison and approach life's events, planned or unplanned, with curiosity, openness, acceptance, and love.

Research into mindful awareness suggests that we can indeed cultivate such love for ourselves. Our approach to mindfulness as a form of relationship with oneself may hold a clue as to how this is accomplished. With mindfulness seen as a form of intrapersonal attunement, it may be possible to reveal the mechanisms by which we become our own best friend with mindful practice. We would treat our best friend with kindness, after all. Attunement is at the heart of caring relationships of all sorts: between parent and child, teacher and student, therapist and patient/client, lovers, friends, and close professional colleagues.

With mindful awareness, we can propose, the mind enters a state of being in which one's here-and-now experiences are sensed directly, accepted for what they are, and acknowledged with kindness and respect. This is the kind of interpersonal attunement that promotes love. And this is, I believe, the intrapersonal attunement that helps us see how mindful awareness can promote love for oneself.

Interpersonal relationships have been shown to promote emotional longevity, helping us achieve states of well-being and medical health (Anderson & Anderson, 2003). I am proposing here that mindful awareness is a form of self-relationship, an internal form of attunement, that creates similar states of health. This may be the as yet unidentified mechanism by which mindfulness promotes well-being.

MEDICAL APPLICATIONS

Sensing the profound importance of the power of mindfulness, Jon Kabat-Zinn, in the late 1970s, began a project to apply these ancient ideas in a modern medical setting. What began as an inspiration during a silent retreat led to Kabat-Zinn's approach to the medical faculty at the University of Massachusetts Medical Center where he taught. Could he take on patients whose situations could no longer be helped by conventional medical interventions? Could he add anything at all to the recovery of those patients who were treated by conventional means? Glad to have a place where these individuals might find some relief, the medical faculty agreed and the beginnings of the Mindfulness-Based Stress Reduction (MBSR) clinic were initiated (Kabat-Zinn, 1990).

The MBSR program brought the ancient practice of mindfulness to individuals with a wide range of chronic medical conditions from back pain to psoriasis. Kabat-Zinn and colleagues, including his collaborator Richard Davidson at the University of Wisconsin in Madison, were ultimately able to demonstrate that MBSR training could help reduce subjective states of suffering and improve immune function, accelerate rates of healing, and nurture interpersonal relationships and an overall sense of well-being (Davidson et al., 2003).

MBSR has now been adopted by hundreds of programs around the world, and research has demonstrated that its use has brought about physiological, psychological, and interpersonal improvements in a variety of patient populations (Grossman et al., 2004). With these consistent findings being so robust, and a rising interest in mindful awareness practices, it wasn't surprising that my own field of mental health would take note and integrate the essence of mindfulness as a basis for approaching individuals with psychiatric disorders.

DISCERNMENT & MENTAL HEALTH IMPLICATIONS

Mindfulness has influenced a wide range of approaches to psychotherapy with new research revealing significant improvements in various disorders with reduction in symptoms and prevention of relapse (Hayes, Follette, & Linehan, 2004; Hayes, Strosahl, & Wilson, 1999; Linehan, 1993; Marlatt & Gordon, 1985; Parks, Anderson, & Marlatt, 2001). Mindfulness can also prevent relapse in cases of chronic depression via cognitive therapy (Segal, Williams, & Teasdale, 2002). Similarly, mindfulness has been used as an essential part of the treatment of borderline personality disorder in dialectical behavior therapy (DBT; Linehan, 1993). Relapse prevention in individuals with substance abuse is also a part of the skills taught by Marlatt and colleagues (2001). The principles of mindfulness are also inherent in the application of contemporary behavior analysis in acceptance and commitment therapy (ACT; Hayes, 2004). One of the first studies to demonstrate that psychotherapy can alter the function of the brain utilized mindfulness principles in the treatment of individuals with obsessive–compulsive disorder (Baxter, Schwartz, Bergman, Szuba, Guze, Mazziotta, et al., 1992). Several books have now been published that review the use of mindfulness and acceptance in the psy-

chotherapy of a wide range of conditions from eating disorders to
anxiety, posttraumatic stress disorder, and obsessive–compulsive
disorders (Hayes, Folette, & Linehan, 2004; Germer, Siegel, & Fulton, 2005; Segal, Williams, & Teasdale, 2002).

The general idea of the clinical benefit of mindfulness is that
the acceptance of one's situation can alleviate the internal battle
that may emerge when expectations of how life should be do not
match how life is (Brach, 2003; Hayes, 2004; Linehan, 1993a). Being mindful entails sensing what is, even sensing your judgments,
and noticing that these sensations, these images, feelings, and
thoughts, come and go. If you have a COAL stance, the rest takes
care of itself. There is no particular goal, no effort to "get rid" of
something, just the intention to be, and specifically, to experience
being in the moment as one lets go of grasping onto judgments
and goals.

Emerging from this reflective COAL mindful way of being is a
fundamental process called "discernment" in which it becomes
possible to be aware that your mind's activities are not the totality
of who you are.

Discernment is a form of disidentification from the activity
of your own mind: As you become aware of sensations, images,
feelings, and thoughts (SIFT) you come to see these activities of
the mind as waves at the surface of the mental sea. From this
deeper place within your mind, this internal space of mindful
awareness, you can just notice the brain waves at the surface as
they come and go. This capacity to disentangle oneself from the
chatter of the mind, to discern that these are "just activities
of the mind," is liberating and for many, revolutionary. At its
essence, this discernment is how mindfulness may help alleviate
suffering.

Discernment also gives us the wisdom of how to interact with
each other with more thoughtfulness and compassion. As we develop kindness toward ourselves, we can be kind to others. By get-

ting beneath our automatic mental habits, we are freed to engage with each other with a deeper sense of connection and empathy.

MINDFUL TEACHING AND THERAPY

A mindful approach to therapy and to education involves a shift in our attitude toward the individuals with whom we work. The active involvement of the student in the learning process enables the teacher to join as a collaborative explorer in the journey of discovery that teaching can be: We can embrace both knowledge and uncertainty with curiosity, openness, acceptance, and kind regard. The teacher does not have to be a source of the illusion of absolute knowledge. Together, educator and student can face the exciting challenge of developing a scaffold of knowledge that embraces the nature of knowing and its inherent context dependence and subtle sources of novelty and distinction.

Viewing an individual in psychotherapy in similar terms may seem new for some therapists. In wrestling with what terms to use in their book on mindfulness and psychotherapy, Germer, Siegel, and Fulton (2005) wrote, "Part of stitching this book together was to arrive at a consistent use of the word 'client' or 'patient.' Our profession has not settled that discussion yet, and we will not either. However, after some exploration, we decided upon 'patient.' Etymologically, patient means 'one who bears suffering,' while client means 'one who puts himself under the protection of a patron.' Since doctor means 'teacher,' it can be said that we are doctoring patients, or 'teaching people who bear suffering.' This meaning is parallel to the original use of mindfulness 2,500 years ago: It is a teaching that alleviates suffering" (p. xv).

With this in mind, we shall also use the term "patient" in this text. This discussion also leads us to the ways in which we'll be addressing both psychotherapy and education as two areas of application of these ideas about the mindful brain. Mindfulness has direct implications for improving people's lives in the classroom and in the clinical setting in addressing various medical and psychological stressors and illnesses.

In their journey to discover an effective approach to treat the important and widespread condition of chronic depression, the renowned cognitive therapists Zindel Segal, Mark Williams, and John Teasdale became intrigued with mindfulness as a skill that might be useful in their efforts (Segal, Williams, & Teasdale, 2002). Initially seeing the benefits of this approach as being a part of attentional skill training, they soon found that the mindful presence of the therapist played a crucial role in the efficacy of the treatment. Their consultations with Kabat-Zinn's Mindfulness Based Stress Reduction (MBSR) clinic led to the ultimate shifting of their emphasis and the creation of Mindfulness Based Cognitive Therapy (MBCT), which proved to be the first demonstration of a form of psychotherapy that could prevent relapse in those with chronic depressive episodes. Their description of this shift is illuminating:

> In our own training, we had been taught that when faced with a difficult clinical problem, we should collaborate with the patient on how best to solve it by seeing what thoughts, interpretations, and assumptions might be causing or exacerbating the problem. We anticipated taking the same approach in developing attentional control training, bolting mindfulness techniques onto this basic therapy framework. However, it became clear from our later visits to the Stress Reduction Clinic that unless we changed the basic structure of our treatment, we would continually revert to dealing with the most difficult problems by searching for more elaborate ways to fix them. Instead, it now appeared to us that the overarching structure of our treatment program needed to change from a mode in which we were therapists to a mode in which we were instructors. What was the difference? As therapists, coming as we did from the cognitive-behavioral tradition, we felt a responsibility to help patients solve their problems, "untie the knots" of their

thinking and feeling, and reduce their distress, staying with a problem until it was resolved. By contrast, we saw that the MBSR instructors left responsibility clearly with the patients themselves, and
saw their primary role as empowering patients to relate mindfully
to their experience on a moment-by-moment basis. (p. 59)

Embracing the acceptance and discernment of mindfulness as a
therapist enables us to become a fellow traveler on this uncertain
path of life. Similarly, as a teacher we can join with the student in
viewing the world through the lens of creative uncertainty that
deeply acknowledges the ever-changing landscape of both the external and internal worlds of our dynamic lives.

WHY THE MINDFUL BRAIN?

By exploring potential mechanisms in the brain that correlate
with mindfulness, it becomes possible to see the connection
among our common everyday view of mindfulness, the educational use of cognitive mindfulness concepts, and the clinical use
in medical and mental health practices of reflective mindful awareness. These sometimes intermixed uses of the term *mindfulness*,
while quite distinct in practice, may actually share common neural pathways. Illuminating these neural mechanisms associated
with cognitive and reflective mindfulness might then assist us in
expanding our scientific understanding further, opening the doors
for asking specific, testable questions. Such neural insights may also
shed light on how to design and implement practical applications
of mindfulness in ways we have not yet imagined. By revealing
how mindfulness harnesses our social neural circuitry, we may be
able to extend our understanding of its impact on physiological
and psychological well-being.

Another important dimension of looking toward the mindful
brain is that by understanding the neural mechanisms associated
with mindful awareness, we may be in a better position to identify

its universal human qualities and make it more accessible and acceptable to a broader audience. We all share the brain in common. Can you imagine a world in which this health-promoting, empathy-enhancing, executive-attention developing, self-compassion nurturing, affordable, and adaptable mental practice was made available in everyone's life?

HOW DO WE KNOW?

In preparing to explore these issues, I have become involved in two ways of knowing: experiential and experimental. I have participated in a number of intensive and direct immersions in mindful awareness in order to sense the power of this important way of being in life. That aspect of the journey, which I will discuss, enables us to view the inner dimension of mindfulness from the inside out. The second way of knowing is equally as powerful, but different: This is the scientific perspective on mindful awareness.

I was invited to teach at a summer research program sponsored by the Mind and Life Institute, which has been pursuing the integration of science and meditation under the leadership of the Dalai Lama. Representatives of other practices, including Christian centering prayer, Taoist tai chi, and yoga attended the Institute: There are many ways to pursue the training of mindful awareness. I was on a panel discussing the clinical applications of mindfulness and the transformation of affect by means of meditation. Before starting, I wanted to get a sense of how much basic neuroanatomy the audience knew so that I could gear the details of my remarks. When I asked, "Who here knows how the brain works?" one of my panel partners, the renowned researcher of affective neuroscience, Richie Davidson, replied "None of us!" We all laughed and realized how correct he was.

The brain is a complex system, and we really don't "know" fully how it works, or indeed how exactly its functions relate to the subjective nature of mind, much less how mindful awareness works. But we do have many fascinating hints as to the interplay of mental experience and brain structure and function. Brain function and mental life are not identical entities. When it comes to exploring mindful awareness, we need to be very humble about saying what we know about the brain's role. But turning with an open mind to the neural aspects of mindfulness can only help shed light onto the associated processes and means of cultivating this important dimension of our subjective lives, an illumination that might further enhance the objective nature of our bodies, relationships, and psychological well-being.

We can say that mind and brain correlate their functions, but we actually don't know the exact ways in which brain activity and mind function mutually create each other. It is too simplistic to say merely that the "brain creates the mind" as we now know that the mind can activate the brain. The process that regulates the flow of energy and information, our definition of the mind, can directly stimulate brain firing and ultimately change the structural connections in the brain.

We can look to the brain for correlations with mental processes, like mindful awareness. These associations are just that: not causal proofs, but two dimensions of reality that ultimately cannot be reduced to each other. For example, Davidson et al. (2003) have demonstrated a shift of brain function to *left* frontal dominance in response to emotion triggers that are associated with an approach state of mind with more positive emotion, as we'll explore in detail in Chapter 10. This left shift in emotion-regulating circuits was directly correlated with the degree of improved immune function. Another study by Lazar, Kerr, Wasserman, Gray, Greve, & Treadway (2005) revealed an increased thickness of two parts of the brain: (1) the middle prefrontal area, bilaterally, and (2) a related neural circuit, the insula, which was particularly thicker on the right side of the brain. The degree of thickness in these areas was correlated with length of time spent practicing mindfulness meditation. Here we see both a left sided and a right-sided correlation with mindful awareness practices (see Appendix III on laterality). Studies of other forms of meditation, such as focusing on compassion, reveal yet other changes, such as increased coordination of firing, especially in the prefrontal areas on both sides of the brain (Lutz, Greischar, Rawlings, Ricard, & Davidson, 2004). An extensive review of many studies (Cahn & Polich, 2006) reveals a range of activations, especially in middle prefrontal areas (anterior cingulate), with mindfulness meditation.

One benefit of turning to the brain for correlations with the mind is that we can actually learn more about the mind itself. In examining the mindful brain, we'll not only review these and other studies of emotion, attention, and executive functions, but we'll be diving into the new territory of social neuroscience. Seeing mindful awareness also as a self-relationship that harnesses the neural circuitry of our social lives may shed new light on the fundamental processes within the experience of mindfulness.

Preliminary research involving brain function hints at the view that mindfulness changes the brain. Why would the way you pay attention in the present moment change your brain? How we pay attention promotes neural plasticity, the change of neural connections in response to experience. What we'll examine are the possible mechanisms of how the various dimensions of mindful awareness emerge within the activity of the brain and then stimulate the growth of connections in those areas. By diving deeply into direct experience, we will be able to shed some light on why research might reveal left-sided changes, right-sided changes, and global impacts on integrative functioning in the brain as a whole.

MINDFULNESS AS A RELATIONSHIP THAT PROMOTES INTEGRATION

Long before we spent time cultivating our minds with reflection, we evolved as social creatures. A great deal of the process of our brains at rest, in default mode, appears to be neural circuitry correlated with understanding others (Gusnard & Raichle, 2001). It is the social circuits of the brain that we first used to understand the mind, the feelings and intentions and attitudes of others. When we view mindful awareness as a way of cultivating the mind's awareness of itself, it seems likely that it is harnessing aspects of the original neural mechanisms for being aware of other minds. As we become aware of our own intentions and attentional focus, we may be utilizing the very circuits of the brain that first created maps of the intention and attention of others. COAL is exactly what parents who provide secure attachment to their children have as a mental stance toward them. We can propose that the interpersonal attunement of secure attachment between parent and child is paralleled by an intrapersonal form of attunement in mindful awareness. Both forms of attunement promote the capacity for intimate relationships, resilience, and well-being (see Chapter 9 for further discussion of attachment).

The outcome measures for studies of secure attachment, and those for mindful awareness practices, have markedly overlapping findings (Kabat-Zinn, 2003b; Sroufe, Egeland, Carlson, & Collins, 2005). I found, too, that many of the basic functions that emerged in these two seemingly different entities were associated with the prefrontal cortex. These functions include regulation of body systems, balancing emotions, attuning to others, modulating fear, responding flexibly, and exhibiting insight and empathy. Two other functions of this prefrontal region, being in touch with intuition and morality, had not been studied in attachment work but did seem to be an outcome of mindful awareness practices (see Appendix III, Middle Prefrontal Region).

The proposal that my colleagues and I had made earlier (see Cozolino, 2002; Schore, 2003a, 2003b; Siegel, 1999, 2001b; Siegel &

Hartzell, 2003; Solomon & Siegel, 2003) was that the relationships of secure attachment between parent and child, and the effective therapeutic relationship between clinician and patient each promoted the growth of the fibers in this prefrontal area.

Prefrontal function is integrative. What this means is that the long strands of the prefrontal neurons reach out to distant and differentiated areas of the brain and body. This linkage of differentiated elements is the literal definition of a fundamental process, *integration*. For many reasons, discussed elsewhere, integration can be seen as the underlying common mechanism beneath various pathways leading to well-being (Siegel, 1999, 2001b, 2006, in press).

How Does Attunement Promote Integration?

When relationships between parent and child are attuned, a child is able to feel felt by a caregiver and has a sense of stability in the present moment. During that here-and-now interaction, the child feels good, connected, and loved. The child's internal world is seen with clarity by the parent, and the parent comes to resonate with the child's state. This is attunement.

Over time, this attuned communication enables the child to develop the regulatory circuits in the brain—including the integrative prefrontal fibers—that give the individual a source of resilience as he or she grows. This resilience takes the forms of the capacity for self-regulation and engagement with others in empathic relationships. Here we see that interpersonal attunement—the fundamental characteristic of a secure attachment—leads to the empirically proven outcome measures we described above.

This list of nine prefrontal functions also seemed to overlap with what I was coming to learn about mindfulness practice. I presented this idea to Jon Kabat-Zinn on a discussion panel (Ackerman, Kabat-Zinn, & Siegel, 2005) and he confirmed the accuracy of the observation of these as outcome measures. He went on to

extend the idea that this list is not just about research–verified outcomes, but it is about the process of mindful living itself.

The excitement of finding a convergence between research in
attachment and in mindfulness has driven me to explore this overlap further. Since that first meeting I have come to learn more
about mindful practice from direct experience and my own clinical
applications as well as by immersing myself in a series of retreats
and research institutes as a participant and as a faculty member.
The journey to learn about these ways of cultivating the mind and
well–being has been thrilling and mind–opening.

In the chapters ahead we'll explore this journey into the mind
and examine what mindful awareness, secure attachment, and prefrontal brain function could have in common.

Chapter Two

BRAIN BASICS

DEVELOPMENT

The nervous system begins in the embryo as the ectoderm, the outer layer of cells that will become the skin. Certain clusters of these outer cells then fold inward to form a neural tube, the spinal cord. This origin of neurons, the basic cells of the brain, on the "outside" and their journey "inside" the body developmentally reveals a philosophical point that the brain originates at the interface of the inner and outer worlds of our bodily defined selves. When we think of the mindful brain, it is helpful to keep this inner/outer interface in mind.

Our brain is the top-most part of an extensive nervous system distributed throughout the body. Whenever we see the word *brain*, it is important to keep this embodied nature as a part of our perspective. The whole nervous system sets up its basic scaffolding, its core architecture, during development in the womb. Genetics are important for determining how neurons will migrate and then connect to each other. In fact, half of our genetic material is either directly or indirectly responsible for neural structure, making genes very important in neural development. As the fetus nears the time to leave the uterus, the connections among neurons are also influenced by experience.

"Experience" for the nervous system involves the activation of neural firing in response to a stimulus. When neurons become active, their connections to each other grow and supportive cells and vasculature proliferate. This is how experience shapes neural structure. Neural firing is the activation of the equivalent of an electrical flow, an *action potential*, down the long axonal length of the cell to the end where it releases either an activating or inhibiting neurotransmitter at the connecting space, the synapse. The downstream "receiving" neuron will either fire off or not, depending on the balance of stimulating or inhibiting transmitters released at that time.

One hundred billion neurons are, on average, linked to each other via 10,000 synaptic connections, which are created by genes and sculpted by experience: Nature needs nurture. These two important dimensions of human development and neural function are not in opposition.

Neurons fire when we have an experience. With neural firing the potential is created to alter synapses by growing new ones, strengthening existing ones, or even stimulating the growth of new neurons that create new synaptic linkages. Synaptogenesis and neurogenesis are the ways in which the brain grows new connections. This growth harnesses both genes and experience to produce changes in the connectivity of neurons: *Neuroplasticity* is the term used when connections change in response to experience.

Experience means neural firing, which can, in some situations, promote the activation of genes, which then leads to the production of proteins that enable new synapses to form and old ones to be strengthened. Research also reveals that experience may stimulate the growth of new neurons. Neurogenesis occurs in which new neurons grow, even in adults. Uncommitted cells in the brain, neural stem cells, divide regularly and have one product of that division continue the stem cell line and the other, "daughter cell," which can be stimulated to grow into a fully integrative neuron in the brain. We know that in adults neurogenesis occurs at least in the hippocampus, and these daughter cells may be stimulated over a period of several months to grow into fully functional integrated neurons (Kempermann, Gast, & Gage, 2002).

NEUROPLASTICITY

Experience can create structural changes in the brain. Often these changes take place at the finely tuned microarchitectural level; for example, when we make new associations within memory. A scanner would be hard pressed to actually detect such changes unless they were quite robust. When Sara Lazar published work (Lazar et al., 2005) revealing structural changes, we need to be aware that this finding would involve significant growth of neural tissue in the brain. If this was a result of experience, then we could see that neuroplasticity could be at the heart of that finding: repeated firing of neurons in specific areas would result in markedly increased synaptic densities in those regions that were activated with mindful practice. The growth of supportive cells and vasculature could also contribute to both the function of those areas and the increased thickness. Mindful awareness is a form of experience that seems to promote neural plasticity.

When we focus our attention in specific ways, we are activating the brain's circuitry. This activation can strengthen the synaptic linkages in those areas. By exploring the notion that mindfulness, as a form of relationship with yourself, may involve not just attentional circuits, but also social circuitry, we can then explore new dimensions of the brain aspect of our mindful experience. (For reviews of social neuroscience, see Cozolino, 2006 and Goleman, 2006.)

In studying changes in the brain in response to experience we can also look toward data from functional scanners (such as fMRI) or electrical monitoring devices (such as EEGs or related tests). Here we would be looking at not just the brain's physical structure, but also the ways in which the brain actually works as a system, revealing how these neuroplastic alterations might produce functional changes. Richard Davidson's finding, that there was a left anterior shift in *function* during emotion-provoking stimuli tests, reveals that mindfulness practice enables individuals to regulate their emotions in a more positive manner with approach rather than withdrawal (Davidson, 2004). The finding that the degree of left brain shift correlated with the degree of positive immune function, enables us to see how mindfulness not only helps us feel good and recover from negative feelings more quickly, but it can actually improve our medical health.

Neuroplastic changes not only reveal structural alterations, but they are accompanied by changes in brain function, mental experience (such as feelings and emotional balance), and bodily states (such as response to stress and immune function).

How would our focus of attention and internal attunement lead to alterations in the circuits of the brain that mediated these functions with mindful awareness? How we pay attention will stimulate neural firing in specific areas, and they will become activated and change their connections within the integrated circuits of the brain.

We will examine how mental activities, such as purposely paying attention to the present moment, actually stimulate the brain to become active in specific ways that then promote growth in those regions. Here we see the notion that the mind is using the brain to create itself. It is this growth, these neuroplastic changes created by the focus of our own minds, that help us see the link between the practice of mindful awareness and the creation of well-being.

THE BRAIN IN THE PALM OF YOUR HAND

Getting to know the brain can feel overwhelming. Recent discoveries in the function of the brain, however, reveal basic principles that actually make it not only understandable, but even accessible and useful, and, if I may go even further, actually fun to get to know your brain.

We have simple diagrams of the brain, complicated maps of neural circuitry, and actual scan images. These pictorial details of brain anatomy can be quite useful. For our explorations of the mindful brain, we need a basic sense of neural locations: the bare bones maps of the brain in Figures 2.1 and 2.2 are a useful place to start.

Another useful tool for viewing the brain is your hand. If you take your hand and put your thumb in the middle and curl your fingers over the top, you'll have a readily accessible and fairly accurate model of the brain. This hand model is oriented such that your wrist represents the spinal cord in your back, the face of the person is in front of your fingernails, and the top of your hand is the top of the head.

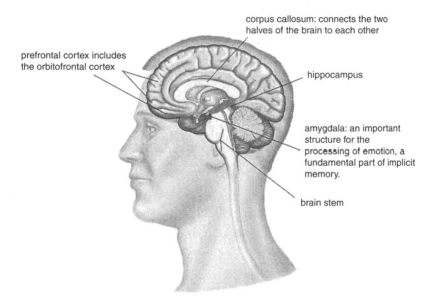

Figure 2.1 Diagram of the human brain looking from the middle to the right side. Some of the major areas of the brain are indicated, including the brainstem, the limbic areas (with the amygdala, hippocampus, and anterior cingulate), and the cerebral cortex (with the prefrontal regions including the orbitofrontal cortex, which, along with the anterior cingulate and other medial and ventral areas, is a part of the "middle prefrontal cortex"). (Siegel & Hartzell, 2003; reprinted with permission.)

Areas of the "middle prefrontal cortex"

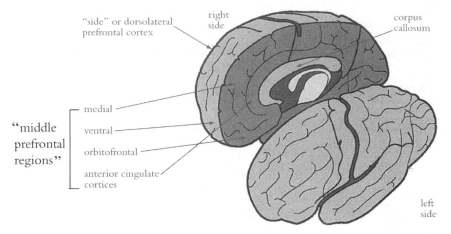

Figure 2.2 The two halves of the brain. This figure also reveals the locations of the areas of the "middle prefrontal cortex," which include the medial and ventral regions of the prefrontal cortex, the orbitofrontal cortex, and the anterior cingulate cortex on both sides of the brain. The corpus callosum connects the two halves of the brain to each other.

The brainstem is your palm, the limbic areas are your thumb (you'd have a left and right thumb, ideally), and your cortex is symbolized by your curved fingers. Let's take them briefly, one by one.

The brainstem carries out important basic processes, such as regulating heart rate and respiration, states of alertness and sleepiness, and aspects of the fight-flight-freeze response. Well developed by birth, the brainstem is the evolutionarily oldest area and is sometimes referred to as the reptilian brain.

The limbic region evolved when reptiles developed into mammals. Limbic zones are involved in attachment (our connections to our caregivers), memory (especially processing events into factual and autobiographical forms), the appraisal of meaning and the creation of affect, and our inner sensations of emotion. The limbic regions also contain the master hormone regulator, the hypothalamus, enabling direct influences to the body proper.

This endocrine connection, along with the brain's influence on the immune system and our bodily states by way of the autonomic nervous system with its brakes/accelerator divisions (the parasympathetic and sympathetic branches) are the direct ways in which the brain and body are intimately interconnected. The limbic zones and the brainstem, the subcortical areas, combine to influence our motivational drives and the activation of our basic needs for survival and for affiliation and meaning.

The cortex is the outer part of the brain, enlarged in mammals. It enables us to mediate more complex processes, such as perception, planning, and attention. With many lobes carrying out different functions, there are varied ways of describing the complex capacities of this region, which is not highly developed at birth and thus is very open to being shaped by experience (Figure 2.3).

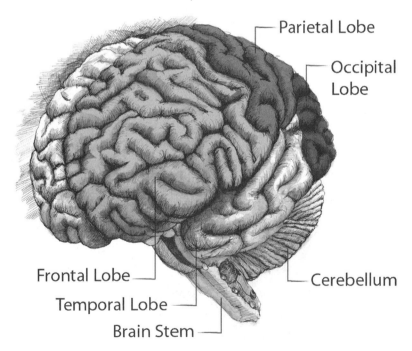

Figure 2.3 The traditional view of the brain: the cortical lobes. (Cozolino, 2006; reprinted with permission.)

The cortex is primarily a six-layer thick folded area made up of gray and white matter. These layers are composed of vertically arranged sets of cortical columns with different clusters of columns often processing a particular mode of activity, such as vision or hearing. These vertical columns are connected to each other with horizontally distributed interneurons that enable cross-talk, the integration of separate modes (hearing, seeing) into a "cross-modal" set of neural firing. It is this linkage of separate areas that creates the important complexity that is our crowning cortical capacity.

In general, the back of the cortex, from your second knuckles backward, carries out perception from the outside world, except for smell and awareness of positions of the limbs. These posterior regions enable human beings to get a sense of the outside world as perceptions.

The front of the brain carries out motor, attentional, and thought-based processes. Our frontal lobes evolved as we became primates. Studies suggest that in mammals, the higher the degree of social living, the more frontal cortical architecture there will be.

The frontal area from your second knuckles to your last knuckles is a region where the first zone carries out motor action, the next zone forward mediates motor planning—the premotor cortex (Figure 2.4). This premotor area was the first region that revealed the finding of the mirror neuron system that enables us to take in the intentions and emotions of others and create those states in ourselves as part of a larger "resonance circuit" (see Appendix III, Resonance Circuitry). We'll be exploring the possibility that this resonance circuitry of our social brain plays an important role in mindful awareness.

Just forward of these motor and premotor areas is the prefrontal cortex. Most highly developed in humans, this prefrontal region mediates many of the functions we consider unique to our species. The prefrontal regions can be divided in various ways that mediate different functions (Figure 2.5). For now, we'll just divide these

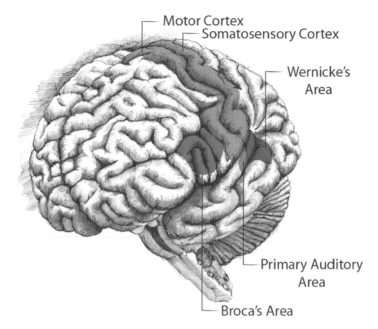

Figure 2.4 The traditional view of the brain: regions of interest. (Cozolino, 2006; reprinted with permission.)

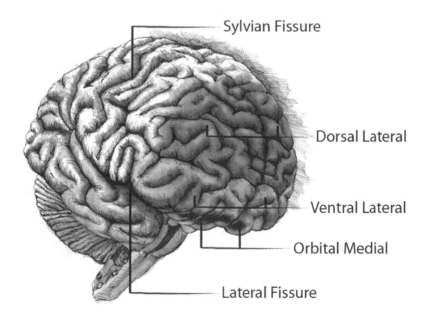

Figure 2.5 Regions of the prefrontal cortex. (Cozolino, 2006; reprinted with permission.)

into two areas: the side and middle prefrontal regions. The areas of the prefrontal cortex generally work as a team, and seeing their function as a system in this way can be quite useful.

The side area of the prefrontal region, the dorsolateral prefrontal cortex (DLPFC), is important for mediating working memory, the chalkboard of the mind, in which we can put something "in the front of our minds." This side area carries out important executive functions that enable self-regulation of our behaviors and help influence the flow of our attention in the moment.

The middle area, from your middle two fingernails up to the knuckles, includes several interlinked regions that mediate those nine middle prefrontal functions, which we will discuss further in the next section. These are the orbitofrontal cortex (OFC), the anterior cingulate cortex (ACC), and the ventral lateral (VLPFC) and medial prefrontal cortex (MPFC). In Figure 2.5 the orbitofrontal and medial prefrontal are combined and labeled orbital-medial prefrontal cortex. In Figure 2.6 their proximity to the anterior portions of the cingulate cortex is revealed.

These midline ventral and medial structures receive direct input from the entire brain and body-proper, especially with contributions from the insula cortex (IC). The insula is the conduit through which information is transferred to and from the outer cortex and the inner limbic (amygdala, hippocampus, hypothalamus) and bodily areas (by way of the brainstem and spinal cord). The middle prefrontal areas appear to utilize the insular data about our emotions and primary bodily state to then create representations of others' minds. The middle prefrontal areas are essential for social communication as well as for self-observation. This region is an important central hub in the social circuitry of the brain (see Appendix III, Middle Prefrontal Function).

Notice how the middle prefrontal region links the body, brainstem, limbic, cortical, and social processes into one functional whole. If you lift your fingers up and put them back down, you may notice that indeed the middle prefrontal areas (represented by

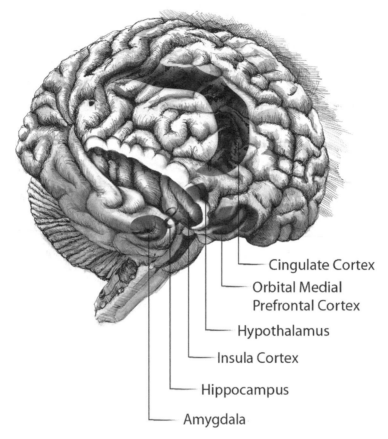

Cingulate Cortex
Orbital Medial
Prefrontal Cortex
Hypothalamus
Insula Cortex
Hippocampus
Amygdala

Figure 2.6 Structures of the social brain. The structures represented here are hidden beneath the surface of the brain. (Cozolino, 2006; reprinted with permission.)

the ends of the two middle fingers) touch everything in the brain anatomically, and that is the nature of neural integration: body-wide synaptic connections that even link us to each other.

An interpersonal neurobiology approach to the ways our social lives help promote well-being views neural integration as the outcome of attuned relationships. Neural integration, the coordination and balance of the brain as separate areas are linked together to form a functional whole, seems to be promoted with the attunement of secure attachments. The proposal here is that perhaps we are gathering some preliminary data to point in the direction that mindful awareness may also promote such neural integration, through a form of intrapersonal attunement.

Awareness of one's moment-to-moment experience creates the opportunity to sense and accept one's own mental experience directly. This state of awareness may harness various regions of the brain, including the important frontal areas of the cortex and subcortical limbic and brainstem areas into an integrated coherent state. Neural integration, carried out in part by these frontal regions, may be essential for creating self-regulational balance. We should keep these prefrontal areas in the front of our minds as we explore how these integrative pathways may serve a crucial role in this important movement toward well-being.

NEURAL INTEGRATION, MINDFULNESS, AND SELF-REGULATION

The concept of neural integration is a very broad, large-system view of how the brain functions. In neuroscience, it is possible to be more microanalytically focused, examining the membranes of neurons, studying neurotransmitters and their receptors, investigating clusters of neurons and their immediately linked neighboring cells. This deep and finely tuned research is important and intriguing. In addition to these crucial microviews, we also can move outward to examine the brain as a whole system. This macroview enables us to not only see the entire brain and body as one functional whole, but to move out further and examine the ways in which signals from one brain/body interact with others within relationships, families, and societies. This is the focus of our work at the Center for Culture, Brain, and Development at UCLA (see Appendix I).

It is always a matter of translation to try to speak at both micro- and macrolevels of analysis. At the Center we must embrace the reality of this spectrum of knowing in order to compile the pieces of the puzzle that can only be assembled when you humbly and respectfully acknowledge the value of these differing points of view. My sense of a whole system view of how two minds become linked within attunement is that this large-system connectivity, neural integration, is at the heart of relational well-being. When we take that neural perspective on interpersonal attunement and consider mindfulness as an intrapersonal form, it is natural to have the sense that neural integration may play a crucial role in mindful states. Neural integration is the linkage of anatomically or functionally differentiated neural regions into an interconnection of widely distributed areas of the brain and body proper. These interconnections take the form of synaptic linkages structurally, and create a form of coordination and balance functionally.

Neural integration likely creates optimal functioning by way of this coordination and balance of neural activation. Coordination means that we monitor and then influence the firing patterns of various disparate regions into a well-functioning whole. Balance implies the activation, deactivation, and reactivation of coupled areas.

One illustrative example would be the balance of such functions as the brakes and accelerator branches of the autonomic nervous system. Here we see that the middle prefrontal regions must monitor the activity of these two inputs (sympathetic and parasympathetic activity) and then be able to actually alter it (shut it down or rev it up).

This is the mechanism of "bodily regulation," the first of our nine middle prefrontal functions. Recall that this is a list of outcomes for secure attuned attachment (the first seven) and also a list for the outcome and process of mindful awareness, what we are proposing as a form of internal attunement. I generated this list while caring for a family in which the mother had sustained an injury, following an automobile collision, to the part of the brain be-

hind her forehead. The family was struggling with the profound
changes in her personality and I was hoping to help them make
sense of this experience and adjust to their new life. I turned to
the basic research literature and asked the question, What functions
correlate with the activity of the middle areas of the prefrontal cortex? (See Appendix III, Middle Prefrontal Functions.)

1. Body regulation, as described above, emerges as the brakes
   and accelerator functions are coordinated and balanced.
2. Attuned communication involves the coordination of the input from another mind with the activity of one's own, a resonance process involving these middle prefrontal areas.
3. Emotional balance implies the capacity of the affect-generating limbic areas to be allowed to have enough activation so
   that life has meaning and vitality but not so much that life becomes chaotic. The middle prefrontal regions have the capacity to monitor and inhibit limbic firing with high levels of
   bidirectional flow from the subcortical limbic to the middle
   prefrontal regions.
4. Response flexibility is the capacity to pause before action.
   Such a process requires the assessment of ongoing stimuli,
   the delay of reaction, selection from a variety of possible options, and the initiation of action. The middle prefrontal regions work in conjunction with the side areas to carry out
   this function.
5. Empathy appears to build on the internal shifts carried out
   by the resonance circuits in which limbic and bodily changes
   are first initiated as we perceive another person's signals.
   Next, the middle prefrontal regions appear to use interoception, the input of these subcortical and bodily states into the
   middle prefrontal region by way of the insula. The data are
   then proposed to be interpreted and that assessment attrib-
   uted to another as a form of empathic imagination of what
   might be going on inside someone else.

6. Insight, or self-knowing awareness, links the past, present, and future. The middle prefrontal cortex has input and output fibers to many areas, in this case regarding cortical representations of autobiographical memory stores and limbic firing that gives emotional texture to the emerging themes of our present awareness, life story, and images of the future.

7. Fear modulation may be carried out via the release of the inhibitory neurotransmitter gamma amino butyric acid (GABA) onto the lower limbic areas mediating fear, such as the extended nuclei of the amygdala. In this way, fear may be learned limbically, but its "unlearning" may be carried out via growth of these middle prefrontal fibers that can modulate that fear (Figure 2.7).

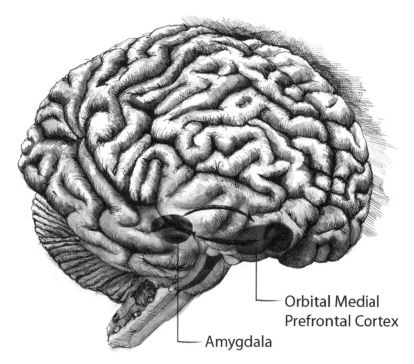

Figure 2.7 The orbital-medial prefrontal cortex: amygdala network. (Cozolino, 2006; reprinted with permission.)

8. Intuition seems to involve the registration of the input from the information processing neural networks surrounding our viscera; for example, the heart, lungs, and intestines. Our body's wisdom is then more than a poet's metaphor, it is a neural mechanism by which we process deep ways of knowing via our body's parallel distributed processing surrounding these hollow organs. This input registers itself in the middle prefrontal cortex and then influences our reasoning and our reactions.

9. Morality: Studies reveal the participation of the middle prefrontal cortex in the mediation of morality. Taking into consideration the larger picture, to imagine what is best for the whole not just oneself, even when alone, is what morality can be seen as entailing. The middle prefrontal region when damaged is associated with impairments in moral thinking leading to a form of amorality.

LEFT AND RIGHT

In Figure 2.2, we can see that the brain is divided into a left and right side. In considering left and right hemisphere distinctions, it is important to avoid "dichotomizing."

In the course of evolution as back-boned animals, the left and right sides of our nervous systems have had different functions (Halpern, Güntürkün, Hopkins, & Rogers, 2005). The benefit of this asymmetry, shared with fish and frogs, lizards and birds, and rats and people may be that with more differentiation, we are able to achieve more complexity of function. Why should left and right, or up and down, be the *same*? As we noted earlier, the brainstem and limbic areas develop earlier than the cortex. Their asymmetries push for a difference in the connectivity of the right and left cortical hemispheres. These emerging structural differences result in some relevant and quite robust differences in function between left and right. The right hemisphere develops and is more active in the first two or three years of life. The left comes on line around the second birthday, followed by a periodic shift in the developmental thrust of left and right in the years ahead. The connecting tissue—the corpus callosum—begins its developmental thrust at this time, lasting well into the twenties.

A general sense of the difference can be pictured by just imagining that the cortical columns of the right hemisphere may have more horizontal linkages between them, making the representational processes more "cross-modal" in that the differentiated processes of one area communicate with those of other areas. This finding, for example, helps us understand why the right hemisphere is better at seeing context and the whole picture than the more detail oriented left hemisphere. In the left hemisphere, the cortical columns appear to work more on their own, which allows for the more in-depth, analytic, problem focused, detail monitoring, and fact accumulating processes of the left.

The streams of input from the subcortical regions feed different sources of sensory data to these two regions, which also helps us understand why such distinctions emerge. People always ask about gender differences, and so here is a general statement, biased in favor of both genders. Female brain development appears to involve more integration, with a thicker corpus callosum that connects the left and right hemispheres. The male brain can be said to be more differentiated, or more specialized, allowing the separate regions to work intensively more on their own. These gross generalizations make me nervous, but that's generally what the science reveals. In clinical work it is important to connect with people as they are, not what statistics say they may be.

The functioning of the left hemisphere is easiest to remember because its functions have four L's: The left specializes in linguistics, linearity, logic, and literal thinking.

In contrast, the right reveals the following features: Nonverbal, holistic, visuospatial, and then a whole host of noncorrelated specialties such as autobiographical memory, integrated map of the whole body, raw spontaneous emotion, initial empathic nonverbal response, stress modulation, and a dominance in the alerting aspect of attention. The right side is thought in some perspectives to mediate distress and uncomfortable emotions and correlates with withdrawal from novelty. The left is seen to mediate more positive affective states and is associated with approach behaviors. The coordination between the left and right in shaping our overall emotional tone may be an important dimension of how mindful awareness alters our affective style (Davidson, 2000). As we have seen, mindfulness appears to lead toward an approach state, with a left sided shift in frontal electrical activity.

When functions are separated, the brain can harness them into a state of connection to achieve more complex and adaptive functions. This is neural integration. This is the way the complex system of the brain, and the mind, may become flexible and create new combinations of functioning. With a left and right hemisphere physically separated and functionally differentiated, we have the opportunity to achieve more adaptive function if we come to integrate them into a whole. This is how, I believe, creativity emerges not from one side or another, but from their integration.

As we shall see, the left hemisphere may have a "narrator" function in which this region serves to linguistically articulate the ongoing story of a person's life. But the "goods" of our autobiographical memories are located primarily in the right hemisphere, and so creating a coherent narrative of one's own life may involve at a minimum this bilateral form of integration. Integrating left and right helps us to make sense of our lives (see Appendix III on laterality for further discussion).

Awareness of the totality of our body's experience may require us to link the right hemisphere's integrated whole-body map with the side prefrontal cortex's activation. In mindful awareness we are often focusing on aspects of our bodily function. This then would involve not only the interoception of the insula and middle prefrontal cortex, but also the whole map of the body represented in the right side of the brain. If in mindfulness practice our mind is filled with word-based left-sided chatter at that moment, we could propose that there is a fundamental neural competition between right (body sense) and left (word-thoughts) for the limited resources of attentional focus at that moment. Shifting within mindful awareness to a focus on the body may involve a functional shift away from linguistic conceptual facts toward the nonverbal imagery and somatic sensations of the right hemisphere. This may help us understand the finding of Lazar that revealed an increase in structural thickness in the middle prefrontal and right insular areas (Lazar et al., 2005).

But if ongoing narration, perhaps even without words in the form of a witnessing awareness or an internal observer, is truly a function of the left hemisphere, then there would be a prefrontal activation on the left side (executive attention with active narrative observation) and perhaps also a right middle prefrontal activation (nonverbal self-reflection and meta-awareness in the medial prefrontal) and right insula activity with viscera representation. This could help us make sense of and synthesize the findings of the left sided/approach shift that Davidson and colleagues have noted (Davidson et al., 2003) and Lazar's middle prefrontal and right-sided insula findings (Lazar et al., 2005). The implications of this line of reasoning need empirical exploration to verify their validity. But this is an example of a way we can draw on existing knowledge of brain function (laterality) to ask testable questions about phenomena (mindful awareness) and general principles (neural integration and well-being) so that we can deepen our understanding of our subjective and neural lives.

"BRAIN" AND "MIND"

Whenever the term *brain* is used in this work, it refers to the brain as an integrated part of the whole body. This reality changes the way we think about the relationship of brain and mind. Because the mind itself can be viewed as both embodied and relational, our brains actually can be considered the social organ of the body: Our minds connect with one another via neural circuitry in our bodies that is hard-wired to take in others' signals.

To examine the relationship of the mind—the flow of energy and information—to the brain—neural connections and their complex patterns of firing—we need to be careful of certain preconceived ideas that might restrict our understanding and bias our thinking. We need to be cognitively mindful: To be open to contexts, embrace novel ways of perceiving, distinguish subtle differences in ideas, and create new categories of thinking in our awareness of concepts in the moment. Here we see that the idea of a cognitive dimension of mindfulness can help in how we think and how we approach learning, even about reflective mindfulness.

The timing and location of neural activation correlates with the timing and characteristics of mental activity. If a person looks at a photograph, his or her brain activity can be monitored with a functional scanner. Activation will be evident in the posterior part of the brain (usually blood flow increases during activation and is visible on a functional MRI scan or as electrical activity on an EEG). The most accurate thing we can then say is that occipital lobe firing correlates with visual or spatial perception.

Why not say the neural activity created the visual perception? If we make causal phrases like this, the erroneous idea is reinforced that the mind is only created by the brain. If we are cognitively mindful here, we need to be open to the truth that seeing the picture actually created the neural firing. The directional arrow goes both ways: The mind can actually use the brain to create itself.

Without cognitive mindfulness, we would miss this bidirectional point. When we examine the nature of our evolution as a species, for example, we find that in the last 40,000 years our species has changed by way of cultural evolution. Culture is the way that meaning is transferred among individuals and across generations with groups of people. How this energy and information flow shifts its patterns across time is what cultural evolution involves. This reality of how we have changed as a species involves not the genetically driven evolution of our brains, but the *mental* evolution of how we collectively pass energy and information among each other across generations. This is the evolution of the mind, not the brain. One view is that for the mind (energy and information flow) to exist it may need to harness the activity of the brain. In this manner, the mind uses the brain to create itself.

This perspective is consistent with the scientific state of our understanding of how mind and brain are related to each other. There is no need to try to simplify the dimension of one reality into that of another. Mind is not "just" brain activity; energy and information flow happens in a brain within the body and it happens within relationships. To visualize this perspective we can say that the mind rides along the neural firing patterns in the brain, and realize that this riding correlates with bidirectional causal influences. Terms such as *mechanisms* or *neurally mediated by* in this text are not meant to imply one directional causality. Neural events are "correlated" or "associated" with mental activities, each influencing the other.

Relationships among people also involve the flow of energy and information, and thus utilize these riding patterns along neural firing as well. This interconnection among brain, mind, and relationships will be a triangle of reality that we will be returning to again and again. With this perspective we can sense a "tridirectional" influence of these three irreducible dimensions.

Relationships shape energy and information flow—as is happening now by these words in your mind. But the brain's activity also directly shapes how energy and information flow is regulated. Right now your brain may be activating certain firing patterns that distract you from paying attention to the text. This would impair your ability to be mindfully aware at this particular moment. There may be a distraction, and this will shape how energy and information flow—the focus of your attention—occurs at this particular moment.

Attention to the present moment, one aspect of mindful awareness, can be directly shaped by our ongoing communication with others, and from the activities in our own brains. Indeed one of the biggest challenges to being present are the top-down patterns of activation in our brains that continually bombard us with neural firing and mental chatter that keep us from being in the moment.

In the next section we'll be diving deeply into the nature of direct experience and mindful awareness. We can keep all of these ideas about brain, mind, and relationships in the back of our minds as we let them go for now and immerse ourselves in the subjective reality of inner life.

PART II

IMMERSION IN DIRECT
EXPERIENCE

Chapter Three

A WEEK OF SILENCE

I'm flying from Los Angeles to Boston for a week-long meditation retreat, and I'm feeling nervous. For the next seven days, I'll be sitting in silence with 100 other scientists at the Insight Meditation Society in Barre, Massachusetts, at an event sponsored by the Mind and Life Institute, an organization devoted to the scientific study of mindfulness and compassion. The event is unique: When before have 100 scientists, most of whom specialize in studying the brain, gathered together to sit in silence for a week and learn "mindfulness meditation"?

I know that teaching mindful awareness to people can markedly improve their physical and mental well-being. At the UCLA Mindful Awareness Research Center, we recently conducted an eight-week pilot study that demonstrated that teaching meditation to people, including adults and adolescents with genetically loaded conditions like attention-deficit/hyperactivity disorder, could markedly reduce their level of distraction and impulsivity. Still, I have no background in meditation, my mind is always busily running on at least 10 cylinders, and I've never spent that much time being quiet.

I told a friend about the silence coming up and he said that talking with other people is his "life's blood," and that connecting with others—the talk, the eye contact, the closeness—was what gave his life meaning. Me too, I said. How will it be to sit completely still for long periods of time, not communicating either verbally or nonverbally (part of the deal) with anybody else for seven days? Why *am* I doing this? I wonder if it's too late to back out of the whole thing.

SCIENTISTS IN SILENCE

There wasn't much for me to do in preparation except pack up warm clothes and shoes for this occasion to be in New England in the dead of winter. I was advised that the best thing I could do to get ready was to tie up all the loose ends at home and work so that in the silence of the retreat, I wouldn't feel the urge to call, email, or write anybody back in my ordinary world. As a psychiatrist interested in the brain and relationships, I can't help wondering what will take over the language-processing areas of my left hemisphere when they, presumably, become silent during meditation? Words are digital packets of information that convey to ourselves and others our models of conceptual reality—how we see and think about the world. They're part of the brain's top-down apparatus for ordering and making sense of incoming sensory information.

But then I think of poetry—a different use of language—which inhibits the strictly hierarchical, top-down left-brain processes organizing our raw experience into a preconceived grid. Poetry, like silence, creates a new balance of memory and moment. We see with fresh eyes through the poet's artistry, which illuminates with words a new landscape that before was hidden beneath the veil of everyday language. Our ordinary language can be a prison, locking us in the jail of our own redundancies, dulling our senses, clouding our focus. By presenting ambiguities, by using words in unfamiliar ways, by juxtaposing elements of perceptual reality in new combinations, by evoking imagery, poets and their poetry offer us fresh, novel possibilities for experiencing life.

Perhaps the silence of this week will do the same for me.

Day One

I arrive at the Insight Meditation Society, where I'll be spending the week with other scientists. After a brief dinner, tour, assignments of daily cleaning duties, and an introductory talk, we've already begun the silence. The idea is to immerse ourselves in the subjective reality of our own minds. With some direction from the insight meditation faculty here, we're to dive deeply into the waters of our own internal sea. The form of mindfulness we'll be learning this week comes from the 2500-year-old Buddhist practice of Vipassana meditation, which is often translated as "clear seeing."

On the first day, we learn to sit in the meditation hall with the brief instructions to merely "watch our breathing." This capacity to focus attention is the first step of mindful-awareness training. When we notice our attention has wandered away from the breath, the instructors tell us, we're to gently return our focus of attention to the breath. That's it. Over and over again. I feel relieved. How hard can this be?

But by the end of the first day of practicing this concentration aspect of the meditation, my confidence level has definitely plummeted. I thought I had what the instructors call "good attention," but, in fact, my mind is repeatedly not cooperating with the instructions to "just focus on the breath." After a few moments it seems I can barely make it through an entire breath without having my mind pulled toward different thoughts like a dog zig-zagging on a walk, drawn this way and that by enticing scents along the path.

Our instructors tell us that this continual wandering is a totally natural part of the mind itself, and suggest we try just to focus on half a breath at a time: the in-breath, then the out-breath. This helps a bit, but my mind still goes strolling off in all directions. This is sometimes called a "proliferation of the mind," we're told—the way the thoughts generate more and more conceptual thinking. The solution to this dilemma, once we become aware that our minds have been hijacked by stray thoughts, is to calmly return to focusing on our breath, over and over and over—at least a million times, it seems to me, during the 45-minute session of sitting meditation.

After each sitting period, we do walking meditation that lasts from half an hour to an hour. While walking, we're to focus on the sensations in our feet and lower legs, step by step. When we notice our minds wandering from the sensation of the steps, we're to bring our focus back to the walking. Same deal: my mind has a mind of its own and goes where it wants to, not where "I" intend for it to go.

Our instructions are expanded more as this first full day goes on. We learn that concentration on the breath will enhance the first step of mindfulness, which is to aim and sustain our attention. By learning to keep our attention focused, we can prevent the constant stream of wayward thoughts, the concepts that comprise our mental processes and get in the way of truly experiencing sensations. Sensation is the gateway to direct experience, they tell us. When we can just see, or smell, or taste, or touch, or hear—our first five senses—then we enter the realm of being in the moment, a distant realm from where I am with all of the clutter in my mind, as I just sit, and walk, and sit, and walk. Getting close to sensation, it seems, is intended to enable us to simply experience, without the interference of thinking.

This first day has been both odd and stressful. Being in silence and out of direct communication with anyone makes me feel a bit stir-crazy. I'm driven to connect, but we're forbidden from communicating with anyone with words or gestures, eye contact, or facial acknowledgments of connection. This is the rule that precludes us from joining in any way, and I feel some part of my brain is aching to reach out to the many who are here. I'm beginning to talk to myself, not just in my head, but out loud. I'm even telling myself jokes and laughing. Then I say "Shhh!" to myself, remembering the rule about the noble silence: No communication with anyone. But how about with myself?

During the practice I try to remember what I told myself before this began: Make every breath an adventure. Now I say to myself, "Make every *half* breath an adventure." But I'm saying this with words, and somehow words have become an enemy, those proliferative concepts that keep me from direct sensation. I'm trapped. I feel confused. I'm feeling the sensations directly, I feel, or I think, but I'm also not giving up the conceptual, word-based dialogue in my head—the words that summarize what I'm doing, like taking a walk, eating an apple—instead of just letting myself *do* it. I've got some narrator in me that just won't quit. "Go ahead, try to just drink that soy milk." S-O-Y M-I-L-K, I read on the carton, the letters jumping into my sight like a long-lost friend. I even have the words active in my mind when sitting and walking in our sessions. This makes me feel that I'm not "meditating mindfully." Maybe I'm just too intellectual and filled with ideas and questions, words and concepts, to be doing any of this.

Day Two

Something shifted today. We get up at 5:15 every day and are in sitting meditation by 5:45. At the end of the first 45-minute session, I had the startling feeling that no time had passed at all. I sat down, began watching my half breath, and before I knew it, the bell had sounded for our 6:30 breakfast. I hadn't fallen asleep, as I was still sitting bolt upright, my head straight, legs still folded beneath me. Then I went for a long, mindful walk in the snow in the forest outside the main building. At one point, I saw this gorgeous vista of a white-blanketed valley framed by a snow-covered limb of a tall pine, icicles dangling down from a nearby boulder. To my surprise, I burst into tears at the vivid sights and smells and cool air on my face, the sound of the wind in the trees and the crunching snow beneath my boots. And then, just as quickly, I heard a thought in my head say, "You'll die one day and none of this will be here for you." My exhilaration vanished in an instant, leaving me distraught. I felt defeated and deflated. It was as if an ancient war were being waged, magnified in my isolated head between thoughts and sensations.

Later, during a brief group meeting, I described this experience to the teacher and wondered if his mindfulness teaching was a form of playing favorites, as if sensations were better than thinking or anything else we might do, perhaps even better than talking with each other. Why were sensations being privileged over thoughts? A teacher said that we'd soon learn that *anything* arising in the mind, from sensations to thoughts, is to be accepted as it comes without judgment. Her instruction was deeply helpful, making me feel there didn't have to be a war in my head between direct sensation and conceptual thinking anymore. Perhaps I could broker a truce between the two. But I was surprised that such a simple instruction could produce such a huge shift in my experience.

With this new perspective in mind, I had a remarkable experience eating an apple at dinner. At each of the meals, in fact in all of our activities besides just the formal sitting and walking practice, we were to be "mindful." What this means is to be awake and aware of what's happening as it's happening. I decided to eat an apple for dessert. Feeling free to think as well as sense, I decided to do a mind experiment of enhancing the experience of eating the apple. I cut a piece and looked at its texture. I felt the skin, the pulp, and the edge where they met. I smelled the aroma and drank in its wafting, expanding scent. I even decided to put the piece of apple to my ear and see how it sounded (yes, I know, ridiculous, but molecules vibrate and that's exactly what sound is, so why not try?). All I could hear was the sound of others in the room, no whirring atoms shaking my ear drum. When I placed the apple slowly in my mouth, I could hear the crunching, taste the burst of flavor, feel the pieces against my tongue and teeth, and then sense the shift as the mashing pieces got smaller, and then moved down my throat, into my esophagus, and down into my stomach.

Feeling free now to allow conceptual thoughts into the picture, I allowed my mind to expand and play with images and sensations of the apple making its way through my digestive system, being absorbed into my body, and becoming an integral part of me. Then I thought about where the apple had come from—the people in the kitchen who (hopefully) washed it, the staff that bought it, the orchard from which it was picked, the tree on which it grew, and the seed from which that tree sprouted. With the freedom to enjoy this imagery, I suddenly felt a sense of wholeness and oneness with everything—the earth, the chain of people, my body.

I floated out of the dining room and wanted to speak to someone, but remembered the silence. A friend had been in the room, but we couldn't talk. I went outside and gazed at the almost-full moon in a cloud-strewn evening sky. I felt a presence next to me and found my friend had come out also, on his way to the sleeping area, and paused a moment by me in the silence under the stars. In that silence, a million words couldn't have said what that shared moment in the moonlight felt like.

Day Three

Today I met with another teacher for a one-to-one meeting. I tried to describe the apple experience. I said that I felt as if there were a flowing river creating my awareness, and this meditation practice was enabling me to go up the current to visit the individ-

ual streams flowing into that river—one stream of sensation, one
of concepts. This image made me feel more at ease with whatever arose in my mind. He answered by telling me that he often
felt that he had "finally gotten it," only to realize that there was always something new to experience in awareness. He suggested
that I might not want to hold on to any fixed idea of "how things
are," but just see what happened.

I felt dismissed and irritated by his response. After this 10-minute
meeting, my head was filled with worded-thoughts and the next
few sessions were difficult. A difficult session feels as if it's going
nowhere; as if instead of feeling the spaciousness of a calm and
stable mind, I'm simply spacing out. Spacing out instead of "spacing in." I get lost in thoughts easily and somehow don't come back
to the breath.

But in the end, this teacher was right. It would get quite a bit
more complicated and would be forever changing. No matter how
illuminating some experiences have been, you can never predict
what the next session will feel like. The mind is always in flux,
and nothing seems to predict anything. The idea is to give up expectation and let whatever happens, happen.

In our group instructions, we've gone from being told to just
watch the breath to also notice sounds and feel our bodies. The
breath is like an anchor point, a place to start, but noticing sounds
gives us a wider expanse. The body scan—sensing each part of
our body one area at a time—enables us to open our awareness
intentionally to the predominant sensations in our bodies. We just
drop into awareness of the body or our senses and take in whatever arises.

Day Four

We're now expanding the field of awareness to move from con-
centrating on the breath to becoming mindful of and receptive
to all that arises, including the experience of mindfulness itself.

Nothing is excluded. But the receptive mind isn't a passive mind. There's a quality of active engagement, not just with the object of attention, but with awareness itself. Yet this active sense isn't strained—it has a flowing, grounded, and intentional quality to it.

An insight that emerged on a walking session today came into my awareness without words. This insight was that deep in mindfulness, it isn't possible to get bored. Words portray a concept, a verbal thought that may articulate even a nonverbal idea. But an insight, like this one, feels more like a shift in internal perspective than a conceptual idea.

There's a strange change today. It feels as if some part of my mind that was aching to connect with others has given up aiming for them and has turned inward toward myself. I feel a surge of awareness of each step, a kind of connection to myself that wasn't there before. No moment is like any other, even step after step after step. I feel with each step the pressure on the ball of my feet transitioning to the sole and then the heel. And then the shift in weight in my legs as the next footstep takes on the pressure of my body. Each step is unique. There's no place other than here, no moment other than now. I'm filled with excitement. I feel a floating sensation on the walking meditation, each moment inflated with a kind of helium from my mind.

I want to tell someone, so I tell myself.

Day Five

We've been working on full mindfulness in experiencing our sensations, feelings, mental activities, and states. One practice is to start with grounding yourself in a focus on the breath and then moving into a more open, expanded, and inquiring state of awareness, which feels something like "bring it on." Whatever comes, will come. We're told that it helps some people to notice a thought or sensation or mental state (without getting sucked into it) by imagining it emerging from a mouse hole in the wall. Others imagine the thought appearing on a video screen that they can turn on or off.

Neither of these approaches worked for me. Instead, my awareness of the present moment emerged in my mind's eye as a valley. Thoughts and feelings and images would float like clouds into this valley, where I could see them, name them ("thinking" or "feeling" or "imaging"), and just let them float off, out of my valley of the present moment. Sometimes a thought would arise without my awareness that it had come and, in an instant, I'd be "lost in thought." There would be no separation between the thought and me. I'd not only be lost in it, I *was* the thought. At those moments, I was no longer in the valley, but had been swept up into the clouds.

When I became aware of my unawareness of my breath, the key was not to get mad or frustrated or feel like a failure, but to just take note of this experience. It also helped to remember what our teachers told us: No matter how many decades people spend practicing mindful awareness, there's always the regular "getting lost in thought" experience. This is just how the mind works. But building mindful awareness helps you see a thought as just arising and floating away. The thought loses its power to kidnap you and make you its captive.

We've also been working on ancient meditative practices for the cultivation of "loving kindness." Loving kindness is a fundamental part of mindfulness meditation and aspires to imbue us with a positive regard for all living creatures, ourselves included, and the world at large. A set of sayings is repeated, beginning with a focus on the self. These are the particular articulations taught by Sharon Salzberg (1995): "May I be safe and protected from harm. May I be happy and have a peaceful and joyful heart. May I be healthy and have a body that supports me with energy. May I live with the ease that comes from well-being." Having an image of yourself in mind can deepen these practices. As these statements are made, the mind's awareness of the body can focus on the heart region, the area just beneath the chest, as one breathes in, and breathes out. Beginning with loving kindness for ourselves is necessary, because if we can't feel it for ourselves, how can we feel it for others?

After focusing on the self, we focus on others. We wish safety, happiness, health, and ease first on a benefactor (someone who's supported us and our development in life), then on a friend, followed by someone about whom we feel neutral. Often an image of that person is useful to have in mind as these wishes are expressed. The next step is harder—wishing these blessings on a "difficult" person in our life, one with whom we may have a challenging relationship. And the next step can be even harder: We're asked to offer and ask for forgiveness. "I ask you for forgiveness for anything I've done or said that's caused you harm or painful feelings." Then, with the same words, one forgives this person.

I chose a friend with whom I'd had a long-standing relationship that had recently ended with confusion and hostility. I pictured his face, saw the troubles that led to our rift, and asked his forgiveness for what had happened between us. It was hard, as he hasn't been forthcoming in trying to make a reconnection. But the exercise, including forgiving him for what had happened, helped me feel a sense of resolution.

I personally found this deeply moving, but several in the group during evening lectures expressed difficulty forgiving those who'd done them harm. For others, this entire "metta" or loving kindness practice was uncomfortable, and some even stopped coming when this was the guided-meditation topic of the session. A number of people later would say that they had a hard time forgiving someone who'd wronged them and hadn't apologized for the transgressions.

Day Six

I'm feeling as if I now have three palpable streams of awareness flowing into my river of consciousness. One is *direct sensory experi-*

ence. These sensations of my body or of my perceptions feel raw and bare. When I walk, I feel the pressure on the heel of my foot, the transition to the ball, the distribution of weight unevenly onto my toes, the movement of my hips as my other leg slowly swings over the center of gravity and my body leans forward, the next heel touching earth, my other foot's toes releasing and taking flight. I'm not observing this as a perception; I'm sensing it. As it's happening in real time, I feel there are no words to describe these sensations, no concepts to analyze and cluster them. They just are their sensory fullness—sights and sounds, inner gurglings, tensions, pressures. I also become quite aware of the second stream—the *conceptual stream* in the idea of walking. I can almost hear the thought—"walking"—in words that aren't quite audible in my mind. But now there's also a third stream flowing that I call the *observer*—the sense that I'm watching myself from afar, out of my head, floating in the hall above me or in the trees above the path where I'm walking.

Each stream—sensation, concept, observer—seems to coexist in the valley of the present moment. I note them, even observing the observer. How odd. At some point, I feel as if I'm losing my mind as my sense of reality crumbles, unraveling before my mind's eye, literally. Or am I actually finding it? I walk on. Step by step, I watch my mind. I sense my steps. I observe my sensing and even sense my observing.

I haven't had a conversation with anyone besides brief moments with my teachers in almost a week. No interactions, no speech, no reciprocity. I'm surrounded by others, but am far away, yet so close. I've been carrying out the assigned job of cleaning our hall's bathroom each day. I dreaded this routine at first, but somehow have come to enjoy it, to even relish the task. There's a kind of connection I feel with the mop, scrubbing the toilet, washing the sink. Day by day, I've come to expect the same sort of reaction from the cleaning fluids, the sponges, the rags. It feels comforting to

know that somewhere in all this there's some sort of predictability. I scrub, the dirt disappears. Magic. But in the open valley of
the present moment, I never know what will arise.

Needing some kind of anchor point during a walk, I think of a
mnemonic for the whole thing. I know we've been told to say to
ourselves, "not now" or "no thank you," to acknowledge an interesting idea and not get swept up in it. But I can't help myself. Or
perhaps I am helping myself. Step by step my shoeless feet are
floating over the wooden floor of this walking room. Step by step.
I think: *Sensation.* Okay. *Observation.* Fine. *Concept.* Good. Each of
these three streams gives me a sense of knowing the present moment, a knowing paradoxically without words, without concepts,
without sensations. This knowing is a kind of subterranean stream
beneath this valley of the present moment, a formless *Knowing*.
How will I ever remember this amazing vision? Then I think,
"S. O. C. K." So, a sock is around the sole of my feet and SOCK is
surrounding the soul of mindfulness, step-by-step, moment-by-
moment: Sensation, observation, concept, and knowing.

Earlier I described three streams of awareness in a question and
answer period and asked if I was losing my mind. When the observer becomes excessively active, I said, it seems to destroy the
direct sensory experience, just as the conceptual thoughts used to
do. "Do I need to get rid of the observer?" I asked. "No," the
teacher responded. "The idea is balance" I can live with that. In
fact, I can float with that. And, of course, on the following walk,
another mnemonic emerges—the ABCDE of mindfulness: A Balance of Concept and Direct Experience. My left hemisphere just
won't quit!

Day Seven

This is the day we "break silence." They've planned a brief,
three-hour period of formal discussion, followed by an evening
meal full of chatter and social connections, during which we

won't be aware of the taste of the food, I imagine, and then a silent evening meditation before going to sleep until tomorrow morning's final meditation and discussion. We first meet in pairs, and I'm dying to describe my experience. I tell my partner about these mnemonics and he likes the YODA one best: You Observe and Decouple Automaticity. This describes the role of reflection in waking us up into mindful awareness: Observation disrupts being on automatic pilot. We laugh about the idea of "YODA's SOCKs." Mindfulness may involve more than just sensing—it may include that capacity to be aware of awareness, to observe experience. When we observe, we can disengage the automatic chatter and less obvious filtering that our emotions and habitual schema create as they distance us from direct experience. Observation feels like the key that ironically unlocks the doors for direct sensation: We observe and note our conceptual mind, and free ourselves to enter the valley of the present moment more fully.

As we emerged from silence, a strange phenomenon seemed to occur that I've subsequently been informed is common, not just with scientists: there was a frantic sense, a kind of party atmosphere, once we could speak after our lonely, silent sojourn. But when we later returned to silence, I felt surprising relief, and an open, spacious sense of my mind coming back to me. I could feel a clearing of my awareness when I knew I wasn't allowed to speak to anyone. That lack of contact freed my mind to be open again, to connect to itself. There's some kind of clarity that comes with silence.

Still, that night, when I called home for the first time in a week, I was glad to connect with my wife and children. And yet, even though things were fine at home, my mind couldn't stop thinking about our conversation, the plans, the tones of voice, things to be done. For the first time all week, I had a hard time falling asleep and awoke several times, just thinking of various things that had evaporated from my awareness during the week. The pull of my regular life made me realize that I hadn't been aware of how much quieter my mind had become.

I'd been drinking hot tea all week long without a problem. After calling home, moving out of mindfulness and back into the frenzy and hustle and bustle of "civilian" life, I burned my tongue. I was thinking of something else instead of being aware of the tea as I was drinking it. Without mindfulness, we can get harried, and burned.

During the brief science discussions about our ideas and experiences on the last night of the week, I couldn't get my head in gear. What struck me was how utterly *conceptual* the conversations felt, and I just wasn't in a frame of mind to reengage in that way. I welcomed the return to silence that last night. On the ride to the airport the next day with two friends, though, I felt we could go into our experience deeply, slowly, without interruption. It felt satisfying to try to put the week into words and share that with one another. I said that it had felt as though some part of my mind that usually connects with others had, by the middle to end of the week, turned its focus onto the only person available: me. As I described my experience, I could feel that they were attuning to me in a way that I'd felt I was attuning to myself during the week. My science mind imagined it was the involvement of the social circuitry of the brain that enables us to resonate with one another that had now become focused on my self. That resonance of internal and interpersonal attunement felt deeply gratifying.

Chapter Four

SUFFERING AND THE
STREAMS OF AWARENESS

One hundred fifty of us, mostly clinicians, were at the Mount Madonna center in the mountains overlooking Monterey Bay in Northern California, to learn from Jon Kabat-Zinn and Saki Santorelli the "Mindfulness-Based Stress Reduction" (MBSR) approach they had been practicing for over 25 years (Kabat-Zinn, 1990; Santorelli, 1999). A number of studies have revealed the findings we've reviewed earlier of improved immune, cardiac, psychological, and interpersonal functioning that are associated with mindful practices (Davidson et al., 2003; Kabat-Zinn, 2003). This is my intensive immersion in mindfulness: two week-long retreats in one month. The retreat of the silent scientists was an immersion in a classical insight meditation experience. Waking early, sitting, walking, sitting, walking—these were done in silence, without any interactions with others.

This week is more of a practicum where we are able to speak with one another for most of the week—except for 36 hours beginning tomorrow morning. These words you are reading now are emanating from a left hemisphere that knows it is about to be forced into dormancy for the next day and a half. Besides not being able to talk, we are discouraged from writing and reading, and even from interacting with each other during that time.

68

Rumi's poem, "The Guest House," is hung on the wall as a beautiful articulation of the sense emerging for me of the heart of mindfulness as these days unfold. The poem begins with the phrase "This being human is a guest house" and urges us to invite all unexpected visitors into our home and welcome and entertain them all. Each morning I read his words and travel down the path past deer and pine to the meeting hall. We meet many guests, inside and out, along this journey we call life.

On the silent retreat we've discussed the vision of YODA's SOCK: the idea that "*you observe to decouple automaticity*"—that observing enables you to distance yourself enough such that you can meet any mental process at the door of your mind "laughingly." The sock is a balance of *sensation*, *observation*, and *conceptualization* that leads to a mindful sense of nonconceptual *knowing*. (Figure 4.1).

If we fight the emergence of mental processes we can engage in a massive internal battle that creates mental suffering. This is the irony of mindful awareness: It is at its core full of acceptance. Without actively attempting to achieve an outcome, it releases us from suffering. Here are some examples to illustrate this fundamental idea.

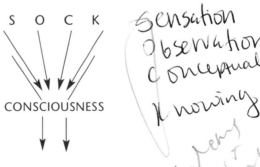

Figure 4.1 The four streams of awareness.

BALANCING ON ONE FOOT

We had a series of exercises that revealed how important mindful awareness can be. I was standing near the center of the room for the yoga exercises. Our teacher gave us instructions to balance on one foot. Standing just beside him, I tried to mirror his actions—but found it very difficult to keep balanced. I felt odd and surprised, given that the day before I had actually done the same exercise on my own during a lecture when I needed to stretch, and held the pose for a long time. What was the difference?

In the mirroring experience, I was focused on creating his movements, the angle of his arm, the height of his lifted leg, even the direction of his head. While this worked for him, it was a secondary "top-down" driven process in which I was not attuned to my own primary needs for balance. The day before, attunement with myself was more directly achieved because there was no one else performing the same balancing act for me to imitate. Today by absorbing his bodily movements I was not attuned to myself. Trying to match him dominated the capacity to perceive my own balance. Here we see that even a perception can serve as a top-down impediment to attuning to ourselves.

It is this imbalance that seems to keep us alienated from ourselves, distant from our own mind. Top-down influences on our perceptual channels twist our capacity to read our own cues. In this case, my awareness needed to "fall into" the domain of sensation for me to achieve internal attunement. All four streams seem to influence our ability to be fully in the moment. Sometimes we need to remember to invite ourselves in, completely, to the guest house of our own mind.

STREAMS OF AWARENESS

As I walked the pebble path I felt the rocks beneath my shoeless feet. In my awareness were the sensations of the stones, the pressure on the soles of my feet, the lifting of my leg, its movement, and then the placement of my foot down again on the pebbles. Here my receptive awareness was taking in the domain of the sixth sense of my bodily sensations and the five senses of the surrounding sounds, sights, smells, and touch.

As I lifted my foot and felt it move through space, I was also aware of the imminent feeling of my foot about-to-be-placed. I stepped forward again and this sensation became more distinct. I could almost feel the pebbles *before* I put my foot down. I had the concept of mirror neurons in my head. I heard the thought, "Oh, this sensation of the pebbles before you step is some awareness of a memory for the future, your mind preparing for next, the perception of this intentional act." So I was both sensing intention and conceptualizing intention. I also observed myself matching a concept with a sensation and "noticed" the process through this observing witness—so I was also observing intention. With all of this going on, a feeling of this awareness was of a sense of knowing, some vague sense of being grounded. But the sensation felt clear. The observation felt distinct. The conceptualizing had its own texture and feel. Even the knowing felt like an emergent process that flowed from the intertwining of the three streams, and perhaps became its own. I sensed, observed, conceived, and knew all within awareness.

Here I sensed a clarity emerging that mindfulness had a "bare" or immediate quality that was not restricted to the physical sensations of the first six senses. This receptive awareness had the spacious quality of being "grateful for whoever comes" and invited them in with openness and laughter. I felt this sense that the observer stream sometimes supplanted receptive awareness, and made life feel detached and unreal, unlived. At other times, conceptualization may make drinking water an idea, and I never really felt the cool liquid flow across my lips and over my tongue, though indeed I was drinking. I imagine there are people who also have a surplus of sensations fill their lives and block out observation and concepts—but this just has never been my fate, though it seems from the outside to be a rewarding imbalance by which to be plagued, at least at times.

And this is the "rub": balance is not the same as simultaneity. Every unexpected visitor does not need to stay in the guest house at the same time. New arrivals come each morning, even forming a crowd. But to treat each guest honorably we need to cultivate this receptive awareness—the spaciousness of our mind—that welcomes them all in their own time.

Immediate experience gives a sense of recognition and familiarity. This "direct experience" can involve the four domains of sensation, observation, conceptualization, and knowing. This may seem strange to you, as it does to me even as I write it. But we can apply each of these streams to have awareness of the other: I can sense knowing, I can know sensing. Perhaps knowing is the outcome of the balance of the first three, and we will explore this possibility as we move along.

What I do recall at this moment is what a battle it was to try to "just" focus on one stream or another back on the silent retreat earlier in the month. This same month? So many moments ago, a month, yet just this one moment is now, and now is just this moment. The mind does change. I couldn't just sense, or just observe: They fought for some kind of attention, like young kids welcoming you home, jumping on your lap to tell you about their day. These streams of awareness seemed to flow fully and freely together when I could enter that receptive state of welcoming them all, in whatever form they came.

SILENCE AND SURPRISE

Why silence? Silence creates a rare opportunity to pause and drop into stillness, to become intimate with your own mind. So often we have things to do, places to be, people to see. In our busy lives our minds are full and reactive. When we start the journey to attune to our own minds by pausing into stillness we enter a new realm of experience that can produce surprise in each moment.

what mindfulness looks like?

One surprise is that the mind is never "empty." It is an oft stated and apparent misconception that the meditative mind becomes a vacuum of activity. Filled with continually generated images and thoughts, feelings and perceptions, the mind is abuzz with activity that never ceases. The mind is a busy bee flitting around its neural hive. Some approach silence thinking that their minds will soon be empty only to find just the opposite to be true. Living next to a beehive of activity is not easy to do. It's even harder to step into it directly.

As the stillness permits the mind to "settle," it becomes possible to be aware of the subtleties in the fine structures of the mind's functions. Stillness is not the same as a void in activity, it's more like a stabilizing strength.

Another surprise is to experience the transient ever-changing nature of the activity of the mind. When busy in the chatter of daily life, our thoughts and feelings can take on an air of solidity and permanence that hides their true effervescent nature. With stillness it becomes possible to peel away this surface solidity to reveal the cloudlike vaporous quality of mental activity.

Surprises are at every corner. Yet another surprise is the ways in which distinct streams of awareness intermix to create the texture of awareness in the moment. The terms *quality of awareness* or *nature of awareness* reveal that awareness itself changes from moment to moment. In my own experience, the directness and clarity of awareness seem to come with a kind of coalescence process in which (I imagine) neural firing clusters appear to resonate with each other to create reverberant loops of reinforcing circuitries. As these loops' reentrant properties literally hum to their mutually created frequencies, it feels as if their self-reinforcement may create a substantial "force" that pushes its way into whatever the neural "conditions" of awareness are. Conditions here do not imply a location, but a function created by the activations themselves. In this manner a clear, direct sensation of awareness can exist for a sensation, observation, thought, or knowingness. But what of awareness itself?

If we state that the quality of awareness in this moment is murky, how are we aware of awareness? Can we have a clear awareness of a murky quality of awareness? Metaprocesses like these, like meta-awareness, give rise to the name of our species, *Homo sapiens, sapiens:* The knowing, knowing ones. We know that we know (Kabat-Zinn, 2003b).

THE RIVER OF CONSCIOUSNESS

Many studies point to the power of mindful awareness to promote well-being in many domains of our lives. Why would this be the case? Why would "nonjudgmental" paying attention, on purpose in the present moment be a good thing? We have seen that nonjudgmental may mean not grasping onto the inevitable judgments that the mind creates from the top-down process of our cortical critics. The decoupling of this automaticity is in many ways what "waking up" to have the time of your life really means.

A visual image of mindful awareness can be one of the hub of a wheel of our mind being open and spacious enough to enable any elements of the rim of the wheel to enter our conscious experience but *not* take it over (Figure 4.2). Any element of the rim

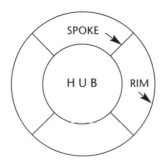

Figure 4.2 The wheel of awareness: rim, spokes, and hub.

can be experienced directly (direct sensory experience of one of the basic senses), observed, conceptualized, and then known. And so the four streams of awareness that feed the river of consciousness into the hub of our minds enable us to have the reflective awareness of something—an emotional reaction, a memory (seventh sense), a tightness in our belly, heaviness in our chest (sixth sense), or a sight, sound, taste, touch, or smell (five senses). We might even have a sense of connection, to ourselves, to others, in a kind of eighth sense, that enables a relational perception.

In many ways it is the filtering of the rims' points (the full seven or possibly eight senses) through the lenses of these streams (sensation, observation, conceptualization, knowing) that then flows into our direct consciousness and makes us fully aware of what we are experiencing. Sometimes this awareness is dominated by one part of the first three: sensation, observation, and conceptualization. At other times this awareness is in a state of balance and then knowing seems to emerge. And so perhaps the balancing of the quartet as they filter data into the receptive hubs of our minds is in fact what shapes the nature of the "quality of awareness" (Figure 4.3).

When we exert the body, the sensation of the sixth sense may become dominant. In that moment, awareness is filled with the somatic input, the wash of bodily sensations, and devoid of linguistic

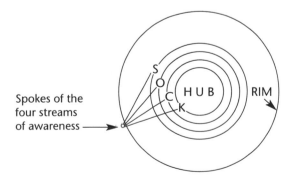

Figure 4.3 The four streams of awareness filtering the flow into the hub of the mind: *s*ensation, *o*bservation, *c*oncept, and *k*nowing.

bounding. If we immerse ourselves in the sensation of a sight we can become lost in the visual beauty and not realize the concept behind what we are seeing. On the other hand, visual input may be easily conceptualized, and our busy cortical pattern detectors may be comparing what we see now with what we've seen dozens of times before. Such a cross-matching process may make it difficult to just see the tree "as it is." Likewise, our left-hemisphere cortical matchmaker will try to connect linguistic representations with visual inputs and categorize and name what we see. This classification process also removes us from the direct sensation of the first five senses. We can still "sense" the thought, but it feels different from sensing the tree. Here concepts dominate the streams flowing into consciousness and the "tree" becomes more category than sensation.

Mindful awareness seems to require a balance of these streams of awareness. Some views may emphasize sensation, but my own direct experience at this point raises the possible importance of all four streams contributing to the clarity and stability of mindfulness.

SELF AND SUFFERING

A question was raised about the "where" of bare awareness. One comment was that it didn't matter *where*, it most mattered *what* the experience was like for the individual. This focus on our subjective experience is important and reminds us that even in postulating the nature of "the mindful brain" we have to be careful not to reify science, neurobiology, or any other scientific discipline.

Knowing about the brain, though, can help us clarify some of these introspective observations and sensations so that the conceptualizations we create are at least consistent with various branches of science. This does not make science better than subjectivity, just different.

Here is a brief summary of the general idea of stress and suffering and their reduction with mindful awareness practices. It is filtered through the interpersonal neurobiology lens in my head, so far as I can tell from direct experience and the existing literature. When the mind grasps onto preconceived ideas it creates a tension within the mind between what is and what "should be." This tension creates stress and leads to suffering.

The role of mindful awareness is to enable the mind to "discern" the nature of the mind itself, awakening the person to the insights that preconceived ideas and emotional reactions are embedded in thinking and reflexive responses that create internal distress. With such disidentification of thoughts and emotions, by realizing that these mental activities are not the same as "self," nor are they permanent, the individual can then enable them to arise and burst like bubbles in a pot of boiling water.

What remains is the essence of sensation, not the menace of imprisoning conceptualization. Not all thinking and habitual emotional reactions are top-down mental events, by any means, but in this model it is these that will create adventitious suffering. Life is full of suffering. There is universal suffering in which we all experience the pain of loss, disappointment, death. But adventitious suffering is the term used for how our minds create our own mental anguish by grasping onto conceptualizations and automatic reactions that pull us out of direct sensory experience. In many ways the quality of our awareness is dulled when we live only in our thoughts and previously sculpted emotions, our concepts and perceptual filters that organize our worldview. But in addition to enlivening our existence, becoming awake to our senses brings us directly into the nature of ongoing moment-to-moment experiences. Thoughts and emotions are fine so long as they do not destroy the capacity for sensory awareness. The idea, I have come to learn, is balance not dictatorship.

And so one role of the senses in our daily lives is to wake us up, to pull us away from automaticity, to sharpen the acuity of awareness so that life is both richer and more present in the moment.

The result of such an awakening is to free the entire being to become more receptive to things as they are. Attunement in the domains of the external world (first five senses), the somatic world (sixth sense), and the mental world of self and others (seventh sense) brings with it a reverberant quality that is both coherent and stabilizing. Attunement means sensing things just as they are within awareness. Our "lived" self resonates in a direct, clear manner with our "awarenessing" self and we "feel felt" by our own mind. We feel this coherent state of attunement within our eighth relational sense.

The flexible, adaptive, coherent, energized, and stable (FACES) flow of mental well-being can be seen to appear as integrated systems emerge across time. *FACES* is the term we can use to refer to this integrated state, a state that may underlie well-being.

Attunement is the process by which separate elements are brought into a resonating whole. Within awareness when we approach things as they are, with COAL as our state of mind, we become internally attuned. This reverberant state enables the self to achieve a FACES flow, embracing whatever arises. Attunement emerges as integration is created.

With moment-to-moment awareness that does not grasp onto judgments, we have the formula for internal attunement across the physical, somatic, and mental domains of reality. This intrapersonal attunement is a reverberant FACES state that illuminates awareness and stabilizes the elements in the focus of our spotlight of attention. Life becomes more vibrant and clear. Mindful awareness feels good, and is good for the whole being and his or her relationships with the world and with others.

As our reflective awareness sheds top-town biasing, the three streams of sensation, observation, and conceptualization blend with the deeper stream of knowing as we are free to flow into our balanced river of consciousness. Disidentification with the objects of attention as the defining features of who we are is created and gives rise to an emerging sense of mindful knowing. This observer-made capacity for discernment is what distinguishes mindful awareness from the notion of "flow" in which we are non-self-consciously immersed in the sensations of an experience (Csikszentmihalyi, 1990). In flow we lose ourselves as immersion in sensation or thought can "carry us away" and we become lost in the automaticity of that stream. At times that may be a good thing, as when we eat, make love, go for a walk, or ponder a problem. But in daily life keeping all four streams in balance may be at the heart of mindful living. In our clinical work with suffering there may be a need to amplify the observer capacity to decouple automaticity (YODA) to begin the process.

Focusing on a pain in a limb, for example, can help to move ourselves toward sensation over a preconceived idea (like "I should have no pain"). But without a robust observer, the pain may remain intense even with the diminishment of the thought. Sensation by itself may give no relief. Mindful awareness of sensation can make all the difference: With a focus on the pain and the activation of an observer, the quality of awareness of the receptive hub can acknowledge the transient and perhaps inevitable nature of the pain itself. Even the thought of "I should be pain-free" can be examined and burst like a bubble over a bath.

Stress and suffering emerge throughout life. With mindful awareness a new possibility is created to reformulate the suffering while not avoiding the sensory experience. Nothing is intentionally blocked; rather all guests are welcome. When a preconceived thought shows up at the door, it can be seen, observed, thought, and known for what it is. In this state of awareness at this moment of writing, all four streams seem to contribute to the texture of awareness, to that receptive hub at the center of our minds.

PRESENT PARTICIPLES

Our silence during this retreat was only 36 hours: I kept on reminding myself not to compare, not to think much about the retreat earlier this month. But the learning from that time shaped my experience—YODA's SOCK kept on filtering through my momentary awareness and I couldn't fight it, I just let it be. I tried to say "not now" but it didn't seem to do much good. So I tried to let the thoughts just be.

The first morning of silence we sat together for what seemed to be a brief 45 minutes. I entered some quality of awareness where not only time seemed to disappear, but the sense of my connection to my body and sensations from the outside world—sounds, light through my closed eyes—all seemed detached, floating as if suspended, weightless, not belonging to anything or anyone in particular. The bells were rung and the announcement was made that it was time to do walking meditation. I couldn't move, or didn't move. I worried about others thinking that I was being arrogant by not obeying directions, but sensed that they'd know somehow that I was in some sort of "choiceless awareness" where my sense of self as usually in awareness now was gone, melted away, unimportant, nonpresent. I noted the worry about envy, and as a teacher had suggested in the earlier retreat, I just noted it gently as "envy thought number one" and it floated somewhere in the distance, not quite gone, but not so important.

I observed this sensation of no "I" in the sensation. I know that sounds strange, and perhaps the whole thing sounds bizarre as I think it would seem to "me" before I had ever experienced this way back after I was dragged by a horse in Mexico nearly 30 years ago now, when I lost my identity, if only for a day, and became more immersed in some other way of knowing beneath the usual top-down sense of "me." For a day I experienced "transient global amnesia" which felt like this: sensations full, identity gone. The identity returned, but I never forgot how "light" our identities really are. A day of intense sensations without the top-down frame of personal identity changed my sense of perspective.

But this was a bit different in texture where even the sensations had no "I" attached to them. In Mexico, I had a feeling of "I" but just in the present, nothing from before seemed available during that day. Now, here, this sense was that things happening were just present participles, sounding, sitting, breathing, awarenessing. I sat through the return of the others from the walking, aware of envy worry number two, noted and dispersed. We sat for another period and when the bells were rung a few seconds later another 30 minutes had passed. I was sitting for over an hour and half without moving an inch. Yet I had moved to the sense of infinity.

SELFLESS AWARENESS

In the retreat they called this state of no "I" a form of choiceless awareness. It felt in my experience more like a selfless awareness in which experiences were all happenings, those present participle verbs that Jon Kabat-Zinn talks about that were just going on, happening, being, emerging. "This being human" felt in this space indeed like a guest house where I could invite all to arise as they would, all welcome, each with its own wondrous texture, even the worries.

After the sitting and breakfast, I found myself for the remainder of the day being aware of thoughts, of constructed concepts and logical forays, into the difference between the observer stream and this selfless or choiceless awareness. I played with the wheel of awareness, trying on different forms in which the hub was created by concentric circles of sensation, observation, construction, and perhaps this nonconceptual knowing to encircle the hub of the mind, our reflective state of mindful awareness (see Figure 4.3). Was the receptive dimension of mindful awareness the same as selfless awareness? Was the choicelessness actually an active form of being receptive? With the lens of observation did the distance of observer and observation permit this spacious freedom from which choice and decoupling from automaticity could occur? What a bunch of conceptual thinking!

The brain aspects of this whole framework were drawn as pictures in my head, not just words but visual images. My left and right cortices were having a heyday. I could see the middle prefrontal regions blocking top-down flow to choose to focus on sensations. This felt like the way I could wander upstream in the valley of the present moment from the river of consciousness to step into the headwater stream of sensation (see Figure 4.1).

I could also dip into the constructed conceptual stream, aware of the thoughts and images that were my internal dialogue and visual artistry, exploring the extrapolated representational world. This stream could be sensed directly, feeling the seventh sense, but it has a different quality of awareness, a different texture, one that feels very much real but wildly interlaced and full of associations just over the rim of the valley's wall.

A step back from the streams of sensation and constructive concepts and there I'd find myself observing, taking the stance of a narrator of the moment. I thought of a young adolescent patient I am treating, using mindful awareness practices, who is so far able to significantly diminish depressive symptoms and avoid medications. Is this the growth of his observer function or his selfless awareness? It felt, in my own observer stream, to be this powerful form of distancing and self-observation rather than a form of awareness that lacks a sense of self. Discussing this later with our teacher, it seemed to him as well that developing the observer or witness form of awareness is indeed a major source of relief for people with mood disorders who learn mindfulness training. The Mindfulness Based Cognitive Therapy (MBCT) approach uses this with great efficacy to prevent relapse in people with chronic depression (Segal, Williams, & Teasdale, 2002).

Somehow that was reassuring: encouraging observation seems a lot more straightforward than helping the average newcomer to this mindful awareness world to entertain embracing selfless sensation. That's just a bit much to ask people to do, or to even think about conceptually, at least at the beginning. "Would you like to jump into an experience where your defining sense of self is transformed?" Probably not.

Back into silence, I found myself relishing the intimacy with my own mind. I know this has only been my second retreat, but I could feel the allure of having time to really get to know one's self.

TIME TO ATTUNE

A fascinating change emerged. This time the observer could deepen that awareness without fighting with direct sensation as had plagued me on the first retreat. This seemed to be growth. As the day went on, in the evening meditations I gave myself permission to have fun: I thought, I felt, I let myself welcome whatever came, as I explored my mind. I started with my body. I noted heaviness in my chest and elected to follow that with inquisitiveness, energy, and curiosity. I wanted to be open to whatever would arise and took on the other trio of concentration, tranquility, and equanimity as my guiding principles. These are the last three of the seven elements of an awakening mind taught to us in the first retreat that also include these first four: mindfulness, investigation, energy, and rapture at discovery.

I let the heaviness in my chest be felt directly, not just through the O of being observed. I dipped into the stream of sensation and found my face feeling heavy. Tears began to form in my eyes, and suddenly, or perhaps gradually but with a tinge of timelessness it was hard to tell the speed, I felt a bellyache. Then I began to sob. I let the sobbing be present, observing it, feeling it, and being curious about it. I sifted my mind, building on the sensations to explore images, feelings, and thoughts. An image of my mother came to mind, and a feeling of both fear and sadness. The thought of her impending surgery next week, the feelings of her as a mother when I was a child, and the possible complications of her operation were thoughts in my mind as the sobbing turned to a stare out in space.

I followed the idea of my mother and put into the front of my mind the intention to go deeply into what this meant for me at this time. An image of a proof sheet of snapshots of my mother and me came into the foreground. I began to sob even more. All the closeness, all the distance, the troubles and the sorrows, and now, as an adult, the longings from the past that remained, these filled my sense of K, my knowing nonconceptually. I just felt them, and knew them—not as sensations alone, but as some amalgam of sense, observation, and thought all stripped of their representational origins and just a clear way of knowing an essence inside me. I told myself I had to be ready to say goodbye to her if there were complications in the surgery, so I made the conceptual decision to see her before that day, and to be present with my father during the operation.

As the walking continued the sobbing subsided, my body felt light, the heaviness in the chest giving rise to a lightness of being, a depth of breath, a freedom in my belly. I would approach this period awake, ready to be present fully for whatever arises.

I don't know how selfless awareness relates to nonconceptual knowing. They feel different: here I "knew" about the overall notion of my mother and love's grief, the sadness of life and of death. But look at this sentence with "I 'knew'" right there. In the choiceless state of selfless awareness, the feeling is distinct. There is a deeply peaceful passive state of floating in which awarenessing is as clouds in the sky, in and out of existence without an anchor. In nonconceptual knowing there is clearly an "I" that knows. And here's the notion: all of these are "real." There is no "better" in losing one's sense of self, of shirking identity and ego, than having a locus of "I," that localized package that creates the me and mine. All are good, each in balance.

And so at that moment I was left with a delicious sense of the four streams of awareness that fed the river of consciousness. Each of these four perhaps encircles the hub of the wheel of awareness, filtering and channeling our experience of now (see Figure 4.2). Even in pure receptivity I imagine we can feel any of the four streams as being predominant. And in those occasions where it becomes clear, even a receptivity that lacks a self is in fact a part of our experience. Knower, knowing, and known become one in that "transpirational" state: We breathe life across all the dimensions, integrating a deep sensation of the interconnection of everything. This sense of belonging remains in the background of potentials, informing the lightness of our being, the "fluffiness" of the clouds we call "self" experience. We don't have to take our bodily defined self so seriously, but we can take it all in, moment by sweet moment.

SEVENTY-FIVE WHISPERS

After emerging from 36 hours of silence, we began with a partner with whom we told our experiences. I started with "I am Dan" and she said "My name is Barbara," and thus we began our return to the personal identity world. Seventy-five of us whispered at once, half of each dyad relating their stories in words, doing whatever we could to translate the nonverbal world into these limited packets of linguistic guests.

That morning we did a number of group exercises that somehow related to this whole discussion, embodying the mind's awareness. First we walked, all 150 of us, quickly in random motions. It was amazing to find how we did not collide. The spaces between shaped our experience, like the spaces between the notes of music making the difference between jazz and rock, classical and schlock. The next exercise was to walk slowly backwards, each time we'd touch another person we'd lean into them for a brief moment and move on. Much like our discursive narrative thoughts in the first experience, here too was a sense of the collision of streams of awareness. Finally we faced outward with our backs toward the geometric center and then all slowly walked backwards into the room. At the end, of course, we were crowded into the center like a beehive leaning in, surrounded, no where to be but there. I felt saddened when we had to break apart, realizing the connectedness to each other and the ways we learn to live as separate entities. The optical delusion of our separateness, as Einstein aptly referred to it. This delusion felt melted away here, and I longed for the reality of our wholeness.

PART III

FACETS OF THE
MINDFUL BRAIN

Chapter Five

SUBJECTIVITY
AND SCIENCE

We turn now to a different way of knowing: The third person data of "objective" science. We have been exploring the direct experience of one person's inner mind, and now we will deepen our understanding by integrating these first-person accounts with various fields of science (third-person accounts), especially the study of the brain.

The reason to add in such an experience-distant set of concepts is that we will be able to see important patterns across large numbers of individuals. These are insights that would not be revealed if one or two people share stories of their experience. Science broadens our vision; it does not replace the power of personal narratives and accounts of experiential knowing.

Roger Walsh's important contributions (1980; Walsh & Shapiro, 2006) suggest that "consciousness disciplines," such as meditation, offer an opportunity to expand our ways of knowing by practical experience that offers new knowledge over intellectual understanding. This disciplined way of focusing on our experience recognizes that there are many subtle variations in consciousness that can be both the object of introspective exploration and greatly expanded through extensive training. Consciousness disciplines acknowledge the limitations of language and abstract thinking and ground ways of knowing in direct personal experience.

In this chapter we will delve into the scientific views of how we experience mindfulness, create a sense of self, and experience time.

SURVEYS OF SUBJECTIVITY

We will now approach science and subjectivity by reviewing a study which put together five independently assembled questionnaires aimed at assessing the subjective experience of mindfulness (Baer et al., 2006). The authors noted that this method offered a way of sensing how researchers broadly conceptualize mindfulness and then enabled them to examine whether there was one central dimension or many facets of mindfulness itself. By pooling the assessment measures together and then giving them at various times to a large sample of subjects (college students), the researchers could address these questions and detect overall patterns of response.

The available questionnaires used were the Mindful Attention Awareness Scale (MAAS: Brown & Ryan, 2003); the Freiburg Mindfulness Inventory (FMI: Buchheld, Grossman, & Wallach, 2001); the Kentucky Inventory of Mindfulness Skills (KIMS: Baer, Smith, & Allen, 2004); the Cognitive and Affective Mindfulness Scale (CAMS: Feldman, Hayes, Kumar, & Greeson, 2004; Hayes & Feldman, 2004); and the Mindfulness Questionnaire (MQ: Chadwick, Hember, Mead, Lilley, & Dagnan, 2005). Each of these surveys has a particular focus, but in general they are each teasing out various aspects of mindfulness from the subject's direct experience.

The detailed approach of Baer and colleagues is an instructive lesson in statistics and assessment and yields a blend of wisdom and astute observation from all of the researchers who developed the individual surveys. The pooled questions were given to subjects in the study and then correlated with other measurements of such dimensions as personality, emotional intelligence, and self-compassion. The conclusions from this pooled assessment in-cluded the following findings.

The predicted correlations among various clustered questions were assembled and five general "facets" or dimensions of mind-fulness were attained. As summarized earlier in the introduction, these included: (1) nonreactivity to inner experience; (2) observing/ noticing/attending to sensations/perceptions/thoughts/feelings; (3) acting with awareness/(non)automatic pilot/concentration/ nondistraction; (4) describing/labeling with words; and (5) non-judging of experience.

Next Baer et al. explored whether these facets were a part of one dimension or actually revealed fairly independent aspects of mindfulness. Statistical sorting and reasoning suggested that mind-fulness is actually composed of multiple facets with somewhat dis-tinct characteristics, with some overlap but quite a lot of inde-pendence, at least in how subjects responded to the questions themselves. One factor, observing, was found in various statistical ways to overlap too much with the others and did not stand out on its own as a separate facet. In this view they came up with a "four-factor hierarchical model" which supported "a hierarchical structure to mindfulness, in which describe, actaware, nonjudge, and nonreact can be considered facets of a broad mindfulness con-struct" (Baer et al., 2006, p. 38).

Interestingly the observe facet was found to be statistically valid as an independent dimension in those subjects with experience of meditation. "Therefore we tested this model in those participants with some degree of meditation experience (n = 190) and found that all five facets loaded significantly on the overall mindfulness construct." This suggested to them "the plausibility of a hierar-chical, five-factor structure to mindfulness among individuals with meditation experience" (Baer et al., 2006, p. 38). More study was suggested to compare this four- and five-facet structure with larger and more diverse subjects.

Correlations of these facets with other measures revealed that the facets seemed to connect with predicted dimensions. For example, act with awareness (the "actaware" facet) was inversely correlated with absent-mindedness and dissociation; "describe" was positively associated with emotional intelligence and negatively with alexithymia (the inability to describe one's internal state); and "nonjudge" was most robustly associated with low psychological symptoms, neuroticism, thought suppression, difficulties with emotion regulation, and experiential avoidance. Interestingly, "nonreact" was most associated with self-compassion and "observe" correlated with openness to experience.

The issue of observe as a facet not panning out for nonmeditators may be, in the view of Baer et al., in part because the act of observing in an untrained mind may be equally fraught with self-condemnation as relief. In other words just being able to observe your internal world without the other facets of mindfulness may not yield the predicted correlations.

Here is a summary of their conclusions, which gives a feeling for this way of thinking: "CFA (Confirmatory Factor Analysis) suggested describe, act with awareness, nonjudge, and nonreact are elements of an overarching mindfulness construct, and three of these factors (act with awareness, nonjudge, and nonreact) were shown to have incremental validity in the prediction of psychological symptoms" (Baer et al., 2006, p. 42). In other words, these three facets were the best predictors overall of lack of symptoms of suffering.

Baer and colleagues found the questions from the original surveys that were most helpful in exploring aspects of mindfulness and sorted these into a set of queries that could tease out these five aspects of mindfulness. What emerged from this analysis was a five facet mindfulness questionnaire to which people responded with a range from never or very rarely to very often or always true. The following is a sampling of these questions as derived from the five-facet questionnaire assembled by Baer and colleagues (adapted from Table 3, 2006; original questionnaire abbreviations appear in parentheses following questions).

Nonreactivity to Inner Experience

"I perceive my feelings and emotions without having to react to them."

"I watch my feelings without getting lost in them."

"In difficult situations, I can pause without immediately reacting." (FMI)

"Usually when I have distressing thoughts or images. . . ."

. . . I am able just to notice them without reacting. . . .

. . . I feel calm soon after. . . .

. . . I step back, and am aware of the thought or image without getting taken over by it. . . .

. . . I just notice them and let them go." (MQ)

Observing/Noticing/Attending to Sensations, Perceptions, Thoughts, Feelings

"When I'm walking, I deliberately notice the sensations of my body moving."

"When I take a shower or a bath, I stay alert to the sensations of water on my body."

"I notice how foods and drinks affect my thoughts, bodily sensations, and emotions."

"I pay attention to sensations, such as the wind in my hair or sun on my face."

"I pay attention to sounds, such as clocks ticking, birds chirping, or cars passing."

"I notice the smells and aromas of things."

"I intentionally stay aware of my feelings."

"I notice visual elements in art or nature, such as colors, shapes, textures, or patterns of light and shadow."

"I pay attention to how my emotions affect my thoughts and behavior." (KIMS)

Acting with Awareness/Automatic Pilot/ Concentration/Nondistraction

"I find it difficult to stay focused on what's happening in the present."

"It seems I am 'running on automatic' without much awareness of what I'm doing."

"I rush through activities without being attentive to them."

"I do jobs or tasks automatically without being aware of what I'm doing."

"I find myself doing things without paying attention." (MAAS)

"When I do things, my mind wanders off and I'm easily distracted."

"I don't pay attention to what I'm doing, because I'm day-dreaming, worrying or otherwise distracted." (KIMS)

"I am easily distracted." (CAMS)

Describing/Labeling with Words

"I'm good at finding the words to describe my feelings."

"I can easily put my beliefs, opinions, and expectations into words."

"It's hard for me to find the words to describe what I'm thinking."

"I have trouble thinking of the right words to express how I feel about things."

"When I have a sensation in my body, it's hard for me to describe it because I can't find the right words."

"Even when I'm feeling terribly upset, I can find a way to put it into words."

"My natural tendency is to put my experience into words." (KIMS)

"I can usually describe how I feel at the moment in considerable detail." (CAMS)

Nonjudging of Experience

"I criticize myself for having irrational or inappropriate emotions."

"I tell myself that I shouldn't be feeling the way I'm feeling."

"I believe some of my thoughts are abnormal or bad and I shouldn't think that way."

"I make judgments about whether my thoughts are good or bad."

"I tell myself I shouldn't be thinking the way I'm thinking."

"I think some of my emotions are bad or inappropriate and I shouldn't feel them."

"I disapprove of myself when I have irrational ideas." (KIMS)

"Usually when I have distressing thoughts or images, I judge myself as good or bad, depending what the thought/image is about." (MQ).

CORRELATING DESCRIPTIONS OF DIRECT EXPERIENCE AND STUDIES OF THE BRAIN

If we are to embrace the nonreducible dimensions of our mental reality, it is of great importance, from the view of neurophenomenology (Varela, Thompson, & Rosch, 1993), to integrate the insights gleaned from second-person accounts of direct experience within these surveys of mindfulness, with the direct experiences from the first-person perspective and the findings of third-person neuroscience.

Our assumptions should be expressed directly; those conceptual top-down cortical influences that shape how we filter input and bias our interpretations of our perceptions can be known and identified to an extent so as to bring ourselves to as clear a vision as possible. We have human minds dancing with our human brains within our social experiences of the shared construction of human culture. Meaning is not some pure invention—we must be humble about the ways in which we sort, select, and sequence symbols into shared systems of knowing. This is the inevitable way we come to know the world through concepts. As we have seen, there is also the direct experience of nonconceptual knowing—but that is a realm of understanding difficult to express in words from one person to another. And taken with its limitations, conceptual maps of the mind can actually be quite useful: Truthful ideas can help us sort through difficult times, alleviate suffering, and promote well-being and compassion. There is no need to throw concepts away, but rather to embrace them for what they truly are—frameworks for knowing.

MINDFULNESS AS A LEARNABLE SKILL

Each of us has a mind with great potential. We have the possibility of creating a world of compassion and well-being and we have the capacity for mindless violence and destruction. A new and second powerful lesson has been in the profound plasticity of the human brain. We can actually focus our minds in a way that changes the structure and function of the brain throughout our lives. As a mindset, being aware of the present moment without grasping onto judgments offers a powerful path toward both compassion and inner well-being. This is what science verifies and what has been taught over thousands of years of practice.

But what is this "practice" that is revealed in the contemplative traditions from around the world? Christian Centering Prayer, yogic practices, tai'chi chuan, and Buddhist forms of meditation have each been studied in recent years, and they appear to harness neurologic and immune improvements in the practitioners' lives. For example, see Field, Fitzpatrick-Hopler, and Spezio's (2006) and Irwin's (2005) studies, and Walsh and Shapiro's (2006) review.

Over 140 scientists from around the world gathered at the Mind and Life Summer Research Institute, held at the Garrison Institute in upstate New York. The program consisted of presentations on meditation of various sorts, with explorations by practitioners, philosophers, psychologists, and neuroscientists. I would hold "office hours" to meet with junior and senior scientists and discuss their research interests and also teach on panels with topics such as mindfulness in clinical work, the treatment of children, emotion regulation, and spirituality. Here I'd like to just highlight some of the exciting ideas that emerged.

In addition to the lectures and discussions, we had extensive readings which delved into the nature of attention, emotion, memory, meditation, prayer, and mindfulness. Three of the scholars there had distributed a paper that provided the most current overview of issues related to the science of training the mind: "Meditation and the Neuroscience of Consciousness" (Lutz, Dunne, & Davidson, in press). Meditation is the training of the mind. For our focus here, we are particularly interested in mindfulness meditation. But there are many forms of mental training that create mindful states that seem to move an individual toward mindful traits. Attentional processes, emotion regulation, and the capacity to observe internally, to introspect and reflect, are all considered trainable skills. Lutz and colleagues (2004) state: "We have already shown that even very brief short-term training in emotion regulation can produce reliable alterations in brain function." In looking specifically at the clinical application of mindfulness meditation training in the Mindfulness-Based Stress Reduction (MBSR) approach, Lutz, Dunne, & Davidson (in press) suggest that:

> The program seems to work by helping the patient to distinguish primary sensory experience (e.g. chronic pain, physical symptoms of anxiety) from the secondary emotional or cognitive processes created in reaction to the primary experience. Individuals are trained to use the mindfulness practice to interrogate the details of their experience and to directly perceive the unstable and contingent nature of the feelings and sensations that are associated with aversion and withdrawal; as a result, individuals are better able to counter any propensity toward withdrawal and aversion in response

to physical or psychological pain. From a neuroscientific perspective, the apparent effectiveness of MBSR practice raises the question of neuroplasticity—that is, does it produce alterations in brain function and structure?

Lutz, Dunne, and Davidson's view of where we are in our search to understand the neural correlates of meditation suggests that, "Despite such a high number of scientific reports and inspiring theoretical proposals . . . one still needs to admit that little is known about the neurophysiological processes involved in meditation and about its possible long-term impact on the brain."

There are universals in meditation, such as a focus on breath awareness. But this initially shared focus then gives rise to other dimensions of cultivating the mind that vary from practice to practice. Mindfulness meditation initiates a self-regulatory mind-monitoring process that ultimately is an awareness of awareness itself.

Breath awareness helps people develop the "aim and sustain" functions of attention. But mindfulness meditation then moves on to a more receptive state where whatever arises is allowed to enter consciousness. The nonjudgmental nature of this process seems to involve a form of awareness of awareness that is more automatic than self-reflection and is sometimes called "reflexivity." Though meditation evolves into an open state, it is not just "empty" or "passive" as a form of withdrawing or going blank.

Mindfulness training can be seen to include the following aspects, as discussed by Lutz, Dunne, and Davidson (in press):

1. Meditation that develops concentration on an object such as the breath;
2. Techniques that cultivate an awareness of subjectivity—of how the mind works—in a manner that deemphasizes the object of the initial focus;

3. One then gains experiential access to the reflexive awareness—awareness of awareness—that is thought to reveal the
   bare aspect of mental processes;

4. As training moves forward there is a deemphasis on subjectivity as well as the receptive state taking in the range of
   experience;

5. This moment in training further enhances access to reflexivity, that automatic awareness of awareness itself; and

6. The practice creates a flow in which the individual moves to
   the point where the bare aspect of awareness is fully realized
   in meditation.

IPSEITY: THE BARE ESSENTIALS

There is a significant distinction made between the narrative
function of relating one's life story with words and the direct sensory experience of the moment. The ways in which our narrative
function is shaped by the context of our telling (to others or ourselves) reveals a profound influence of top-down processes which
can obscure direct experience.

In formal mindfulness meditation training, practitioners deal directly with this narrative "subject" as teller of story, into an immersion in "bare awareness" or a sense of the essential nature of
the mind. Lutz, Dunne, and Davidson (in press) suggested that the
formal term for this experience of life without the trappings of
our constructed self is *ipseity*—our essential way of being beneath
the layers of thought and reaction, identity and adaptation. "Essential" here implies an invariant quality, a grounded essence of
our being that is not just a function of the transient contexts that
come and go in our lives. The authors stated that:

> Ipseity is the minimal subjective sense of 'I-ness' in experience,
> and, as such, it is constitutive of a 'minimal' or 'core' self. By con-
> trast, a narrative or autobiographical self (Legrand, in press) encom-

passes categorical or moral judgment, emotions, anticipation of the future, and recollections of the past. This explicit sense of narrative or autobiographical self is often characterized as occurring in correlation with an explicit content, or object, of experience. It also appears to be dependent in some fashion on ipseity, inasmuch as the narrative self is in part based upon that minimal subjective sense of 'I-ness.'

Addressing the movement of highly trained meditators toward ipseity, Lutz, Dunne, and Davidson stated:

> Finally, at the highest level of practice, what we have described as a "de-emphasis" of both object and subject moves, at least theoretically, to a point where no elements of objectivity or subjectivity—whether in the form of conceptual structures, categories of time and space, or some other feature—remain in the experience. . . . Traditions recognize only a small number of practitioners as having truly reached this level of practice.

It may be that mindfulness gives a hint of this state, even though living it fully is only realized by the few. If this is the case, we can envision ipseity as an aspect of the deep knowing that emerges as a stream of awareness, one without concepts, but one which may be perfectly compatible with having a "subject" and an "object" that are experienced with a sense of bare essentials, beneath top-down layers, but still retain a sense of an experiencing "I." In other words, our *ipseitious self* retains a sense of agency and is open to experiencing the full range of awareness extending from bodily sensation to a non-dualistic sense of the world where the boundaries of the body no longer define where "self" begins and ends.

SELF-REGULATION

Why bother getting in touch with your essential nature? Mental training that enables you to access ipseity, to get a sense of the essential "you" beneath narrative and memory, emotional reactivity and habit, liberates your mind to achieve new levels of well-being.

With the dissolution of automatic patterns, the mind seems to be freed to acquire new levels of self-regulation. This is the power of mindfulness to alter our affective responses. Being closer to an open sense of one's essential nature creates a "facility to regulate one's emotions such that one is less easily disturbed by emotional states. The mind is also said to be more sensitive and flexible, and the cultivation of positive states and traits is therefore greatly facilitated" (Lutz, Dunne, & Davidson, in press).

James Austin's two in-depth integrations (1998, 2006) offer a beautiful example of the blending of first-person direct experience with explorations into the scientific insights into the brain. In Austin's view, "you cannot probe deeply into the phenomena of such states without uncovering properties of fundamental neurobiological significance. Indeed, one finds that meditative experiences not only are reflected in the findings of neuroscience but that these two fields are so intimately interrelated that each *illuminates* the other" (Austin, 2006, p. 23). Austin's experience in deep forms of meditation revealed that they "not only drop out the psychic self but their insights transform the rest of one's prior existential concepts about what constitutes reality" (Austin, 2006, p. 25). The wisdom gleaned from sensing, for example, that we are all a part of the interconnected whole is a mindset that can inform our ways of seeing and being in the world. Austin went on to describe the importance of these insights and the effort to bring science and contemplation together when he stated, "We shall need all the help we can get from neurobiologists to live mindfully in the present moments of this next millennium" (p. 24).

Lutz, Dunne, and Davidson (in press) reflected on the importance of this integration, and the realization that well-being and compassion can be intentionally acquired, when they state that the scientific evidence confirms that:

> Many of our core mental processes such as awareness and attention and emotion regulation, including our very capacity for happiness and compassion, should best be conceptualized as trainable

skills. The meditative traditions provide a compelling example of strategies and techniques that have evolved over time to enhance and optimize human potential and well-being. The neuroscientific study of these traditions is still in its infancy but the early findings promise to both reveal the mechanisms by which such training may exert its effects as well as underscore the plasticity of the brain circuits that underlie complex mental functions.

A GATHERING OF SCIENTISTS

Two months before I journeyed to the silent retreat I spent 10 days continually immersed in mindfulness and the brain through attendance at a number of meetings.

At the Society for Neuroscience meeting in Washington DC there were 36,000 attendees and over 17,000 presentations. The opening keynote address was given by the Dalai Lama who addressed the issue of blending science with contemplative practice. Someone asked him what he would do if the science proved tenets of Buddhist meditation were inaccurate. His response was that they would then have to revise Buddhist practice and thinking. Even though there were many "satellite rooms" available in which people could sit close to a large video screen for closed circuit live viewing of the speech, tens of thousands of the neuroscientists waited patiently in line for two hours to try to get a seat in the actual (huge) room in which he was to speak. One could interpret that effort to be present as a sign of some curiosity if not a longing to be in the presence of an open mind.

I participated in that neuroscience meeting and listened to as many of the presentations as I could manage (not quite all of them) after attending three days at a Mind and Life conference in which the Dalai Lama met with other contemplatives and a host of neuroscientists to explore the relationships among meditation and science. It was clear that our understanding of how meditation may affect the brain is in its infancy. There were presenta-

tions on the power of mindfulness meditation to shift brain laterality toward the left where more positive and approach states were
mediated, and ways of preventing the negative mental states of
clinical depression. Mindfulness meditation had been shown to be
a powerful tool for focusing the mind, and it seemed in my own
experience to be generating an increased ability to attend to the
nonverbal signals of others. After my silent retreat, that is exactly
how it felt: I was tuned in to the most subtle of responses. Why
would being silent for a week make you more sensitive to others?

Perceiving another's non-verbal signals is followed by a process
that appears to involve both the insula and the related middle prefrontal region's activity to interocept, interpret, and attribute one's
own internal states with those of another person. Interoception
draws on the capacity of the mind to focus awareness on the internal state of the body. The insula transmits data from the body
to the brain (Carr, Iacoboni, Dubeau, Maziotta, & Lenzi, 2003) and
may directly be involved in the experience of "looking inward,"
which is inherent in every culture's contemplative practice. In fact,
we have a map of the whole body that is only represented on the
right side of the brain. Attending to facial expressions, and other
nonverbal signals such as eye contact, tone of voice, posture, gestures, and timing and intensity of responses, are all right hemisphere sent and perceived. In this way, looking inward for a week
at the totality of my body experience, at my own nonverbal bodily
states, may utilize the right sided aspects of prefrontal and insular
functions. So here we see the beginnings of "how": The practice
of looking inward, of reflection, activates the insula and the middle
prefrontal regions, especially on the right side of the brain.

As we've discussed, Lazar et al. (2005) found that long-term mindfulness meditators had not only increased middle prefrontal thickening, but they had enlargement of the right insula. These findings
are consistent with what we know about the fundamental processes
of interoception. Given that these structures also enable us to have

mindsight—the capacity for seeing the mind in ourselves and in others—Lazar's research suggests that mindfulness meditation might alter the very structures of our brains responsible for empathy and for self-observation. This may be the link between the practice of looking inward and reported enhancement of the ability to connect with others. (See Appendix III, Relationships and Mindfulness.)

ENHANCING THE ODDBALL: EXPANDING SUBJECTIVE TIME AND DISABLING CORTICAL INVARIANT REPRESENTATIONS

Attuning inward also seems to change our experience of time. Do we have any idea of why that might be true?

Another presentation at the Society for Neuroscience meeting focused on how to expand subjective time. Tse (2005) designed a brilliant perceptual experiment in which subjects were shown a series of images in a pattern that consisted of carefully spaced geometric shapes. As these shapes emerged and disappeared on the screen, subjects were asked to relate their awareness of how much time had passed. What the study revealed was that when an "oddball"—an unusual shape that does not fit the previously established pattern—appeared, subjects experienced time as slowing down. The conclusion was that the increased "density of information" created by the oddball was the key to understanding this subjective sensation that time was expanded.

In everyday life we have the experience of a certain amount of information being perceived and processed per unit of time. This is information density. When an oddball appears we focus more intently upon this unusual shape or stimulus because it does not match our prior expectations. Expectations are processed in cortical memory. The outer bark of the brain, our neocortex, is arranged in cortical columns or clusters of vertically arranged piles of cell bodies that enable memory to shape perception.

In the brain the six-layered neocortex appears to have both input and output fibers that create a bidirectional flow of information within the column itself. When we bring in sensations, say, of seeing a flower, the visual data is taken into our lower levels (layers 6 and 5 as it moves upward from sensory input to ultimate "processing") and then brings them up the cortical layers toward the higher areas where ultimately we may "perceive" the object being examined. But the cortex also sends information back down essentially from the higher levels (layers 1 and 2) toward these lower "input" layers. The result is as if two waves of information processing come crashing in the middle regions (the equivalent of layers 3 and 4) where we ultimately blend the two information streams (Hawkins & Blakeslee, 2004).

We "know" what a flower looks like from prior experience, from memory, and our cortical top-down processing sends that expectational bias downward to alter incoming perception. "Alter" means that we do not need to pay such close attention. This is called top-down processing. We label the object "flower" with our left cortex, and we move on. Jeffrey Hawkins and Sharon Blakeslee (2004) labeled this top-down influence as an "invariant representation," in that we have an invariant image of the category of flower. Invariant representations allow us to quickly assess the nature of our environment and move along to what we are trying to achieve. Prior learning helps us become more efficient information processors by having readily available invariant representations that continually bombard our sensory inputs with, "I know what that is, let me help you out with a model of what we have already seen!"

But in many ways such learning oppresses our raw sensory experience by muddying the waters of clear perception with prior expectation. As we grow into adulthood, it is very likely that these accumulated layers of perceptual models and conceptual categories constrict subjective time and deaden our feelings of being alive. Without the intentional effort to awaken, life speeds by. We habituate to experience, perceiving through the filter of the past and

not orienting ourselves to the novel distinctions of the present
(Goleman, 1988; Langer, 1997).

Our invariant representations lessen the information density
because they establish filters that constrain what we actually see.
If there were to be a new flower, we might miss it because we are
anticipating the old flower. Waking up and "smelling the roses"
is, literally, telling the invariant representations of our brains to
take a break.

When we awaken with mindful awareness could the possible
shutting down of the top-down invariant representational flow
actually alter the density of information as we come to experience more fully our sensations? Perhaps this is how mindful awareness may increase information density and expand the subjective
experience of time.

We see more, hear more, smell more. By inhibiting invariant
representations, we enable the densely packed incoming sensory
data not to be generalized nor its details minimized. Once this enhanced incoming data is created, what before was "just a flower"
can become the one-of-a-kind flower that it actually is. With such
a mindful awareness of our moment-to-moment experience, everything can become the oddball. When invariant representations are
shut down, the ordinary becomes extraordinary. We can propose
that mindful awareness enhances the oddball by making each moment unique as it dissolves the top-down constraints of invariant
representations. Without mindful awareness, patterns of sensation
are set as background in the cortical two-lane highway of top-down
invariant representations as they cloud the edges and blur the focus of the incoming data. This blurring of focus is self-generated,
created by memory, and automatically attempts to ready us for action by drawing on the past so we know what to expect.

It is in this way that mindful awareness, paying attention in the
present moment without grasping onto top-down invariant judgments, is literally a way of calming the past's intrusion on our ex-

perience of the present. When we awaken our minds we expand the subjective time of our lives. Our experience of time is expanded as the densely packed sensations of each moment are no longer muted and blurred. If you take a moment and just sit quietly for a minute, notice what arises in your awareness, your sensations in your arms and legs. Just notice the sounds filling the air around you. Much of what you may sense now was there before, but pausing, becoming receptive, changes time and one's whole sense of the world and yourself. Reflection opens the doors of sensation. As we move forward we can embrace this silence in the spaces between the words of the explorations ahead. Dissolving our own invariant top-down representations can be achieved with mindful intention.

Chapter Six

HARNESSING THE HUB:
Attention and the
Wheel of Awareness

In this chapter we will explore the central role of attention in shaping how we act with awareness and come to learn to observe the nature of our ongoing mental lives. To intentionally bring something into awareness means that rather than just registering input from sensory organs (light input to the eye, pressure sensors activated in the foot) into the primary sensory cortical regions toward the back of the brain, we engage in an active search process, a purposeful seeking of perceptual data in the field of awareness.

With mindful awareness we have more than just awareness of sensation: If we say we are observing ourselves having the sensory experience, that observational stance embeds meta-awareness that includes more of the brain than the posterior perceptual columns and the side prefrontal region. Metacognition is correlated with middle prefrontal activation, as is self-observation. In this way, mindful awareness has been shown to activate middle prefrontal regions to a greater degree than forms of meditation in which sustained focus on one target (internal word or external object) is the task (Cahn & Polich, 2006).

The metacognitive dimension of mindful awareness involves more complex secondary associational cortices, such as those in the middle prefrontal region, that carry out our witness awareness function and permit us to be aware of being aware. It should be said here as well that mindfulness is much more than a relaxation technique: We can become stable and clear, and we can be engaged and ready for action. It is the sense of presence, not relaxation, that embodies the essence of mindful awareness. But how does this middle prefrontal involvement distinguish simple direct sensory experience from a form of sensory awareness that also includes observation of experience? This question is the ultimate issue about the difference between being aware, and being mindfully aware.

The power of clinical interventions to reveal their important positive effects comes with mindful awareness practices, not with simple awareness. In this way, the distinctive component of mindfulness is crucial for us to grasp.

A mindful mode of awareness may be mediated beyond the side and posterior regions bringing simple awareness and may be correlated with the integrative activations of the middle regions of the prefrontal cortex—the areas we have discussed, including the orbitofrontal, anterior cingulate, and ventral and medial prefrontal cortex. This middle prefrontal region involves metacognition (thinking about thinking), being aware of awareness. It is also fundamental to the range of the middle prefrontal functions we have discussed earlier (see Appendix III).

A research study on the "framing effect" (De Martino, Kumaran, Seymour, & Dolan, 2006) revealed that when subjects were presented with two different versions of a gambling problem, those that could "see through" the verbal biasing utilized their middle prefrontal areas during the task. Those that "fell for" the bias, who responded on automatic, did not catch the trick and did not activate these midline areas. In this study, for example, stimuli were presented such as, "If you gamble in this way you have a 40% chance of keeping your money" rather than "If you gamble in this way you have a 60% chance of losing your money." Activation of these middle prefrontal regions (orbitofrontal and medial prefrontal cortices [OMPFC]; see Figure 2.3) seemed to pull the subject out of automatic, into a more reflective state that could take into account a broader perspective of the problem at hand. Though this is not a study of mindfulness, we can see that the role of these middle prefrontal areas revealed in this and other studies suggests that these regions play an important part in disengaging us from top-down influences, such as prior expectations and our own emotional reactions.

The middle prefrontal regions are an important contributor to self-observation and metacognition: We can have an image of ourselves in the past, present, and future and we also map out the nature of our own mind's activities. It is here where we see the potential neural contribution to the idea that mindful awareness is more than simply being aware: In mindfulness, we actively perceive our own mind and are aware of our awareness.

NEURAL DIMENSIONS OF ATTENTION

Research is beginning to examine the attentional networks that may be involved in mindful awareness. At this point we do not have definitive data to suggest how focusing attention in the present moment may harness neural circuits in a particular way, nor why these potential attentional mechanisms would result in such improvements in physiological, psychological, and interpersonal well-being.

Much of the research on attention is focused on tasks that are active in nature: attending to a stimulus, flexibly altering attention when stimuli change unexpectedly, handling conflictual streams of information. Mindful awareness has a different quality; within a mindful state there is a process of receptivity and meta-awareness that seems quite different from the active stimulus-driven attentional processes studied in these investigations. Nevertheless, it may be helpful to have this research on active tasks as a background because it represents the state of the science at this point.

The idea that there is not just one form of attention is generally accepted today. There are three generally agreed upon aspects of this process, which regulate the flow of energy and information: executive, orienting, and alerting. As the mind itself can be defined as an embodied and relational process that regulates the flow of energy and information, attention is absolutely central to mind.

Amir Raz and Jason Buhle's review (2006) of types of attentional networks reveals the complexity of the state of our understanding. In their words, "Cortical and subcortical networks mediate different aspects of attention; without the modulatory influence of subcortical areas, the brain would not attend effectively" (p. 370). These systems of attention have cortical areas that specialize in them; the subcortical regions have been less studied, but serve as a deep source of motivation, drive, and arousal in the brain itself. Clearly these subcortical processes likely are at play in the bodily focused work of mindful awareness. We come to the sense of mindfulness not just as a focus of attention, but as a way of being: It is likely more than a stimulus-response cortically mediated attentional process.

Raz and Buhle go on to suggest that "as neuroimaging begins to unravel the effects of practice on brain substrates cumulative findings suggest that these attentional networks can be modified. Introducing attentional training in preschools or childcare centers could be an educational innovation" (p. 370). The crucial issue is that attention, so central to the mind itself, is not some fixed process. As mentioned earlier, our Mindful Awareness Research Center's pilot study was able to show that mindful awareness training over an eight-week period could significantly improve the executive functions of attention in adults and adolescents with genetically loaded forms of attention-deficit hyperactivity disorder (Zylowska, Ackerman, Futrell, Horton, Hale, Pataki, et al., submitted).

Lidia Zylowska and her colleagues at UCLA created an eight-week pilot program that offered the basic mindfulness meditation techniques similar to what we discussed in Chapter 3 on the silent retreat. As we've seen, this form of insight meditation is based on the general approach of first having individuals focus attention on their breath. When they notice their attention shifting to something else, as it invariably does, they are to gently return their attention to the breath. Over and over again, this practice of returning the attention to the target of focus seems to develop the "aim and sustain" capacity of the mind's attention. A focus on the body via a "body scan" and on the feet in walking meditation broadens the attention to bodily sensation as an anchor and enables the individual to reorient attention when it strays. Loving kindness exercises are also offered. As we've discussed, when mindfulness is seen as a form of internal attunement, it is natural to view these intentional states of compassion from loving kindness exercises as reinforcing the essential state of loving connection—with oneself and with others.

After an eight-week group experience of two and a half hours each, meditation lasting from 5 to 15 minutes, the attentional capacities of these individuals were measured and compared to baseline before the intervention. The executive functions of the participants were shown to be markedly improved over baseline. As this was only a pilot study, there was no control group and we cannot say that these results were caused by anything in particular. Future work needs to utilize a controlled, blinded version in which we can determine what combination of aspects of the experience—group support, mindfulness skills, parking on the UCLA campus—may have contributed to the clear success of this pilot effort. Subjects not only reported an enhanced sense of well-being, but their tests revealed an increased capacity to focus their attention and resist impulses. The important possibility illustrated here is that attention is a trainable skill.

Given that attention is central to the mind and behavior, finding ways to train attention is a crucial aspect of both education and therapy. Attentional training would involve ways of intentionally focusing the mind to engrain new patterns of aiming and sustaining attention. Both computer-assisted and meditative techniques may prove effective in training the attentional networks in the brain (Raz & Buhle, 2006; Wallace, 2006). We will review the three dimensions of attention that are fairly well accepted in the scientific literature.

Alerting

Alerting involves sustained attention, vigilance, and alertness that create the ability to enhance and maintain readiness to respond as a preparation for anticipated stimuli. Alerting can be phasic (specific to a given task) or it can be intrinsic or tonic (a general state of control of arousal levels). When we think of readying our minds to be open to what arises, that would likely be a form of alerting.

Imaging studies support the idea that the frontal and parietal regions, especially on the right side of the brain, are essential for this sustaining aspect of alerting. The right dorsolateral prefrontal cortex (DLPFC, the side part, right side) seems to function as a monitor of performance or arousal levels and regulates them as a form of executive attention (see below). The anterior cingulate cortex (ACC) and other midline prefrontal areas may collaborate in these regulatory functions as well, enabling response flexibility. The right inferior parietal region becomes active with alerting to both internal and external stimuli.

Orienting

Orienting is the capacity to specifically select certain information from a variety of options in a process of scanning or selection. Most of the research in this highly investigated area has been carried out on visual stimuli and so the findings of brain structures may be quite specific to this modality of perception.

The neuroanatomy of orienting involves areas of the brain specific to the form of stimuli presented. In research paradigms involving vision, areas such as the pulvinar, superior parietal lobe, superior colliculus, the junction between the temporal and parietal lobes, and the superior temporal lobe are all activated. The superior parietal cortex has been reported to be especially important in voluntary shifts of attention (see Figure 2.3).

Executive Attention

Executive attention has many features with descriptions such as *selective*, *supervisory*, and *focused attention*. Conflict resolution among competing stimuli is also an essential aspect of executive attentional control. "Effortful control" is a phrase used to describe the nature of this executive function. The general processes under the regulation of this form of attention are related to "planning or decision making, error detection, new or not-well learned responses, conditions judged to be difficult or dangerous, regulation of thoughts and feelings, and the overcoming of habitual actions" (Raz & Buhl, 2006, p. 374). It is here where we can begin to imagine the power of mindful awareness to decouple automatic habitual thinking within the framework of executive attentional control.

Brain imaging investigations have implicated the role of the anterior cingulate cortex (ACC) as a crucial node in the executive attention network. The ACC can be considered the chief operating officer of the brain because it allocates attentional resources. Various aspects, dorsal and ventral, of the ACC play differing roles that link body, affect, and thought. In general, the ACC serves to determine the distribution of an attentional focus and to be involved in the regulation of emotional arousal. Here we see the physical reality of the anatomical linkage between thought and information processing with the bodily and limbic generation of affect. The ACC may be especially involved when there is a conflict in attentional response. Under certain situations of more complex conflicts, the ACC may also link with the DLPFC, a linkage that might also tap into the deeper subcortical systems such as the locus coeruleus and the ventral tegmental areas.

Research on mindfulness meditation reveals the state involvement of ACC activation (Cahn & Polich, 2006). Meditation in general appears to involve the induction of alpha and theta waves on EEG which some suggest accompanies a sensation of stability and calming.

From a developmental perspective, the period between 3 and 7 years of age appears to be a profoundly important time for the acquisition of executive attentional functions, raising the notion that interventions may be best initiated at this time. As the child nears puberty, a resurgence in the growth of synapses begins and there actually may be a diminishment in the efficiency of cortical processing at this time (Casey, Tottenham, Listen, & Durston, 2005). During the adolescent years, the prefrontal areas undergo a great deal of remodeling in which neural connections are pruned and functions carried out by this region may be labile and become dysfunctional under stress. As we grow through this period, more complex metacognitive capacities become available and may enable teenagers to think in much more complex and ultimately self-observant ways.

Though attentional regulation develops during these early years, mindfulness skills may also be of use in helping adolescents and adults to develop more effective executive attentional mechanisms as discussed earlier (Zylowska et al., submitted). The reasoning, as we've seen, is that focusing attention in specific ways can stimulate neuronal regions that are prime candidates to help mediate such neuroplastic changes in response to mindful practice.

Rueda, Posner, and Rothbart (2005) stated: "Effortful control serves as the basis for the development of more reactive to more self-regulative behavior. Systems of effortful control may contribute to this development by providing the attentional flexibility required to manage negative affect, consider potential actions in light of moral principles, and coordinate reactions that are under voluntary control (Rothbart & Rueda, 2005)" (p. 575). In examining the neural structures involved in such self-regulation, the ACC as we've seen plays a major role: "The main node of the executive attention network, the ACC, is part of the limbic system and is strongly connected to structures involved in processing emotions" (p. 578).

In development, Rueda and colleagues propose that "Altogether, these data suggest that the brain circuitry underlying executive functions becomes more focal and refined as it gains in efficiency. This maturational process involves not only greater anatomical specialization but also reduces the time these systems need to resolve each of the processes implicated in the task" (2005, pp. 586–587). The authors go on to discuss the use of Attention Process Training that can lead to improvements in executive attention (Sohlberg, McLaughlin, Pavese, Heidrich, & Posner, 2000), and posit that preliminary findings "suggest that the brain mechanisms associated with attentional control can be improved by training, and that this improvement produces a benefit in behavioral measures of competence. Given the connection between attention and self-regulation, plasticity of the neural system underlying executive attention opens a window for fostering self-regulation in young children" (2005, p. 589).

The overlap between attentional regulation and executive functions is revealed in the structural and functional aspects of the middle prefrontal areas. For example, the ACC seems to be involved in the reduction of negative affective states and it interacts with other midline structures, such as the medial and orbital areas of the prefrontal cortex (see Figure 2.6). In situations involving anterior cingulate dysfunction as a result of brain damage, marked changes more severe but qualitatively parallel to certain aspects of a proposed "low road" process (Siegel, 1999) have been described. Devinsky, Morrell, and Vogt have stated: "Behavioral changes following anterior cingulate cortex lesions included the following: increased aggressivity . . . emotional blunting, decreased motivation . . . impaired maternal–infant interactions, impatience, lowered threshold for fear or startle responses, and inappropriate intraspecies behaviour" (1995, p. 285). Following brain injury, an individual's experience revealed that "The social consequences of combined anterior cingulate and orbitofrontal cortex damage can be devastating . . . there was a disconnection between the intellectual understanding of the images and the autonomic expression with anterior cingulate cortex and orbitofrontal lesions. . . . The cingulate and orbitofrontal cortex are important in linking emotional stimuli and autonomic changes to emotional stimuli, and the behavioral changes that follow such stimuli" (Devinsky, Morrell & Vogt, 1995, p. 292).

When we combine these research perspectives on the anterior cingulate and orbitofrontal regions with the role of the medial prefrontal cortex in enabling awareness of one's own and others' mental processes, as well as regulating affective response (Decety & Chaminade, 2003; Frith & Frith, 1999), we see that executive processes in the brain correlate with the midline structures we've labeled as the "middle prefrontal" regions. It is the development of these areas that seems crucial for emotional and social functioning, as they form a central node in the ways in which self-regulatory aspects of the mind correlate with structures and functions in the brain.

AN OVERVIEW

One can see that there is some overlap in neural function between the frontal attentional networks of executive and alerting capacities and the more lateral and posterior stream of orienting.

There is controversy over how much overlap and interaction these systems have with each other, but in general there seems to be agreement that these three domains function as organized aspects of the heterogeneous nature of attention.

When a person practices some form of mindful awareness training, the initial components would be to aim and sustain attention. These functions would fall under the alerting (sustain) and orienting (aim) dimensions of attention. Naturally the individual needs to have the intention to carry out such an aim and sustain, and therein lies the executive aspect of attention.

As mindfulness training evolves, it soon gives rise to a more receptive process of becoming aware of the nature of the mind and awareness itself. This more open awareness may not match well with the active object-focused analyses of attention in the existing literature at this point in time, though it likely correlates with middle prefrontal metacognitive functions.

Further research on mindful awareness is needed to examine more fully these attentional processes, and the results are not in as yet as to exactly what aspects of neural plasticity, of change in response to experience, will be harnessed by mindful awareness.

STATES & TRAITS: EFFORTLESS MINDFULNESS

Mindful awareness over time may become a way of being or a trait of the individual, not just a practice initiating a temporary state of mind with certain approaches such as meditation, yoga, or centering prayer. We would see this movement from states to traits in the form of more long-term capabilities of the individual. From the research perspective, such a transition would be seen as a shift from being effortful and in awareness to effortless and at times perhaps not initiated with awareness.

Mindfulness without awareness? The idea here is that the open and receptive state of being, taking in whatever is, may be initiated before awareness, but then will involve awareness as reflection emerges in a person's moment-to-moment experience. This effortless process can be seen as "automatic" and so we could misinterpret this as being another example of being asleep, of being a prisoner of top-down influences. But the engagement of middle prefrontal functions as an effortless trait has quite a different quality from just being a passive recipient of old, memory-shaped top-down judgments. The middle prefrontal functions are alive, engaging, metacognitive, self-regulatory, connecting, and integrative. What would it be like if we could engage these middle regions without the involvement of the side region, at least for the moments when an experience initially takes place? Here we see the benefit of distinguishing regions of the brain, such as the side from middle prefrontal areas. We could imagine well "trained" middle prefrontal circuits that have been reinforced by mindful practice and living. With these in place, a mindful state could be achieved even without the side (DLPFC) region evoking working memory at that initial time. This could be effortless mindfulness.

If we practice mindful awareness and develop the state of utilizing our middle prefrontal regions with intentional effort in the practice session, it may be that this initial conscious, side-prefrontally activated state may induce the neuroplastic changes that lead to this mode as a trait. The trait of mindful awareness may then have the more effortless quality of middle prefrontal engagement without the side prefrontal region's active attempts to consciously create that state: Mindfulness just is, even without our efforts to make it so.

When we recall that the middle prefrontal region is profoundly integrative of body, brainstem, limbic areas, cortex, and the social world of others' minds, we then can realize how this effortless mindful awareness may be created. As a person's brain grows with mindful awareness practice (involving side prefrontal cortex effort), the neuroplasticity enhances the growth of the integrative middle prefrontal fibers. As they grow with practice, the individual achieves the trait of effortless mindful living.

In mindfulness there feels as though there are multiple states engaged, which intertwine in differing ways to enable this focus on present experience, the disengagement from top-down judgments and habitual emotional reactions; and a meta-awareness that permits some deep knowing about the whole flowing process. Though we may consider the idea of a mindful trait as being effortless, it does not mean that we are unaware of its fullness in the moment. Effortlessness and awareness are not opposites. In this way, the movement from an effortful state to an effortless trait does not diminish awareness though it may shift the quality of the "awarenessing" sensation.

As we have discussed, structural (as opposed to functional) scans of the brain of mindfulness meditators in one study revealed thicker middle prefrontal areas and the right insula (Lazar et al., 2005). It could be that the practice of mindfulness meditation activated those regions and made their anatomical bulk larger; or it could also be that individuals with larger regions in those areas are more likely to meditate. Thickness did correlate with years of practice, supporting the possibility that this indeed is a result of the practice of mindfulness meditation, not just an associational finding. Increased cortical thickness could be due to greater branching of the neurons themselves with increased linkages to other neurons, increased volume of supporting cells in those brain regions, or increased local blood vasculature. Each of these possible contributors to "thickening" would represent important dimensions that could enhance neural function. Though not a prospective controlled study, which is needed, these findings are at least consistent with the idea that repeated activation of a set of circuits may enhance the synaptic connectivity—and hence thickness—in those activated regions.

With enriched neural connections, the processes carried out by those interconnected areas become more readily available to the person's day-to-day, and moment-to-moment, life. What was an effortful practice becomes an effortless way of being. This is how a state can become a trait. (See also Appendix III, Developmental Issues.)

THE MIND'S WHEEL OF AWARENESS: A METAPHOR FOR MINDFULNESS

One way I have found it helpful to teach students and patients about this spacious quality of mindful awareness, is to consider the mind's "wheel of awareness" as a visual metaphor for the functioning of the mind. We discussed this view briefly in Chapter 4 and here we will explore more fully the aspects of awareness and possible neural correlates in this metaphoric image of the mind.

On the outer rim of the wheel of awareness we have anything that can enter our focus of attention (Figure 6.1; see also Figure

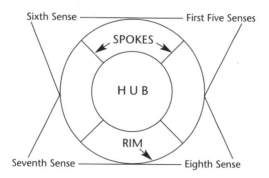

Figure 6.1 The wheel of awareness (rim, spokes, and hub) and the sectors of the rim: first five (outer world), sixth (body), seventh (mind), and eighth (relationships).

4.3). Each point on the rim represents the potential object of awareness, from one's foot to one's feelings. The spokes emanating from the central hub symbolize our ability to focus attention on a single point on the rim. The hub at the center of the wheel of awareness symbolizes the spaciousness of the mind that can engage a spoke on a particular point on the rim, or be receptive to whatever arises along the rim as it enters the hub.

The Rim

The first five senses bring in information from the outside world, enabling us to sense this physical domain of reality. When we become aware of the first five senses, we take in points along that sector of the rim that represents this physical plane of knowable aspects of the world outside our bodies: These are our first five senses.

Our sixth sense sector of the rim includes sensations in our limbs, our body's motion, the tension or relaxation of our muscles, the state of our internal milieu, including our organs such as the lungs, heart, and intestines. These bodily aspects of potential awareness serve as a deep source of intuition and shape our emotional state. The neural net processors around our internal organs directly influence our reasoning. The hormonal state of our bodies and the tension of our muscles in our limbs, torso, and face, each contribute directly to how our interior world shapes our feelings. We use the process of interoception to perceive these important sixth sense inputs, bringing them into our sensorimotor awareness via spokes from the hub to our sixth sense sector of the rim.

The seventh sense enables aspects of mind—thoughts, feelings, intentions, attitudes, concepts, images, beliefs, hopes, dreams—of oneself or others to be brought into the focus of attention. This capacity to perceive the mind can be called "mindsight" and enables us to gain deep insight and empathy. Mindful awareness contains the metacognitive processes that enable both awareness of awareness and the focus of attention on the nature of the mind itself. These reflective practices directly develop our mindsight abilities. This seventh sense even enables us to ultimately become aware of the mental nature of even the first physical-domain related six senses.

As we develop our sense of the mind, we come to realize the opacity of previously transparent representations: We can appreciate that awareness of the color of a flower is a product of our minds. Rather than destroying an appreciation for sensory experience and pleasures, such a meta-awareness can enable us to rejoice in the mystery and majesty of the mind's creations.

An eighth "relational sense" can also be proposed. This sector of the rim represents our sense of relationship, our connection, with some being. When we attune with another person, for example, we can become aware of this resonant state that is created within the relating. The eighth sense is how we are aware of "feeling felt" by another and enables us to feel a part of the larger whole. Human relationships, prayer, meditation, and perhaps even membership in group social behaviors, such as religious rituals or even athletics, might enable people to feel that they "belong" and have membership with others. It may be that when we attune to ourselves within mindfulness, we become aware of that reverberant connection of our ongoing living self and our witnessing awareness. We have become friends with our self, and our eighth sense would enable us to be aware of that feeling. As we have seen, this resonance may involve our awareness of our own intention. This intentional attunement may be at the heart of resonating relationships of all sorts.

The Spokes

The spokes of the wheel of awareness represent the intentional focus of attention on some aspect of the rim. During walking meditation practice, one focuses a spoke on the sensation of one's feet and legs. We can build the skill of concentration by a practice on the focusing on one chosen object at a time: the breath, our steps, the moves of our body in tai chi or yoga. We can also focus on a part of the body, or a picture. Focusing the mind, and returning to the object when our attention wanders, is the practice of developing our "aim-and-sustain" function of concentration. We strengthen the hub's capacity to send a spoke to an intended target on the rim. This skill of concentration is the building block of mindful awareness, a necessary but not sufficient characteristic. Having a strong set of spokes is important but not enough to create mindfulness.

A stimulus can enter our awareness and draw our attention to it. This is called "exogenous attention," and often occurs in the busy lives we lead with people and technical gadgets. A cell phone can go off and its sound can come into my ears and draw my attention to it, pulling from the rim a spoke that I haven't initiated. In a drawing we would illustrate that with an emphasis on the point on the rim and then a less bold spoke. This is the pull of exogenous attention—modern society's technological challenge. In multitasking we would see numerous spokes pulling simultaneous data in from various aspects of the rim.

With mindful awareness, the hub of the mind represents the executive function that enables us to return to what we have intended to be doing. We can send out another spoke to return our attention to the object we desire to be the focus of our attention. This capacity to have single-pointed, self-initiated attention is sometimes considered "endogenous" attention in that it comes from one's own intention, not the pull of an exogenous source. Others use this term to signify just "looking inward" or being drawn to focus on the internal world. The research in attention is filled with mixed use of terminologies (Raz & Buhl, 2006), and so we'll stay close to our wheel metaphor for visual clarity. Here we are using the term *endogenous* to refer to the initiation of a focus from within, no matter what sector of the rim the spoke is aimed at as a target of attentional focus. The aiming of the spoke is initiated by the executive functions of the hub.

The Hub

The choice to refocus our attention and the capacity to realize that our attention has wandered seem to be essential aspects of mindful awareness. The hub of the mind's wheel of awareness embeds this capacity to keep track of the target of attention and then to alter attentional focus to comply with desired goals. In this way we can say that mindfulness involves the hub of the mind and that mindful awareness practices likely develop or strengthen the hub.

As we practice mindful awareness with effort, we purposefully train the mind by again and again returning attention to our target (concentration training of aim and sustain that strengthens our single-pointed endogenous attention) by monitoring the process of attention itself (mindful meta-awareness). This single-pointed and meta-awareness practice forms a foundation for creating a mindful state of awareness. Repeated states of mindful hub activation over time can likely induce neuroplastic changes that transform the hub's executive and integrative circuitry. This development and strengthening of the hub enables effortful states of practice to become effortless traits of living. Mindful awareness training strengthens the hub of the mind and makes mindfulness a way of being, not just a practice.

Harnessing the Hub

Mindfulness can be seen to involve the fullness of function in the ways that we shape our sensory flow, the feelings in our minds we call affect, the nature of our thoughts, and our sense of ourselves. How could a specific form of awareness embrace such a wide range of complex processes? What is it about mindfulness that makes it have such an impact on the wide array of human activities, from education to law, parenting to romance?

Mindfulness embraces the most central aspect of how we define our mind, which is the core of our subjective life. The embodied and relational process that regulates the flow of energy and information—the mind—is exactly what mindfulness shapes. This state of being, this particular form of being aware, is all about regulating the flow of energy and information—in our bodies, and in our relationships with others.

EXECUTIVE FUNCTION & SELF-REGULATION

The science of attention uses the concept of executive function as an aspect of the mind that directly governs a broader notion of self-regulation, and self-regulation is how we shape the many domains of our existence, from states of arousal to patterns of response. In the field of psychopathology, self-regulation is a crucial concept in studying the development of well-being and mental illness.

Executive functions involve a range of cognitive and emotional processes that permit a balanced form of self-regulation. Thoughts and feelings are intertwined in the brain, and it is therefore not surprising that an integrative function like self-regulation would involve the capacity to monitor and influence our many layers of mental activities, from how we pay attention to how we feel. Here we see the important overlap of what are sometimes considered separate processes of thought, emotion, and attentional focus. In the brain itself we see that these dimensions merge as one process, revealed in this executive function, a self-regulating dimension that governs these three aspects of our mental world. The hub symbolizes this executive self-regulation.

In our pilot study of mindful awareness meditation training (Zylowska et al., submitted) we found that the executive functions that enabled the subjects to inhibit impulsivity and to achieve more cognitive flexibility, were greatly enhanced. This would be seen as being due to the flexible nature of a strengthened hub of the mind, the essence of executive function. The hub of the mind enables us to be reflective. Within reflective awareness we can describe three dimensions: receptive, self-observational, and reflexive awareness.

Receptive Awareness

The hub of our mind also represents a reflective form of awareness in which we can choose, with intention, to be receptive and open to whatever "comes to mind in the moment." How does this differ from exogenous attention in which our mind is pulled toward some stimulus, internal or external? In this receptive state, we are intending to be aware of the fullness of awareness, noticing our five senses, our bodily sixth sense, our mental seventh sense, and our relational eighth sense. With exogenous attention, we are becoming distracted from our intended state of attention, pulled away from our present awareness to become lost in the object of distraction.

Receptivity is an intentional state of openness to whatever arises. We as yet do not know the specific neural correlates of receptivity, but we can propose an overall brain state of neural integration connecting body, brainstem, limbic regions, and cortex that may help paint a possible picture of what may be occurring in this state of mind. As we have discussed, the middle prefrontal regions may play a central role in mediating such neural integration. Such an accepting state creates a flexibility in self-regulation that may enable an individual to profoundly shift out of old habitual ways of adapting and reacting. Receptivity may in this way directly contribute to the disruption of automatic top-down influences on present experience. In mindful awareness we can transition from being reactive to becoming receptive.

Self-Observational Awareness

Accompanying this receptive state is a separate but equally important capacity for self-observation. This reflective observational function is an active exploration of the nature of experience. Self-reflection, focusing observation on the self, has been consistently found to involve activation of the regions within the middle pre-frontal areas (medial prefrontal and anterior cingulate cortex) (Beitman, Viamontes, Soth, & Nitler, 2006; Decety & Chaminade, 2003). Reflective observation enables the individual to have an engaged process of observation in which the contents of the mind are placed not only in awareness, but are approached with a sense of investigative interest. When this self-reflective state is integrated with receptivity, it has the features of curiosity, openness, acceptance, and love (COAL). The perspective of self-understanding within this COAL frame of mind can directly create ways of knowing that can be transformative.

Reflexive Awareness

A term sometimes interchanged with the word *reflective* is the idea of a *reflexive* awareness. Being reflective as we are defining it here includes reflexivity as one of its dimensions. Some authors use the terms synonymously; others view *reflection* as an active, conscious, effortful process whereas reflexivity, as we will also use it here, is automatic, effortless, and nonconceptual. Reflexivity, as we have discussed in the previous chapter, implies a more immediate capacity of the mind to know itself, without effort, without conscious observation, without words. This reflexive quality helps us to understand the nature of awareness of awareness: The reentry of sensing one's own processes, of being aware of being aware. We can view reflexive awareness as the more automatic meta-awareness within the larger framework of reflection.

The metacognitive learning emerging from the reflexive dimension of mindful awareness may be a result of this reentry loop that creates neural maps of the mind before conceptual understanding. Neural correlates of metacognition reveal the central role of the middle prefrontal regions. The growth and reconstruction of this area during adolescence may help us understand how these reflexive functions both emerge and then become temporarily disrupted during this important period of change in an individual's life.

The overall reflective process can embed more conceptual and linguistic functions in the brain than the reflexive component alone. With self-reflection, any aspect of the self—the moment, memory, plans for the future—can be observed and mental notations made.

With the dimension of reflexivity there is a direct knowing of the process of knowing. There is no particular frame of mind that intends to create reflexive knowing—it just emerges with this level of metaprocessing. The process itself is the object of its own awareness.

In the larger picture you may be able to see that reflexive awareness of awareness may accompany the experience of reflection on the self. Both of these processes are a fundamental part of how we create mindsight, our capacity to perceive the mind itself.

Attunement and Attention

One proposal we can make is that the process of attunement creates a neural state of integration that forms the foundation of the receptive dimension of reflective awareness. Within interpersonal integration, when we come to "feel felt" by another person, we feel not only aligned with the other, but our brain likely establishes a state of what Steven Porges has called a "neuroception" of safety (Porges, 1998). Porges' polyvagal theory proposes that our nervous system evaluates the state of threat or safety of a situation and activates the brainstem's vagal and autonomic nervous systems to respond with either a sense of open receptivity with "safety" or with two aspects of "threat." One response to an assessment of threat is a state of *fight-flight* with sympathetic accelerator activation and readiness for action; the other is one of *freeze* with parasympathetic firing creating a state of collapse.

With attunement between two people creating a sense of safety, we can suggest that Porges' proposed activation of the myelinated "smart" vagus occurs with the softening of facial muscles, relaxation in vocal tone, and opening of the perceptual system to receive input from outside itself. Myelination creates more rapid neural signal transfer, and with the neuroception of safety this branch of the vagus nerve activates and supports the individual becoming open and approaching others. This receptive state of mind has the qualitative sense of exactly what we are discussing when we view the receptive dimension of reflective awareness.

Porges proposes a *social engagement system* that "provides a system for voluntary engagement with the environment with special features associated with the prosocial behaviors of communication" (1998, p. 850). The activation of this vagal system may involve the release of the hormone oxytocin and its distribution throughout the body with sensations of positive states associated with physical touching and proximity. We can extend these interpersonal mechanisms into the view of internal attunement by imagining what we can term as a "self-engagement system" that activates a form of intrapersonal communication that is embedded in a similar sense to Porges' interpersonal notion of "love without fear" (Porges, 1998, p. 847). *Love without fear* is a wonderful phrase capturing a COAL state of mind in mindful awareness.

Taking this to the next step, we can now suggest that internal attunement may activate the same neural circuitry involving the myelinated vagus in a state of safety as we create a loving relationship of self-engagement with our own direct experience. If we envision how the brain is actually able to have a map of its own ongoing state embedded in midline prefrontal structures (Decety & Chaminade, 2003; Decety & Jackson, 2004), we can then create an image of how this internal attunement might shape attention. We map our experiencing self within neural firing patterns of lived-self representations within the middle prefrontal area. We then observe these intentional states, as we'll discuss in more detail in Chapter 8, in a manner that actually primes our perceptual system for what will happen in the next immediate moment. This internal matching process of observed and anticipated, akin to what happens between two people in attunement in which they have resonance of their states, creates a state of neural integration.

The key here may be the ways in which we have a sense of our intention that directly links to our perception of moment-to-moment lived experience, the ways we engage the self with curiosity, openness, acceptance, and love (without fear). With this open, receptive part of reflection, we are freed to resonate with our own authentic experience.

When secondary influences impair this matching, then internal attunement does not occur. But when mindful awareness can disengage those top-down impediments to clear sensing, as we'll discuss in depth in the next chapter, integration occurs, internal attunement is created, and the neuroceptive assessment is one of "safety." This may be the way in which internal attunement alleviates suffering and creates a stabilizing sense of being connected to both moment-to-moment experience and to our authentic sense of self. In this evaluative state of safety, attention becomes open and receptive. The qualitative feel of such an open state is the foundation of love.

Tucker, Luu and Derryberry address a related perspective when they note that "Decety and Jackson (2004) have proposed that empathy requires three primary components: (1) a sharing of another's affect, (2) the maintenance of a separate self-representation, and (3) flexible mechanisms of emotional self-regulation to allow engagement of the differential perspectives of self and other. In reviewing neuroimaging findings related to empathic processing, Decety and Jackson cite evidence not only of brain activations that appear to mirror the experience of the other, but midline frontal activity (posterior cingulate, anterior cingulate, and frontal pole) that appears to reflect self-regulatory mechanisms integral to the shifting of self-other perspectives" (2005, p. 707).

If we apply this analysis to the notion that the self-other shifting in mindfulness is actually between self-as-observing and self-as-experiencing, then we have a neural formula for self-empathy, or internal attunement. Here the social circuits of the brain are focused on the experiencing self as an "other" that can be understood, received without judgment, and attuned to with a sense of resonance by the observing self. Tucker and colleagues also note that it is these same social circuits linking cortex and limbic areas that overlap with the executive control networks of attention as we have discussed earlier in this chapter in the work of Rueda, Posner and Rothbart (2005).

In sum, we are proposing that mindfulness involves a form of internal attunement that may harness the social circuits of mirroring and empathy to create a state of neural integration and flexible self-regulation. The sense of safety that is established with internal attunement then initiates receptive awareness in which executive attention is open to whatever arises in the field of ongoing experience. This is the reflective state of awareness that is at the heart of mindfulness.

Awareness with Intention

The reflective qualities of receptivity, self-observation, and reflexivity are each a part of mindful awareness and are not randomly achieved but are established with intention. Mindfulness is a form of paying attention in the present moment, *on purpose.* Though we may have acceptance without targeted goals per se, a nondriven form of attention, this is a way of being that is quite enveloped in a fullness of intent.

Instead of just being a passive observer or scribe of the experience of awareness, this purposeful reflective state may actually alter the flow of awareness itself. In this way, receptivity, observation, and reflexivity are all contributors to the way the mind changes within mindful awareness.

When we think of the example of engaging in autobiographical reflection, an activity we engage in regularly with patients in therapy, we can see the importance of this characteristic of awareness with intention. When people get lost in leftover issues there is a quality of spacing out into the details of their autobiographical memories. This has an exogenous feel to it, of the past imprisoning the person in the present. They have lost receptivity and reflexivity even as they pursue self-observational explorations.

In contrast, people can engage a more intentional state of mindful awareness in which they can be purposefully receptive, open to whatever arises in the moment. In this reflective state they can choose to engage their autobiographical memory stores, inviting whatever comes into awareness to come fully: Sensations, images, feelings, thoughts. In a mindful state we can SIFT through the mind's rim with intention and openness, ready to sort through anything that comes into our field of awareness. Observation enables us to sense and know the self; reflexivity creates awareness of awareness; receptivity permits the COAL state to suspend judgments. The healing that emerges with this reflective form of memory and narrative integration from a mindful exploration is deeply liberating.

Chapter Seven

JETTISONING JUDGMENTS:
Dissolving Top-Down Constraints

D irect experience gives rise to the sense that mindful awareness involves the dissolution of the influences of prior learning
on present sensation. This is the way we diminish the effects of
automatic top-down processes and it enables us to create that state
of "nonjudging" experience. We will see that this process also involves the reflective capacity of "observation" as we decouple our
responses from automatic pilot.

THE SCIENCE OF TOP-DOWN

In a helpful review of cognition and the brain, Engel, Fries, and
Singer (2001) suggested that:

> Classical theories of sensory processing view the brain as a passive,
> stimulus-driven device. By contrast, more recent approaches em-
> phasize the constructive nature of perception, viewing it as an ac-
> tive and highly selective process. Indeed, there is ample evidence
> that the processing of stimuli is controlled by top-down influences
> that strongly shape the intrinsic dynamics of thalamocortical net-
> works and constantly create predictions about forthcoming sen-
> sory events. (p. 704)

These *top-down* influences come in many forms, with researchers
using this term, and its opposite, *bottom-up*, in sometimes confus-

ing ways. I will use *top-down* to imply how engrained brain states can impinge on emerging neural circuit activations and thus shape our awareness of ongoing experience in the present moment.

In Engel, Fries, and Singer's view, this is considered a dynamicist perspective in which top-down refers to a process in which "large-scale dynamics can have a predominant influence on local neuronal behavior by 'enslaving' local processing elements" (Engel, Fries, & Singer, 2001; p. 705; Haken & Stadler, 1990).

We experience top-down influences each moment of our lives. With the process of mindfulness, we can awaken from automaticity to not be "enslaved" by the large-scale dynamics set up by earlier experience and embedded in beliefs in the form of mental models of right and wrong and judgments of good and bad. Top-down influences also come in less abstract forms, such as intense emotional reactions or bodily responses derived from prior learning.

These top-down influences have had huge survival value in our evolutionary history in that they enable the brain to make rapid assessments and carry out efficient information processing to then initiate behaviors that enable the organism to survive. Generation after generation, the more top-down rapidity of judgment, the more likely it was in many ways that we could survive as a species.

Our personal history also may reinforce top-down processes. If every moment of our lives we approached experience as if it were a baby's first step, we would never walk to the market. We must make summations, create generalizations, and initiate behaviors based on a limited sampling of incoming data that have been shunted through the filters of these mental models. Our learning brains seek to find the similarities and differences, draw conclusions, and act.

In quality of life issues, these top-down automatic filters, if too dominant, can unfortunately keep us from feeling alive. If most of life is shuttled into a previously existing category of reality, it can get pretty routine and dulled as we mindlessly move through our experiences. Top-down can make minor differences disappear and nothing becomes the "odd-ball": Subjective time is not expanded, but contracted. Having the time of our life may literally depend on dissolving these top-down enslavements and enhancing our sensitivity to the novelty of everyday living.

In the brain these top-down influences may be revealed in the structure of the neocortex. "Network architecture could constitute an 'implicit' source of top-down influences as, for instance, the topology of lateral connections within cortical areas is known to embody stored predictions that have been acquired during evolution and through experience-dependent learning" (Engel, Fries, & Singer, 2001, p. 714).

Top-down processes are defined as "intrinsic sources of contextual modulation of neural processing." These influence all levels of systems, including planning, working memory, and attention. They are put into action via large-scale groupings of neurons in widespread areas including limbic, parietal, and frontal regions. These areas and their higher-level representations embedded in both explicit and implicit memory (facts and autobiographical memory; beliefs and mental models) can continually influence the entrainment (or activation/coordination) of the processing of new perception and new information. As these activities are "entrained" they are literally shaped in the patterning of their activations by the top-down effects. This is enslavement.

The gist of these considerations is that neural firing patterns of large assemblies of neurons are influenced by past learning and by inherent developmental features, such as one's constitutional temperament. Reaching toward a deeper essence of one's self would directly move against these top-down influences as mindfulness moves us closer to the bare awareness of experience. Notice that both "higher" cortical thoughts and "lower" bodily and emotional reactions are components of this secondary top-down processing. In this perspective, "bottom-up" would refer to a more primary sensory experience that accesses ipseity, our more basic, core self experience.

On a practical level, if our past top-down influences create an internal set of "shoulds," then becoming enslaved by these beliefs without meta-awareness would make us prey to being quite judgmental about ourselves and others. The receptivity, self-observation, and reflexivity of reflection each help dissolve top-down influences.

THE SCIENCE OF BOTTOM-UP PROCESSING

Although mindful awareness is more than simply being aware of our senses, the direct route of sensation is an important component of direct experience. As we dissolve top-down influences to give us direct experience within our attentional focus, we move toward such simplicity and access ipseity at the heart of mindful living. When we "come to our senses" as Kabat-Zinn (2003b) notes, we become grounded in a mindful way of being that opens our hearts to ourselves and to others. A brain perspective on this experience of being fully present in the moment can shed some light on the path of bottom-up processing to liberate us from the prison of top-down.

Each of our eight senses has primary neural circuitry in which we (1) perceive the outside world through our first five senses, (2) have interoception of our bodily sixth sense, (3) achieve mindsight for the mental processes of our own and others' minds in our seventh sense, and (4) have a direct sensation of our resonance with something larger than our day-to-day adaptive self in our eighth sense. Living within the directness of these eight senses enables us to be grounded in the physical world, the body, our mind, and our relationships.

At the simplest level of experience, "bottom-up" processing likely entails a linkage of the neural activity of these eight senses with our dorsolateral (side) prefrontal cortex as we become aware of the core of our being, of our ipseitious self. Living in this core gives a grounded sense of being fully present and open to the moment-to-moment arising of whatever offers itself from the rim of the wheel of awareness. Here the hub of our mind is spacious and receptive.

Bottom-up can be achieved through direct focus on any of the eight senses, but perhaps the most effective early steps are to begin with the body (Ogden, Minton, & Pain, 2006). We sense our breath, for example, becoming aware of the in-breath, the turn of inhalation to exhalation, and then the out-breath. Within this rhythmic cycle of life, this ever-present interface of our body with the outside world, we bring awareness and create a resonance of connection between attention and corporeal self. We ride the wave of the breath with our mind, sensing the miracle of being alive, of being able to sense the very air that sustains this wondrous journey we call life.

Soon the sounds surrounding us fill our awareness and invite us to taste each of the five senses. In our MBSR training (Kabat-Zinn, 1990) we taste a raisin, a single raisin, for well over five minutes. Who could guess the intricate folds of a shrunken grape? In one training at our Mindful Awareness Research Center, after the raisin exercise, something seemed to shift in my brain and when we went to lunch immediately afterwards, the salad on my plate became a journey of discovery in my palate, my ears, my nose. I couldn't participate in the discussion at the table, could barely even speak to let them know why I wasn't able to join them in the verbal exchange. I was there, with the salad, the tastes and sounds and smells and textures slowly filling my awareness with each morsel. I couldn't help but giggle, the transformation was so full, and so freeing. It was a "long lunch," now I see, as I was eating a plate of "odd balls."

Bottom-up brings us into now. I taught some basic reflection skills of mindfulness to a patient recently (reviewed in Chapter 13), and after she practiced these just a few minutes each day she said, "Wow—this feels like my soul just went back into my body. It's amazing! When I get all lost in my head all I need to do is watch my breathing and then, whoosh, my soul comes sliding back in. It feels so different, and so good."

Turning to our senses brings the world and our bodies into direct, simple sensory fullness in our awareness. When the richness of the textures of that bottom-up world become a part of our lives, it soon creates a quality of experience that lends itself to knowing when the seventh and eighth senses are also felt with direct bottom-up simplicity. Sensing the mind's thoughts, feelings, memories, beliefs, attitudes, intentions, and perceptions is clearly less grounded in the physical world than our first six senses. So how do we know when our senses are freed as much as possible from being compromised by the secondary forces of top-down? There is no easy answer, from experience or science, but the gut feeling of this is akin to knowing when our awareness of the life of the mind, or of our relationships within the eighth sense, has a bare bones grounded quality. There is nothing to shed, no clouded lenses to clean, no jungle of defense and adaptations to reveal. Just being. Just this thought, this emotion, this sense of connection. This is how the "S" of the SOCK of our streams of awareness brings in data straight from whatever sector of the the rim we are focusing upon (see Figure 4.3).

Mindfulness clarifies bottom-up by its intricate dance of receptivity, self-observation, and reflexive awareness. Indeed, immersing ourselves in direct sensory experience can be a gateway to developing mindfulness skills. In this way, mindful awareness is not itself "just bottom-up," as it seems that ipseity by itself cannot disengage the top-down enslavements so prevalent in our adult lives. Within mindful awareness we develop all four of the streams of awareness to help us sense directly, observe, conceive, and know. Mindfulness is an intricate process involving discernment that enables us to detect and shed the impediments to direct experience. With mindful awareness we can sense directly and revel in life's fullness because this reflective capacity is the integrator of much more than the glorious simplicity of bottom-up sensation.

CORTEX AND CONSCIOUSNESS

In discussing mindful awareness, we need to look at what it really means to be aware, to be "conscious" in our lives.

Neurodynamics

The study of neurodynamics gives us an extremely useful view of how large-scale complex systems, such as the brain, might create states of ever-changing firing patterns that could correlate with our subjective experience of consciousness. Cosmelli, Lachaux, and Thompson (in press) have provided an in-depth look at this field:

> One of the main outstanding problems in the cognitive sciences is to understand how ongoing conscious experience is related to the working of the brain and the nervous system. Neurodynamics offers a powerful approach because it provides a coherent framework for investigating change, variability, complex spatiotemporal patterns of activity, and multi-scale processes (among others). Consciousness is an intrinsically dynamic phenomenon, and must therefore be studied within a framework that is capable of rendering its dynamics intelligible.

Neurodynamics views the brain as a complex system with self-organizational properties. As such a dynamic entity, the brain is both an open (rather than a closed) system and capable of chaotic states of activation. One of the essential aspects of this approach is to examine large-scale patterns of change in neural assemblies. In this view our understanding of consciousness, still in its infancy, will require complex assessments of electrical patterns of activity in widely distributed regions.

For example, Evan Thompson and the late Francisco Varela (2001) offered a three-dimensional model of consciousness as summarized by Thompson and colleagues (Cosmelli, Lachaux, & Thompson, in press) "Neural processes relevant to consciousness are best mapped at the level of large-scale, transient spatiotemporal patterns, the processes crucial for consciousness are not brainbound events, but comprise also the body embedded in the environment." These emergent processes reveal that those essential for consciousness "span at least three cycles of operation" that cut across brain-body-world divisions. These include regulatory organismic cycles, sensorimotor coupling between organism and environment, and cycles of intersubjective interaction. This "last type of cycle depends on various levels of sensorimotor coupling, mediated in particular by the so-called mirror-neuron systems that show similar patterns of activation for both self generated, goal-directed actions and when one observes someone else performing the same action" (Rizzolatti & Craighero, 2004).

In this perspective, "consciousness" is seen as extending beyond a merely personally experienced awareness emanating from a brain, to involve embedding a "consciousing" self in the embodied and relational world. This overlaps beautifully with our definition of the mind and also enables us to see how "sensorimotor coupling" may be an essential neural correlate of awareness (see also Chapter 9).

Invariant Representations:
Secondary versus Primary Flow

Within the brain we have seen that our six-layered cortex takes in new sensations from the bottom-up, registering this primary form of neural firing pattern in the sixth and fifth layers. Even these inputs are filtered by the thalamus, and so we know that these neural firing patterns are already quite removed from the sensed "thing itself" but are a neural translation, from the get-go, of some sensory input. We call them "primary" because they are the initial input into the cortical stream, even long before awareness. We can sense light, touch, taste, sound, smell; we can sense the state of our bodies and position of our limbs, the tension in our muscles, and the expressions on our faces; we can even sense the mind itself, experiencing directly thoughts and images, hopes and dreams, memories and worries about the future. We can possibly even sense our relationships—in resonance or dissonance—through some cortical assessment of these internal states in our eighth sense.

Primary sensory experience of these eight senses, even before awareness, involves a neural firing of the primary areas that encode them. These primary input areas include the posterior cortex for the first five senses, except for smell; the somatosensory region and other areas of the posterior cortex, as well as the midline prefrontal areas for interoceptive data, which has been taken in from the flow of neural firing through the insula; middle prefrontal activation creating a sense of self-awareness of mental processes, including self-observation and metacognition; and perhaps the mirror neuron related circuits and midline prefrontal systems for a sense of resonance and connection (see Appendix III).

To enter into consciousness, these "primary cortical sources" of the eight senses then need to be functionally connected to the side (dorsolateral) prefrontal area for us to become aware of their content. This is a general sense: something in awareness involves some linkage via this side prefrontal region. The sensory process can be occurring "beneath awareness," in which case these primary areas can be activated but just not linked to the side area.

The side and midline prefrontal regions work as a team to enable awareness not only to give us a specific quality of consciousness, but also to enable us to regulate the subsequent internal and external responses. With awareness we can choose the outcome of our response. This makes awareness not just a factor influencing our knowledge: Awareness alters the direction of our future activations.

The findings that the left prefrontal cortex seems to be activated with mindfulness practice is an important data set in our exploration of the dissolution of top-down processes (Davidson, 2004; Davidson et al., 2003). We can integrate Davidson's findings with prior work by Michael Gazzaniga and others regarding the narrator function of the left hemisphere (Gazzaniga, 2000). Though often associated with logic, language, linearity, and literal processing, the left hemisphere also appears to be dominant for the narrative drive to tell a story of events. In earlier work (Siegel, 1999; 2001b) the view has been proposed that the left hemisphere's drive to narrate and the right hemisphere's dominance in storing autobiographical memory require an integration of left and right for our life stories to be coherent.

For mindful awareness we can propose that the shift toward a left prefrontal dominance with mindfulness-based stress reduction may well be associated with not only an approach state but also the engagement of the "describe/label" aspect of the narrative dimension of the left hemisphere's function. Our experience of life will be quite different if we approach rather than avoid the contents of our own mind. Being able to describe in words enables us to share what is inside with others, and often even more effectively with ourselves.

Narrative begins as a non-linguistic process (Damasio, 1999) and appears to be embedded in the brain's inherent inclination to sort, select, and assemble the myriad representations within its vast neural networks. Long before words, our brains are creating nonverbal narratives, assemblies of selected neural network firing patterns that then serve to order our sense of the world. Even perception, at its most fundamental level, is an assembled process.

Attention helps selectively guide the process of information flow. Assemblies of neural representations in nonverbal clusters of neural nets, these unworded narratives help organize the "information" that is actually flowing. In turn, conscious attention, awareness of a specific sensory domain, can then enable the mind to sample these assemblies and then order them, selecting certain ones and discarding others.

When awareness, involving the side prefrontal region, is coupled with the metacognitve flexibility, self-observation, and bodily regulation of the middle prefrontal regions, then we have the opportunity to actually disengage automatic clusters of firing patterns.

With this fuller sense of mindful awareness beyond simple awareness, we can disengage the earlier established probabilities of firing those top-down invariant representations that have been created within memory and shape and limit ongoing sensation.

Mindful awareness is fuller than mere attention to the present moment, a simple awareness, which does not necessarily involve our middle prefrontal regions. This is a hypothesis capable of empirical investigation to verify its claim. It seems that being aware of the sensations in the present is quite likely to just have a person experience the automaticity of top-down influences without any chance of intervening because without meta-awareness these invariant representations are transparent—they are not seen as activities of the mind but "taken at face value."

Mindful awareness, in contrast, permits the decoupling of automaticity (you observe and decouple automaticity: YODA). It may be that the dimensions of "reflection" involved in mindfulness embed receptivity, self-observation, and reflexivity to create the capacity to decouple automatic invariant influences, and may be essential for mindful awareness. This can help us clarify the role of "observation" as a clearly delineated facet only for subjects with experience meditating because it may be more highly refined, and therefore detectable on a survey, with skill development.

With active observation, we would expect this: Observation would have a left hemisphere bias. The narrator function and observing "witness" of the left side of the brain may correlate with the approach state with a resultant engaged observer function detecting and disengaging previously transparent top-down influences. With this view, then, we could see a left prefrontal shift as enabling the layers of mindful awareness to disentangle the automatic firing in other areas of the brain.

REDUCING TOP-DOWN ENSLAVEMENTS

What lies beneath top-down influences? How do we actually "see directly?" We have explored one view of awareness as being composed of four streams: sensation, observation, conception, and knowing. Where would the top-down influences shape those streams? It seems that observation would be some witnessing neutrality that might enable a clear, if disconnected, vision to be created of the internal process of awareness itself.

Conception is filled with influences from invariant representations. Perhaps in cognitive mindfulness there is an attempt to loosen the constrictions of premature "hardening of the categories" (Cozolino, 2002), but still, our scaffold of knowledge is shaped by language and semantic structures of learned associations. And sensation? As we have seen, the road from direct sensation to assembled perception is filtered by top-down biases that shape our ongoing experience based on what came before.

Nonconceptual knowing may be a deeper flow of representations that rests beneath the radar of invariant influences. As we saw in Chapter 5, ipseity is the bare self that may exist beneath top-down influence. It could be that nonconceptual knowing is in fact accessing this state of being, this ipseity of our essence. If that is the case, then the knowing stream of awareness, along with direct sensation before perception and the observer, may be how we come to sense what lies beneath the influence of top-down enslavements.

Dissolving preconceived ideas and reactions, those ever-present top-down influences on ways of experiencing reality, is a challenging process. Even dropping these ideas about how to drop these ideas creates a seeming paradox. The issue is at least addressed with direct experience. With access to direct experience in that mindful state, a bare essence was felt and other processes could then be observed as being the mental activity of the mind that indeed they are.

It is a lifelong challenge, and perhaps the brain's architecture as a sense making, pattern detecting, associational anticipation machine makes that challenge inevitable. At this particular point in my own development, I have the top-down influences of my layers of streams of awareness fully in view. Perhaps one day they'll disappear and I'll tell you about it—but as my old dear professor Bob Stoller (1985) once wrote, "Maybe then, in a hundred years, sitting on my haunches like a Zen master, I shall finally write a clear sentence. But it will have no words" (p. x). Right now, in this moment, this is just the way I experience it. Streams in a valley. A beautiful sight, but a concept of distinct streams they are, a concept I can share with you through these words.

Kabat-Zinn (2003a) addressed this challenge of conceptual knowing in an articulate manner when he described how a teacher of mindfulness-based interventions needs to practice mindfulness personally:

> How will one know how to respond appropriately and specifically to their questions if one cannot draw on one's own lived experience not just on book knowledge and concepts, when the practice itself is all about seeing clearly and transcending (not getting caught up in and blinded by) the limitations of the conceptual mind while, of course, not rejecting the conceptual mind or the power and utility of thought within the larger context of awareness? (p. 150)

The challenge to work within a clinical or educational framework of goal-directed actions with a mindful approach seems quite paradoxical. "All that would be required would be to shed one set of lenses for a while and bring a fresh set, or what we might call the 'nonlenses' of original mind, to bear on what is unfolding moment by moment within one's own experience, that is, through bare, non-judgmental, non-reactive, non-conceptual attention" (Kabat-Zinn, 2003b, pp. 441–442). Here again we see the important notion of dissolving top-down influences in order to enter a state of reflective mindful awareness. Such a state requires that people "intentionally suspend their usual frame of reference, their cognitive coordinate system, for a while, and simply practice watching their own minds and bodies" (p. 441).

The "cognitive coordinate system" is exactly what mindful awareness can dissolve. Exactly how this is actually accomplished I'm not sure anyone knows. But I would like to expand on the proposal that the unique capacity of this state of reflection with its receptivity, observation, and reflexivity is what seems to be at play in enabling us to disentangle ourselves from our own automatic top-down mental processes.

At that moment of top-down influence we can imagine that Engel, Fries, and Singer's (2001) notion of enslavement would occur in which the power of large-scale assemblies (embedding the concept) would directly influence and dismantle the sometimes perhaps more fragile nonconceptual knowing stream.

Literally in the brain we could imagine becoming aware of nonconceptual knowing as correlating with activation of cell assemblies that begin to oscillate with a certain frequency as they reinforce their firing in a reentrant loop that ultimately can enter consciousness when enough integrative complexity is achieved by them. This allows "k" (knowing) to be sensed directly—enough to feel it, to remember it, to come up with SOCK, and to be convinced enough of its reality that I report it to you in words.

As the "c" (concept) comes on the neural assembly scene, the reverberation of that top-down concept-based oscillation of distal neurons enslaves the firing of the "k" assemblies and functionally they dissipate. In the brain this would occur by engrained patterns of cell assembly connections reinforced by repeated activation from prior experiences: I have come to learn how to think in concepts. I have not only learned it, I have been "emotionally rewarded in school and home" for it, which enhances the neuroplasticity strengthening the connections of those top-down invariant conceptual representations. There is nothing "wrong" with that, it is just the reality of the strength and automaticity of top-down influences.

If I can be fully mindful, I may be able to sense those influences directly. There is some way in which in that conditional open state, these influences manifest themselves in awareness and then, as mentally noted, they just seem to dissipate. How a mental note does enable this to happen would be an exciting process to understand. One clue may be in the limited resource capacity of attention: If I am noting, I am altering the power of automatic influences to dominate. Mindful awareness creates discernment, a potent de-coupler of automatic firing.

If we aspire to seek freedom from the "shoulds" and automatic misbeliefs that hold sway over our lives, learning to reinforce the assemblies of ipseity, of bare awareness, of nonconceptual knowing, of the core self, is exactly what is on the teaching docket. We can, in fact, train the mind to reinforce deeper ways of experiencing the world around and within us. We do not have to be enslaved by top-down influences. This is the process of getting beneath belief to the basics of awareness.

ACCESS TO IPSEITY: LOOSENING THE GRIP OF PERSONAL IDENTITY

The mind is making judgments as we breathe. Letting go of the grasping onto judgments seems at the core of a nonjudgmental stance. Each stream of awareness seems to uniquely support becoming nonjudgmental: "Just sensing" enables me to embrace the experience, as it is. I could sense sensations—or sense observation, or concepts, or even nonconceptual knowing. Yet observation seemed essential as well to introduce some dimension of disengagement, an uncoupling of what might have been a cascade of reactions and counterreactions that now I could just observe, not just sense. This seems to be a major contribution of mindfulness over "just being aware." But to achieve all of that, it seemed that I needed the concepts given by the teacher to embrace it all, even the words that could give voice to the present participle nature of mental reality: thinking, feeling, sensing. Instead of becoming lost in a memory, I could say (this is a word-expressed concept) "remembering" and the image would float off like a balloon or burst like a bubble. Describing and labeling with words—conceptual processes—is a fundamental part of mindful awareness.

And so, for me, awareness of sensation, observation, and concept enabled automaticity to be decoupled. But during the week of silent retreat it became clear that these three streams did more than give me that freedom in the moment, it opened a subterranean stream of awareness, that spring of nonconceptual knowing, that somehow held it all together.

In silence at first I felt I could lose my mind, as all of my usual external anchors were gone and the ship of my psyche lost its moorings. But as time went on it seemed that I came instead to find my mind. Yet it felt somehow quite familiar, as if meeting someone who "has loved you your whole life" as Derek Walcott the poet says, yet has been taken for granted. Attuning inwardly felt like a welcome home celebration. Our personal identity is filled with adaptations to a lifelong list of experiences from our earliest days forward. In many ways, the layers of memory that embed these events and our ways of coping with them form a scaffold of neural connectivity within the brain that serves to organize our lives. This organizational structure we call "I" is filled with the top-down influences we have been exploring. These invariant representations have been reinforced by emotional arousal which

enhances neuroplasticity. They have also been a part of a reentry
loop in which we carry out behaviors based on a certain identity,
and the world responds in a particular way to us. We then respond
back to how others treat us, and that in turn engrains our patterns
of processing and solidifies our personal identity even further.

The mind emerges from this matrix of memory shaped by interpersonal and embodied patterns of energy and information
flow. We can see then that both synaptic connections (memory)
and interpersonal responses (social interactive habits) converge
upon a personal identity that we then carry around with us as a
transparent cloak that constrains how we live our lives. Mindful
awareness is an opportunity to make the cloak of personal identity visible, to see beneath its surface textures.

From this reflective vision, we can see identity for what it is, an
organizational structure that has helped us survive and adapt to
our lives. Underneath this cloak may be found a feeling of what
Milan Kundera has called the "unbearable lightness of being." Its
lightness may in fact be so unbearable as to have most people cling
to the cloak of identity to avoid sitting fully in what initially may
feel like the chaos of ipseity. Our personal identity is real, but it's
not the whole deal. This awareness can change your life. Accessing ipseity creates freedom as it enables us to experience life with
a sense of novelty and emergence. In many ways the restricted cohesiveness of personal identity can give rise to the flexible coherence of the ipseitious self.

The power of mindful awareness to promote physiological, psychological, and interpersonal well-being seems to emerge from
this freedom it can offer from the prison of rigid identification
with the habits of one's own mind. These identity-driven sets of
memories and expectations, these life narrative themes and emotional patterns of response, often drive us to conform to their huge
scaffolding that filters and forms our perceptions.

The issue does not involve the removal of an individual's life
story or identity, but rather creates a coherent life story that en-

ables him or her to become free of constraints from the past rather than devoid of access to memories of who that person has been. "Feast on your life" the poets tell us. Mindfulness can clear the way to do just that.

POSSIBLE NEURAL CORRELATES OF IPSEITY

Without judgments, what are we? If we "just" are curious, open, accepting, and even loving, where has our identity gone? These may sound like curious questions, but it seems that top-down influences like judgments, memory, emotional reactivity, and identity do not so readily loosen their grip on our minds. What are we without them? The benefit of jettisoning judgments and infusing experience with freedom is that life becomes much more rewarding, engaging, exciting, flexible, and physiologically healthy.

We have seen the basic idea: Things as they are clash with things as our top-down invariant processes expect them to be. We shove sensation through the filter of the past to make the future predictable. In the process, we lose the present. But because the present is all that exists, we have lost everything in the bargain. It seems as simple as this. But it isn't so easy to undo because top-down influences that enslave bottom-up living have potent neural connectivity backing them up—much more powerful than the uncertainty of living in the here-and-now. And for this reason being mindful requires intention, and courage.

Let us take a look at how this dismantling process might occur in the brain. A sense of how mindfulness dissolves top-down influences emerges when we combine the view of large-scale assemblies and the nature of self-identity. Within the cortex we're proposing that the directional flow of top cortical layers onto the input from the lower layers might be "disrupted" with a new integrated state of neural assembly we call "mindful awareness."

One neural finding may help shed light onto how this may occur. In transient global amnesia the individual has the temporary suspension of a sense of personal identity. In my case, an injury to the head led to the temporary disabling of the axonal firing patterns in the frontal areas of the cortex, which is thought to be the mechanism whereby consciousness is fully intact, but personal identity is not present. This is more than just transient disorientation following a concussion. In this state there is sensation without the top-down shaping of prior experience through the cloak of identity. This functional state reveals that the brain can experience raw, direct sensation without the personal identity constraints that usually filter ongoing experience. Here a blow to the head can disengage the functional assemblies that embed self-identity.

When we think of the nature of global amnesia and the ways in which mindful awareness gets "beneath" top-down influences of self-identity, we can sense the ways in which those neural tracts become disrupted within the cortex to disable the usual neural net patterns of firing that bias our ongoing perceptions through the filter of "selfhood." As mentioned in Chapter 4, when I experienced that transient state of global amnesia after my own accident years ago, the focus of my attention could aim clearly on ongoing sensation. We know that working memory, the "chalkboard of the mind," has a limited space in which to hold representations in the front of the mind. This working memory process involves the side part of the prefrontal cortex (DLPFC). As other regions of the brain's activities become functionally linked to this side prefrontal area, through the filtering area called the thalamus, the representations of that more distal region enter our momentary consciousness. Perhaps in global amnesia the contribution of cortical networks of self no longer impinge on the filtering bias as streams of neural inputs feed into this thalamocortical sweep. Freed from that space-consuming input, sensations come in rich, raw, and relatively unbiased forms.

My personal experience after the accident suggests that such inhibition of the top-down influence of self-identity on ongoing sensation is possible, at least with functional disruption. For this reason I wonder if in fact one could develop a form of mental training in which that same kind of cortical disruption of top-down influences could be intentionally achieved. We could maintain our deep sense of a core self, of ipseity, while noting and disengaging from the restrictive senses of an "I" that smother our lives and keep us from showing up fully in the present.

Could mindful awareness actually create a functional disengagement of the large-scale assemblies that usually create our self-identity? As states of mind themselves are considered to be correlated with assemblies of widely distributed clusters of neurons, we can imagine how certain states of consciousness (such as mindfulness) might directly interfere with the assemblies of top-down influences such as personal identity. If this particular set of assemblies becomes activated, that includes not only side (for consciousness) but middle (for reflexivity, self-observation, receptivity, self-regulation, resonance) prefrontal areas, could it be that the frontal areas disrupted in global amnesia could also be shifted in mindful awareness? Studies of cortical disruption with transmagnetic stimulation can support this view of how the complex system of our brain can alter its states of organizational flow (Engel, Fries, & Singer, 2001; Meyer-Lindenberg, Ziemann, Hajack, Cohen, & Berman, 2002). Could these regulatory prefrontal areas shift such large scale assemblies of identity and other top-down invariant representations? If such a shift influenced the thalamocortical sweep, believed to shape what enters our state of awareness, we could imagine how our conscious experience of self might be significantly altered.

What theoretical viewpoints can we draw on to support this proposal? James Austin (1998, 2006) has written about a relevant but distinct process called "kensho" in his in-depth explorations of the relationship between Zen Buddhist practice and neuroscience. As a neurologist, he comes equipped with professional experience with disturbances in neural functioning; as a practitioner of Zen, he has experienced the subjective side of delving into altered states of consciousness. Austin (2006) wrote:

> Once you pass beyond this simple distinction of the self into soma and psyche, it then becomes easier to understand some differences between states of consciousness. For example, the early, superficial states of absorption drop out the sense of the physical self. On the other hand, the later states of kensho not only drop out the psychic self but their insights transform the rest of one's prior existential concepts about what constitutes reality. Kensho made it easier for me to envision the separate "*I-Me-Mine*" operations within my own self with greater objectivity and to recognize how deeply I had been overconditioned. (pp. 24–25)

Austin wrote about the brain's two different sets of circuits, which he referred to as "egocentric" and "allocentric" circuitry. He postulated that the neural networks important in the construction of an autobiographical narrative self might be shut down during this state of kensho. Such circuits might involve the thalamus, sitting at the top of the brainstem and serving as a relay port through which much of perceptual input passes. Input from the deeper structures of the most basic self, at the brainstem level of the reticular activating system, could then "gate" this flow directly and alter how we perceive a sense of egocentric or allocentric focus. He suggested that the intralaminar nuclei of the thalamus may be involved in the creation of hyperawareness in kensho that can increase a form of "fast-frequency synchrony" in more distal regions, such as in the cortex. These thalamic nuclei could then shape the process of reentry that promotes a form of resonance within the loops from cortex to thalamus and back to cortex and thus alters the functioning of the egocentric and allocentric networks. These proposals, he acknowledged, are in need of empirical validation.

Newberg reported a finding that at moments of "peak" states during meditation in Buddhist practitioners and during nuns' prayer there was a common decrease in activity in a region of the brain that helps define our bodily boundaries, the parietal cortex (Newberg, D'Aquili, & Rause, 2002). While the specific nature of the subjective states achieved is unclear in this work, it does suggest the notion that a correlate with the shift of a bodily sense of self in certain practices may be found by examining cortical regions associated with our experience of identity.

We can also turn to general discussions of the neural correlates of consciousness for further insights, as with Walter Freeman's (2000) fascinating discussion of consciousness and the brain. In his section entitled "Neocortex as an Organ of Mammalian Intentionality" he stated:

> Recent findings obtained by recording EEGs from the scalps of volunteers . . . indicate that cooperation between the modules of each hemisphere . . . shows that sensory and limbic areas of each hemisphere can rapidly enter into a cooperative state, which persists on the order of a tenth of a second before dissolving to make way for the next state. The cooperation depends on the entry of the entire hemisphere into a global chaotic attractor. (pp. 229–230)

What this suggests it that large-scale assemblies are coordinated in rapid order to create a sense of awareness in the moment. Freeman (2000) further offered that:

> [his] hypothesis is that a global spatiotemporal pattern in each hemisphere is the principal correlate of awareness. The interactive populations of the brain are continually creating new local patterns of chaotic activity that are transmitted widely and that influence the trajectory of the global state. That is how the content of meaning emerges and grows in richness, range, and complexity. . . . So the whole hemisphere, in achieving unity from its myriad shifting parts, can sustain only one global spatiotemporal pattern at a time, but that unified pattern jumps continually, producing the chaotic but purposeful stream of consciousness. (p. 232)

If certain aspects of frontal assemblies were not recruited into the "interactive populations" that enter a "cooperative state," we can imagine that a mindfulness-induced form of intentional access to ipseity could be created. Just as transient global amnesia has the bare awareness of ongoing sensation without top-down constraints of identity, so too could mindful awareness omit those aspects of frontal "modules" from being recruited into the assemblies of ongoing conscious experience.

The rapid sense of direct experience, that items shift in awareness, may be illuminated in Freeman's discussion of timing. If every tenth of a second our brains are capable of assembling states of activation that create a "now" sense of awareness, then it would be quite possible to have rapidly fluctuating experiential immersions in, say, the four streams of awareness. Consciousness then could embed reverberating assemblies of five rounds of the four streams, all within two seconds. The subjective feel of that two-second period might seem like a simultaneous presentation of each of the four streams. But in fact, if Freeman is right, the tenth of a second profile on some monitor might instead appear as if they were global spatiotemporal jumps, not the seemless flow of streams of awareness.

Interestingly, Daniel Stern's analysis from a range of thinking (2003) inferred that five to eight seconds in general is what we can consider the duration of the subjective sense of a present moment. What this means from the neural point of view is that we could have at least 50 instantiations of "states" all in the present moment! For my experience of streams of awareness, this means that in one present moment I could have had between 12 and 20 rounds of each stream giving me a deep sense of continuity and clarity in this "being in the present moment."

As the river of consciousness flows within mindful awareness, we may be able to stabilize our states in our internal experience. With stabilization ongoing, sensation may become more vivid, the details more available for absorption, and ultimately accessible for description and sharing with each other in these word forms.

As one gets closer to sensation beneath top-down, closer to the bare self we are calling ipseity, we can imagine the brain would entrain that state—making it more likely to be able to be achieved in the future. In mindful awareness, then, we can propose that ipseity is not some "better" state that attempts to get rid of personal identity. Instead we can suggest that mindfulness broadens identity by giving neural access to the direct experience beneath invariant top-down influences. In this way, the trait of mindfulness may disengage the large-scale assemblies of top-down layers so that we can "simultaneously" experience ipseity alongside personal identity. With such a trait, our previously restrictive personality patterns may become more flexible and, ultimately, transformed.

The assembling of selected modules that bring ipseity to awareness is a skill. This learned ability does not require disappearing from one's daily life, but it may require showing up for it in a new way.

NONJUDGMENT

To jettison judgment, we need to disengage the reentry loops that reinforce top-down processing. We have seen that the dynamic definition of top-down influences refers to the way that these "higher" processes, like self-identity, carry out a takeover mission called enslavement in which they shape the "lower" perceptual processes in the moment. This shaping is automatic and persistent in our day-to-day life. But with mindful awareness we can propose that something quite profound happens. Beyond just "sensing in the moment," mindfulness involves the powerful facets of nonjudgment and the description of internal states that are coupled with meta-awareness, knowing the mind as the mind itself. We have seen that the reflective combination of receptivity, observation, and reflexivity can be proposed to massively alter the nature of large-scale assemblies of neurons involved in consciousness. Giving us access to ipseity, such shifts can enable us to not grasp onto judgments.

It is this alteration that dissolves the automatic nature of top-down processes, making them available as visible rather than transparent mental activities that then can be observed, noted, and allowed to disengage from their enslaving influences.

With the practice of such disengagement of these automatic processes, we could imagine strengthening the connectivity among cells needed to create such a coherent state of mindfulness. As an individual engaged in mindful awareness continues to practice, that assembly of bare awareness, the ipseity-imbued clear access to a core self, would become more readily accessed. Over time, the capacity of that large-scale assembly of mindfulness to effectively, efficiently, and perhaps (eventually) effortlessly engage itself and dismantle top-down influences would become a trait of the individual's "personality." In research terms we would see this as lasting changes in such observable traits as the flexibility of affective and cognitive styles and patterns of interactions with others.

Here we would see that the functional linkages creating cell assemblies across widely distributed areas would be the key to identifying neural plastic changes in the brain. As we explore how internal attunement and neural integration may alter these large assemblies, we may be able to get a glimpse of how they facilitate the capacity of the mind to get closer to bare awareness beneath the top-down influences that keep us from clarity.

TOP-DOWN WORDS AND THE POETRY OF MINDFULNESS

As this journey into mindfulness has evolved, I have become more acutely aware of something I could not have put words to in the past, the nature of presence. Years ago I came across the work of an Irish Catholic scholar/philosopher/poet named John O'Donohue. His work, *Anam Cara: A Book of Celtic Wisdom* (1997) struck a deep chord in me. His prose read like poetry, depicting the deep nature of our longing to belong. In particular, I was moved by his discussion of the importance of solitude as a way of gathering oneself, of regaining a sense of balance. I was able to attend a seminar with John O'Donohue and on the second day of that Oregon retreat I told the story of my evening the night before. It was a blistery cold autumn evening and I hiked down the tattered stairs to the rocky beach below. The sky was studded with the intermittent glow of distant stars peaking through the clouds. As my eyes adjusted to the dim starlight, I could see the edge of the tide moving its serpentine path up the beach for miles along the base of the steep cliffs hugging the shore. As I walked past a hollow in the rocks I heard a sudden sound, my heart pounding me out of my star-gazing daze. I turned toward what seemed to be a cave in the cliff and imagined an intruder, or a bear, or some kind of menace. My hand gripped the flashlight and my thumb put pressure on the switch. As I peered into the darkness, I realized that shining the light would actually make it more difficult to see clearly. I'd be undoing the adjustment to the dim light that created my night vision.

I held the flashlight in front of me and could imagine its beam shedding a concentrated glare into the cave. While that limited view would have exquisite detail, I'd lose the big picture of the whole scene.

Fear drives us to shine a focused beam of light onto what we think we must know, to keep us safe, to give us a sense of truth, of keeping the world the way we think it should be. We have words and ideas that frame and form the field of awareness that dull our senses, shaping what we think we know, in thoughts, about what can be known. But the real truth is that those "cognitive contraptions" help structure a neural attempt to make sense of a complex world, only to then entrap us in the very structures that we have created.

As we grow, we run through our lives with those spotlights of attention that selectively focus on only what we need to be doing. Without the night's mind vision of being, we lose sight of the real and big picture. We lose the essence of being, the core of being present. Presence is the bare awareness of the receptive spaciousness of our mind. Beneath the layers of adaptation to survive in the world remains a powerful mind vision that enables us to be receptive to whatever is. It is this presence that mindfulness re-creates. This is a re-creation because children early on have this receptivity, this playfulness of being. Recreation, in its deepest sense, is a re-creation of a playful state of presence.

When we feel presence in others we feel that spaciousness of our being received by them. And when we reside in presence in ourselves, others and indeed the whole world are welcome into our being.

When I presented this story to John and the other mystics, as John calls his students, we had gathered in the small hall overlooking the sea and laughed at the idea of my being attacked by a mountain goat. The parallel to life was clear: we imagine a sense of danger and then we create our conceptual constructs to save us, our personal identities to define and confine us, so that we'll know and be able to predict, to control the outcome of this wild journey we call life.

Letting go of such top-down influences is the art of mindful awareness. The receptivity of presence permits us to unleash the shackles that automatically enslave us. The fear, so often unspoken, is that without that structure we'll lose our minds, go insane, fall prey to attackers, and die.

Words are the cognitive contraptions we use to work our way through the world of uncertainty. Words can free us: as symbols they are essential to distance us from experience enough to compare and contrast and reveal patterns in a complex universe. Seeing those patterns with ideas framed in our mind also enables us to communicate those insights to others. In these ways words are a wonderful gateway to understanding and sharing.

Yet words can also entrap us. If we do not recognize the limitations of their boundaries, if we see them as real, their top-down influences on our lives can be devastating. We can come to believe that "intelligence" is something we are either born with, or not. We can think that "we" are good and "they" bad. We can even feel that "I" is something so real and important that "you" don't matter. In each of these ways, our linguistics lock us in, trap our minds, cloud our vision. But poets have found a way to use words to free our minds, to clear our vision, to create mindfulness in the moment. The art of the poet is to bring presence into our lives. With poetry we sense the world in a new light. I felt the directness of the words of poetry at the retreat, words that did not seem to "represent" anything other than the essence of what they said, some primary presentation of what they spoke. And when I took the time to be present with myself and journey along the sea, the words that emerged seemed to come directly from somewhere beneath the layers of an everyday "me."

Hearing poetry feels integrative. The science of language and the brain reveals that while the left hemisphere specializes in linguistic language, the right takes a dominant role in words with ambiguous meaning. Also, the imagery evoked by poetry seems to more directly activate the primary visuospatial processes of our brains, also a specialty of the right hemisphere. In these ways, a poet may be artfully inducing an integrated state that melts away the simple secondary enslavements that everyday top-down usage of words can become.

In several seminars, inviting people to focus on their breath for a few minutes enabled them to have a deeper appreciation for the impact of poetry (O'Donohue & Siegel, 2004, 2005, 2006). The mindful state, even if just a hint of it is created by a few moments of silent breath awareness or poetry reflection, seems to create a receptive presence of mind. By "presence" I mean quite specifically the state of receptive awareness of our open minds to whatever arises as it arises. Presence is an invitation to experience directly.

In the presence mindful awareness reveals, top-down constraints that filter, distort, limit, and restrict sensation are minimized. I want

to say that they are eliminated, but perception, as we have discussed, is never "the thing as it is." There is no immaculate perception. But it seems that mindful awareness does permit us to get
as close as we can to clear vision, that there is some kind of "ground
of being" or some grounded receptive state, some spaciousness of
the mind, that is as free from top-down filter constraints as is hu-
manly possible.

Poetry may dissolve those secondary influences because the
words of poems do not "stand for something else." Poems have
words, and as linguistic packets they must be symbols of something other than the squiggly lines or vibrations of sound waves
of which they are made. But I sense that what is meant by this
proclamation is that as words they are as direct as can be.

Just as presence is as "pure" a form of receptivity as the mind
can muster, the words of poetry have that same bottom-line
essence to them. In an intimately integrative way, poems transform
our minds with direct experience. To be open to experiencing
the message we need to be in at least a state of intentionality to
receive. But poems can also *activate* a state of receptive mindful
awareness. I believe that they do this by directly stimulating the
four streams of awareness that flow into our river of consciousness to create a mindful presence. Poems evoke a *sensory* immediacy that is at the ground of mindful awareness. Poems enable us to
observe with clarity as they show, but do not tell. The imagery and
sensations of poetry seem to put old conceptualizations on hold—
and can even burst our cognitive contraptions at their roots as they
create new *conceptual* frameworks of experience. And poems give
birth to a new way of *knowing*.

AN OPTICAL DELUSION

In our daily lives our brain decodes patterns of experience into
concepts that in turn shape the nature of our perceptions. Sensory

data emerge up into our cortices' lower levels and then are molded by secondary influences from the upper cortical layers. The cortex seems to have an innate push to sort, select, and sequence bits of data to make sense of what it is experiencing, moment by moment.

The concept of self is one such molding influence of this sorting process. Under normal conditions, we continue to see self as separate, as clearly defined. But when these usual inputs and reinforcements to our top-down concepts are undone, we perhaps can begin to see more clearly that we all share some fundamental connection to each other. With this clarity the interconnectedness of all things becomes readily apparent. Albert Einstein referred to an "optical delusion" of our separate nature, a delusion we needed to struggle with to help "widen our circle of compassion." Here is what Einstein said in a letter to a rabbi who requested help on what to say to his daughter who was coping with the accidental death of his other daughter, her sister (Einstein, 1972):

> A human being is a part of the whole, called by us "Universe," a part limited in time and space. He experiences himself, his thoughts and feelings as something separated from the rest, a kind of optical delusion of his consciousness. This delusion is a kind of prison for us, restricting us to our personal desires and to affection for a few persons nearest to us. Our task must be to free ourselves from this prison by widening our circle of compassion to embrace all living creatures and the whole of nature in its beauty. Nobody is able to achieve this completely, but the striving for such achievement is in itself a part of the liberation and a foundation for inner security. (p. 165)

This may be a reality that is hard to grasp through the lens of the top-down model of personal identity we carry around with us each day, the concept of a separate self. As we come to get closer to the ipseitious self beneath those adaptations, as we find a way to attune to our own minds, an emerging sense of freedom and inner security becomes available in our lives.

Chapter Eight

INTERNAL ATTUNEMENT:
Mirror Neurons, Resonance, and Attention to Intention

In this chapter we will deeply explore the possible neural correlates of the process of resonance, as we expand our view of mindfulness as a form of internal attunement.

Mindfulness involves attuning our attention to our own intention. Of course, mindfulness itself is an intentional state, so we could say that this creates the following tongue twister: An intention to pay attention to intention to be mindful. This appears to be a reentry loop of mental reinforcement that lies at the heart of the experience. Intention to attend to intention.

From a complexity point of view, such resonant states create a special condition in which the system is said to move toward maximal complexity. In relationships we study the way two people attend to each other's intentions in the process of attunement. The mathematical probability theory underlying this perspective suggests that when an open system moves toward complexity in such an attuned, resonant state it is the most stable, flexible, and adaptive. As we've seen in Chapter 4, if we add the other characteristics of coherent and energized, we get flexible, adaptive, coherent, energized, and stable (FACES). The word *coherence* itself is the acronym for its own features: connected, open, harmonious, engaged, receptive, emergent, noetic, compassionate, and empathic. The less familiar of these, *emergent* and *noetic*, mean that something arises with a sense of freshness and novelty as emergence; and that we have a sense of deep authentic knowing with noesis.

There is a set of neural circuits, the mirror neuron system, that links perception and motor areas in the creation of representations of intentional states. This system, along with other areas such as the insula, superior temporal cortex, and middle prefrontal regions, form the interconnected "resonance circuitry" (Figure 8.1; see Appendix III, Resonance Circuits). The resonance circuits have been shown to not only encode intention, but also to be fun-

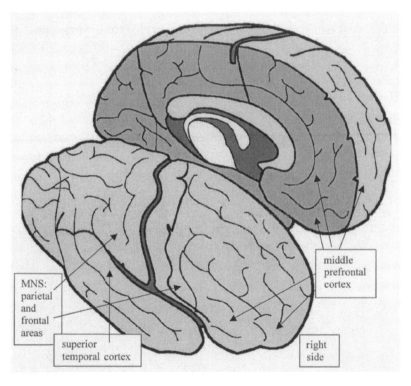

Figure 8.1 The "resonance circuitry" includes the mirror neuron system (MNS), the superior temporal cortex (STC), the insula cortex (IC, not visible on this drawing, but beneath the cortex linking these areas to the inner limbic region and the body below), and the middle prefrontal cortex. (See Figure 2.2 and Appendix III for specific details.)

damentally involved in human empathy, and also in emotional resonance, the outcome of attunement of minds.

A SYSTEM THAT MIRRORS MINDS

Researchers in Italy were studying the premotor area of a monkey's cortex. When the monkey ate a peanut, a single neuron being monitored with an implanted electrode fired off (Gallese,
Fadiga, Fogassi, & Rizzolatti, 1996).

Fine, that is what they were studying, so it wasn't a big surprise.
What happened next has changed the course of our neural insight
into the mind. When the monkey *watched* someone else eat a
peanut, that same motor neuron fired off! This implies that the
motor neuron in the front of the brain was connected to the perceptual areas in the back of the brain, in this case the visual system. At a minimum this is an example of sensorimotor integration, an interesting but not startling finding. The exciting finding
was that this integrated system only becomes active when the motion being observed is *goal-directed*. If you wave your hands in front
of the monkey there will be no activation of mirror neurons. The
mirror properties imply that the carrying out or the perceiving of
an intentional act, a goal-directed behavior, activates this set of circuits: Monkey see, monkey do.

As these mirror properties were discovered in humans by Marco
Iacoboni and others, including the original researchers, Rizollatti
and Gallese, it became clear that the *human brain creates representations of others' minds* (Gallese, 2003; Iacoboni, in press; Iacoboni,
Koski et al., 2001; Iacoboni, Woods et al., 1999; Rizzolatti &
Craighero, 2004; Rizzolatti, Fogassi, & Gallese, 2001). At a neural
level, we embed in our brains not just what we physically see, but
the mental intention we imagine is going on in someone else's
mind. This is big news: Mirror neurons demonstrate the profoundly social nature of our brains.

Marco Iacoboni and I work together at the Center for Culture, Brain, and Development, at UCLA (http://www.cbd.ucla.edu; see Appendix I). There we provide a research and educational program for undergraduate, graduate, and postdoctoral students in interdisciplinary thinking and investigation. Mirror properties of the nervous system provide an important window into examining the nature of culture and how shared ritual behaviors within our families, schools, and communities enable us to resonate with each others' internal states, including intentions.

Iacobini carried these ideas further into the realm of empathy. He and his colleagues were able to demonstrate (see Carr, Iacoboni, Dubeau, Maziotta, & Lenzi, 2003) that the mirror neuron system, located in various cortical regions such as the frontal and parietal lobes, and relating directly to the superior temporal area, would not only be able to represent intentional states of others, but could mediate the basic mechanisms of emotional resonance so fundamental to relationships.

These outer cortical processes of perception and representation of intentions become linked to the more central limbic/emotional processing and bodily state shifts by way of the insula. The insula serves as an information highway responding to mirror neuron activations by engaging bodily and limbic firings to match what the individual perceives in another person. The insula links mirror neuron activation in perception to the alteration in bodily and emotional states that we call emotional contagion in science, or emotional resonance in plain language. Resonance, as we have said, is the functional outcome of attunement that allows us to feel felt by another person.

We use our first five senses to take in the signals from another person. Then the mirror neuron system perceives these "intentional states," and by way of the insula alters limbic and bodily states to match those we are seeing in the other person. This is attunement and it creates emotional resonance. The mirror neuron system interacts directly with the insula and other regions, such as the superior temporal cortex, to create what we are calling a "resonance circuit" (see Figure 8.1 and Appendix III, Resonance Circuits). Mirror neurons link perception and motor action directly and interact intimately with these related areas to create a functional circuit that can create behavioral imitation, affective and somatic resonance, and the attunement of intentional states. The input of these processes directly influences the middle prefrontal areas, which are thus also included as part of the resonance circuitry.

Empathy draws on these bodily and limbic shifts in a process called "interoception" in which we perceive inward—using what we've called our "sixth sense," so that we come to sense what we ourselves are feeling in our own body. As we use the prefrontal cortex to carry out interoception by way of the input back-upward from the insula (relaying data from our limbic and our bodily areas), we can then be in a position to carry out the hypothesized functions of interpreting our state shifts and then attributing these to others. Interoception, interpretation, and attribution are the proposed steps of empathy carried out by the prefrontal region in this "insula-hypothesis" model of Iacoboni and colleagues (Carr et al., 2003).

As Iacoboni and I were presenting the clinical implications of this view to over 500 mental health practitioners in San Francisco (Iacoboni & Siegel, 2004), the audience was eager to understand not only the science, but what could be done with this information in clinical terms. At the very least, these discoveries confirmed a clinician's intuition that relationships are fundamental in a person's life and well-being. But these findings also verified the importance for each of us to be attuned to our own internal states in order to attune to others. Here is where mindfulness, empathy, and interoception seem to overlap. Each may reinforce the other.

The discovery of mirror neurons also revealed the ways that our brains are able to create representations of other people's minds.

This is a crucial view of how we are linked to each other on the mental plane of reality—our seventh sense, mindsight.

Empathy requires that we reflect on our internal states. The mirror neuron system and related regions' creation of emotional resonance shifts the limbic and bodily states so that the prefrontal region can reflect on those changes and create compassionate (feeling with another) and empathic (understanding another) responses. When we sense that resonance, when we become aware of being attuned, there may be the eighth sense we have been discussing in which we feel the state of our relational resonance. In this way, the resonance circuitry involves all eight senses and participates in creating a coherent state of mind.

MIRROR NEURONS AND MINDFULNESS?

Four interrelated dimensions of our social brain's mirror neurons, and related regions that comprise the resonance circuitry, might make it likely that this system is involved in the experience of mindful awareness.

Social Circuits and Personal Reflection

The first is that it seems reasonable to assume that we use the social circuitry of the brain to create the mindful states of awareness. As we discussed in Chapter 1, given that our evolution as a species has largely been influenced by our highly social ways of living and surviving, it is likely that these social networks were created long before we had "time" to have inner reflection in our lives.

Our brains are the social organ of the body, and the way human beings have survived thus far has been related to the ways in which we use our minds within social settings. Could this social brain be embedded in how we function in solitude? Certainly, psychologists such as Lev Vygotsky (1934/1986) and writers such as John Dewey

(1933), and George Herbert Mead (1925) had been championing the idea of the social nature of our minds in the early part of the 20th century. Dewey and Mead both discussed the importance of reflection in our social lives. Dewey even used the term *reflective intelligence* to articulate the way that we can awaken our minds and stop living on automatic (1933). In other words, these writers proposed that we utilize the social in engaging the personal.

More recent work in brain imaging suggests that our capacity to have an image of our own mental processes and to image those of another within what can be called "mindsight" are intimately interwoven (Siegel, 1999, in press). These findings support the notion that we neurally embed a sense of others within circuits similar to those where we create a sense of ourselves (Decety & Chaminade, 2003; Keenan, Wheeler, Gallup, & Pascual-Leone, 2000).

And so, standing on the shoulders of giants, we can look ahead and imagine that the social nature of our brains may have something to do with our minds in solitude—as when we are immersed in mindful awareness practices.

Attending to Intention

A second major idea that points to the possible role of the socially based mirror neurons and superior temporal cortex is that this system enables us to create *maps of intention*. In a social setting we map the intentions of others. What if we conceived of this same resonance circuitry as enabling us to make neural maps of our own intentional states? Mindfulness involves a curious, open, accepting, and loving stance toward awareness of awareness. In addition, we focus on our own intentional states. This is how we activate our proposed "self-engagement system" that enables us to be receptive to our own experience, attuning to ourselves moment-by-moment (see Appendix II).

As I would ponder these ideas while working with patients, I came to sense the maps of their intentions in my own mind. An understanding of transparent and opaque processes helps to explain this phenomenon. As mentioned briefly in Chapter 7, when mental activity happens without our sensing it as an event of the mind, it is referred to as *transparent*. When metacognition enables us to sense that mental activity as a product of our minds, it is said to be *opaque*. Raising awareness of a process, like a representation of intention, sensitizes our minds and primes the metacognitive process to identify that experience as a mental activity. We now know that in fact we can indeed come to sense internal representations as the mental maps that they are: This is how what before was a transparent seamless sense of something becomes an opaque representational process and observed as a mental function, an activity of the mind. Turning transparent processes into opaque activities is a way of describing discernment.

With practice and direction, we can become aware of the contents of our own mind as being just that: mental contents. As one parent of a young patient of mine once said, after experiencing this difference in our family session, "I never knew my feelings and thoughts were just activities of my mind and not all that I am!" With this emergence of meta-awareness, the power of mindfulness to dissolve the top-down influences of automatic living becomes engaged. As we attune to ourselves internally, our own intentional states become opaque. This attention to intention may directly involve the mirror neurons and superior temporal cortex.

Internal Resonance

A third dimension pointing to the possible role of mirror neurons is their proposed role in emotional resonance. Educated as an attachment researcher, I know that resonance is the underlying mechanism beneath the attuned communication between parent and child in secure attachment. As we have discussed, mindful awareness can be seen as a parallel form of intrapersonal attunement. If this is true, then it might be that our own mirror neurons and related areas utilized in interpersonal communication might enable us to resonate with ourselves. Both inter- and intrapersonal forms of attunement might similarly involve the mirror neuron system in the larger resonance circuit we have proposed to involve the insula and superior temporal regions as well as some aspects of the middle prefrontal cortices.

If attunement were indeed a central mechanism of both mindfulness and attachment, it might help explain why the middle prefrontal functions we have discussed might be well developed for both secure attachment and for mindful awareness practices. Recall that the middle prefrontal region receives the input via the insula from the limbic and bodily resonance as mediated via the mirror neuron system. It is these very areas, in fact, that Lazar and colleagues found were thicker in individuals with mindfulness meditation practices (Lazar et al., 2005).

Sensory Implications of Motor Actions

The fourth aspect of mirror neurons that suggests to me that they might be intimately involved in mindfulness, is a little known aspect of them that becomes evident in their actual functioning in the brain. Essentially the linkage of the perceptual areas with the premotor areas enables the perception of a goal-directed act to be linked to the readying, or priming, of the premotor planning area of the brain. This linkage is representation of intention.

As we shall see, the representation of intention is central to what some researchers consider the heart of emotion (Freeman, 2000). In this way, how we tune in to each other's intentions gives us a feeling of emotional closeness. How we attune to our own state by attending to our own intentions would create a kind of internal emotional closeness, or "becoming our own best friend." This is the internal attunement that yields such a powerful sense of a coherent mind. Let's dive more deeply into how this may emerge in mindful awareness.

INTERNAL ATTUNEMENT

Mirror neurons and the superior temporal regions create representations of intention by responding to goal-directed actions or expressions. From prior experience, the brain comes to learn what is coming next. Memory research reveals how the brain is an associational organ, making linkages among its widely distributed clusters of neurons. Donald Hebb (1949) is often paraphrased as saying that "neurons that fire together, wire together," meaning that the associational linkages at one time become reactivated in the future. This is the fundamental basis for memory.

But the brain is also an anticipation machine. The brain's fundamental architecture as a parallel-distributed processor enables it to learn from experience and anticipate the next step in a sequenced pattern of stimuli. Over time the brain learns how such things as gravity work, so that "what goes up, will come down" is a learned eventuality. Interestingly, the brain early on also makes a distinction between inanimate and animate objects. There are actually special regions of the brain, such as in the superior temporal cortex, that activate only with "biological motion." This superior temporal sulcus region activates in response to a living organism's motion through space—living organisms move with intention. (See Appendix III, Resonance Circuits for further discussion of the superior temporal cortex.)

The mirror neuron system and superior temporal cortex are tuned in to intentional acts. This resonance circuit carries out its mathematical deductions by way of anticipation of what will happen next in biological motion. Iacoboni (2005) described this process as a "predictor of the consequences of a motor plan" (p. 634), meaning that the brain anticipates what the sensory changes will be based on the motoric movement of the organism being observed. We can refer to this important function as SIMA (sensory implications of motor action).

SIMA enables the brain to prime itself for the next anticipated event. SIMA creates in us, through the mirror neuron system's linkage of perception and motor action, a neural process that readies ourselves to not only anticipate, but to carry out the same action ourselves! This is how we social creatures can have such coordinated lives together. It's how we learn to dance, engage in a kiss, participate in social rituals, and find empathic attunement with each other. What would happen if we engaged our SIMA and the attunement of intention dimensions of our social resonance circuitry as we focused on our self? We can propose that as we embed an image of what is happening *now* with an automatic readying for what is *next*, the brain is representing an intentional state. This is how we are aware of intention. Notice how this automatic anticipation is a form of priming, not a prefrontal planning process. Priming readies us for the emerging now that peaks over the "horizon of the future" (Stern, 2003). In the next *now*, what happens actually matches what our mirror neuron system anticipated and the coherence between that anticipation and the map of what actually came to be creates a profound state of coherence. If this is a part of mindful awareness, we can refer to this as "reflective coherence."

SIMA would allow for this matching of what is happening right now with what intention embeds will happen in the immediate next now. This is not a preoccupation with planning for the future, this is the unavoidable state of "moment-by-moment" awareness, where each moment is matched with what happened in the immediate past. The timing of this would be the order of 10s of milliseconds and would create a state of neural integration yielding the mental sensation of coherence. This is intrapersonal attunement.

BREATH AWARENESS

One example of intrapersonal attunement would be the practice of breath awareness. You are aware of your in-breath. The mirror neuron and superior temporal areas, as a part of the resonance circuits, automatically—through SIMA—anticipates the out-breath. With a beat of time, the out-breath indeed comes and there is a match between what was anticipated and what is happening. That matching creates coherence. Naturally the awareness of the out-breath entrains an anticipation of the in-breath, which when it comes, integrates SIMA with here-and-now awareness and reflective coherence is created. This may be why the breath is such a powerful, and common, focus of mindful awareness. It is also interesting to note that each relaxed half breath takes about the interval Stern (2003) defines as the present moment.

We could predict a similar process for nonmoving objects of attention, like a rock or even a mental image of a person or deity. In this case the SIMA creates a stationary image of what is anticipated with that intentional state. The point is that the neural representation of self-intention enables the SIMA process, with mindful awareness, to create reflective coherence.

We pay attention, focusing awareness on a very specific mental process: our own intentional state. This focus of awareness, when created in a process of clarity, then creates a dual-matching system in which we have a neural map of intentions (a product in part of our mirror neurons and superior temporal cortex) and we have the sensory map of the carried out action in our focus. Whether that sensory map is moving, as in our awareness of breathing, or stationary, as with an image, we create a match between sensory map and intentional map.

Further, we actually have a recursive map of ourselves maintaining a focus of attention, intentionally, on our intentions. Breathing in, breathing out, we have a match of *ourselves* as the focus of attention, and the map of ourselves with the intention to attend, and the anticipated next step in the sequence: During the out-breath we are readied for the in-breath, and then it arrives, and the mapping matches. With the in-breath the same anticipatory priming occurs, the match takes place, and with continued intentional attention, the sequence repeats. That matching set of maps creates integration and a deep feeling of wholeness, of harmony.

This may be why something as "simple" as breath awareness has been found in so many cultures as a basic approach toward well-being.

Breath is a fundamental part of life. Breathing is initiated by deep brainstem structures and is impacted directly by our emotional states. Yet breath can also be intentional. And for all of these reasons, breath awareness brings us to the heart of our lives. We come to the borderline between automatic and effortful, between body and mind. Perhaps for each of these reasons, pathways toward health include the mindful focus on the breath as a starting point on the journey.

Sensation and intention are dual representations mapped coherently on each other. The SIMA priming of the mirror neuron system and related areas then is a proposed mechanism by which we can imagine that mindful awareness might create internal attunement and coherence in the mind. Such a resonant state may have a deep sensation of fullness and stability that comes with coherence, that resonant and harmonious state of mind.

ATTENTION TO INTENTION

Two of the essential elements of all mindful awareness practices appear to be an awareness of awareness itself and a focus of attention on intention. We have examined the metacognitive process of self-monitoring and have seen that it is associated with activation of the middle prefrontal regions. But how do we really pay attention to intention? We can imagine that intention, as a mental state of the internal world, is likely also to be assessed by self-reflective middle prefrontal circuits.

When we surmise another person's intention, we have "figured out" his or her internal state by the perception of the person's patterns of action (Decety & Chaminade, 2003; Decety & Jackson,

2004; Frith, 2002). Frith put it this way: "Activity in the anterior cingulate cortex and medial prefrontal cortex is associated with awareness of our own actions and also occurs when we think about the action of others" (p. 481). He goes on to propose that "the mechanism underlying awareness of how our own intentions lead to actions can also be used to represent the intentions that underlie the actions of others. The common system enables us to communicate mental states and thereby share our experiences"(p. 481).

Intentions create an integrated state of priming, a gearing up of our neural system to be in the mode of that specific intention: we can be readying to receive, to sense, to focus, to behave in a certain manner. Intention is not just about motor action. For example, if we have the intention to be open, our brains likely will create a priming of areas involved in the inflow of neural firing of sensation from the five senses, interoception of the sixth sense, mindsight of our seventh sense, and relational resonance in our eighth sense. This intention to be open, not the receptivity alone but the *intention* to be receptive, is itself something which can be perceived by the mind. This is the perception of intention.

Intention is a central organizing process in the brain that creates continuity beyond the present moment. Although we have seen that an emotion can be viewed fundamentally as a process reflecting neural integration (Siegel, 1999), intention seems to have many features overlapping this integrative function. William Freeman (2000) supported this view as he stated that "a way of making sense of emotion is to identify it with the intention to act in the near future, and then to note increasing levels of the complexity of contextualization. Most basically, emotion is outward movement. It is the stretching forth of intentionality . . ." (p. 214). He addressed the neural dimensions of this emotion/intention correlation, stating

the frontal lobe refines and elaborates the predictions of future states and possible outcomes toward which intentional action is directed. The dorsal and lateral areas of the frontal lobe are concerned with logic and reasoning in prediction. The medial and

ventral areas are concerned with social skills and the capacity for
deep interpersonal relationships. These contributions can be summarized as foresight and insight. (Freeman, 2000, p. 225)

Could these medial and ventral frontal areas then enable attunement of intentional states to promote a "deep relationship" with
others as well as with oneself? Here we see that emotion woven
with intention correlates attunement to intentions with emotional
resonance. If we attend to other's intentions, we create interpersonal attunement. As we attend to our own intentions, we create
internal attunement. Intentional states integrate the whole neural
state in the moment. When we tune in to intention, in others or
in ourselves, we are attuning our state with that of the "being"
with whom we are focusing our attention. Because the resonance
circuitry not only detects intentional states but creates them in the
self, attention to intention creates attunement. When we pause
and reflect, attending to our intention, we are creating the foundation for internal attunement. When we pause and take the time
to become open to another person's intentional state, we are creating interpersonal attunement.

THE IMPORTANCE OF INTENTION

Why would intention be so pivotal in our lives? Intentions tie a
given moment of life together, link actions now with actions of
the immediate next moment, creating the underlying "glue" that
directs attention, motivates action, and processes the nature of our
reactions.

Freeman (2000) discussed the important nature of intention and
awareness by exploring their fundamental role in defining emotion and shaping the unfolding of our neural states.

The crucial role that awareness plays, according to this hypothesis,
is to prevent precipitous action, not by inhibition, but by quench-
ing local chaotic fluctuations in the manner described by Prigogine,

through sustained interactions acting as a global constraint. Thus awareness is a higher-order state, one that harnesses the component subsystems and minimizes the likelihood of renegade state transitions in them. . . . This is the part of intentionality in which the consequences of the just-completed action are being organized and integrated, and a new action is in planning but not yet in execution. Consciousness holds back on premature action, and by giving time for maturation, it improves the likelihood of the expression of the long-term promise of an intentional being in considered behavior. (pp. 232–233)

When we monitor someone else's patterns of behavior, our resonance circuitry creates an integration of perceptual and motor neural maps—what we call a representation of their intentional state.

The brain harnesses the pattern-detecting representations of action to create an image of the other person's mind. The mirror neuron system links patterns of perception of goal-directed actions (behavior with intention and predictability) to the individual's motor circuits so that he or she can be ready to carry out a similar action. The larger resonance circuitry also enables us to know what "is on the other person's mind" by examining the neural network activations of our own brain and body proper. Such imitation and mind sensing has tremendous survival value for us as a socially complex species. We take in others' movements and expressions, anticipate the sensory implications of their motor actions (the SIMA process), and then create representations in our brains that embed these cross-time patterns of what "was" into priming in our brains of what we anticipate will happen "next." What would happen if we matched our self-state with our perceptions of our own emerging self-state, moment by moment? The feeling of this may be the unfolding process of mindful awareness.

As mindfulness entails a focus on one's own intention, we could consider this a form of awareness in which we are sharing our own mental states with ourselves. Sharing mental states is the underlying experience within secure attachment between child and parent that promotes resilience. Mindfulness can be seen as a way of developing a secure attachment with yourself.

In mindful awareness, the attention to intention creates an important resonance, moment-by-moment, of what is and what was anticipated. The readiness for the immediate next event is actually the object of attention, so what comes next now matches what the brain was primed to anticipate. This attunement to our own state of intention, I believe, creates the reverberant sense of fullness of experience as we mindfully sip tea, walk, breathe, or open our minds to whatever arises. This is the power of mindful awareness to create a new internal world of coherence and richness of direct experience.

SOME SMALL HINTS

Months after I sat in silence I served as a faculty member at the Mind and Life Summer Research Institute I mentioned earlier, where over 140 scientists had gathered from around the globe to explore scientific perspectives on contemplation. Three presentations were made of subjects that included data from studies of entering a mindful state of awareness of the breath (Brefczynski-Lewis, 2006; Lazar, 2006; Short, 2006). Although the authors were understandably searching more for attentional and regulatory circuitry, in all three studies the researchers independently found that an area connected to mirror neurons, the superior temporal region, was activated simply with breath awareness. Other studies (Lazar, personal communication, June 2006) would also reveal that these areas were activated along with middle prefrontal regions (see Appendix III, Resonance Circuits). This activation correlates with our proposed resonance circuits.

These existing imaging findings support the proposal that mindful awareness, even of just the breath, may indeed activate our resonance circuits, including the superior temporal areas, in conjunction with the insula and middle prefrontal regions of the brain. Further research will be needed to validate this proposal and replicate these empirical findings.

At that same meeting, a piece of second-person data also emerged as a hint in this direction of thinking about mindfulness as a relational skill. A powerful moment of teaching happened there on a panel I shared with two Buddhist monks. An audience member had asked the monks a fairly direct and personal question, which they elected to answer directly, even after we gave them a polite exit. Their heartful thoughts about contemplative life and suffering filled the room with a sense of clarity and authenticity. You could feel the intention from them to respond to the caring intention of the questioner. And you could sense their desire to connect with everyone in the room. The receptivity of their response and the intense focus of the audience was electrifying. One student spoke up after their statements, his eyes full of tears, and said something like, "This feeling I have now after you've spoken so deeply from the heart about what we all struggle with makes me feel so connected to you. This feels exactly like when I meditate, so clear and so full." I spoke with him afterward and could sense the way he had noticed this parallel of feeling himself seen by the monks, and seeing them himself. It seemed to me (in my biased and primed state, of course) that he was sensing this parallel between inter- and intrapersonal attunement.

We can also turn to direct issues about the social circuitry of the brain for further hints as to the relational view of mindfulness. Mark Johnson and colleagues (Johnson, Griffin, Csibra, Halit, Farroni, De Haan, et al., 2005) addressed issues related to social circuitry.

One of the most important functions of the brain is to identify and make sense of the behavior of other humans. As adults, we have regions of the brain specialized for processing and integrating sensory information about the appearance, behavior, and intentions of other humans. Although a variety of regions can be activated by any complex perceptual or cognitive task, a subset of areas appear to be largely dedicated to computations on social stimuli, including the superior temporal sulcus (STS), the fusiform "face area" (FFA), and orbitofrontal cortex. (p. 599)

Sara Lazar (personal communication, June 2006) found that during mindfulness meditation, the orbitofrontal cortex and superior temporal region, the gyrus just adjacent to the anatomically and functionally related sulcus, were both consistently activated (Figure 8.2; Figures A.1 and A.2; Appendix III, Resonance Circuits). This lends support to the notion of mindfulness being a relational process. The STS, as we have mentioned, is part of the resonance circuitry, along with the mirror neuron system, the insula, and the middle prefrontal areas.

Further, studies (Uddin, Kaplan, Molnar-Szakacs, Zaidel, & Iacoboni, 2004) have revealed that mirror neuron areas become activated to a high degree when subjects are viewing a gradually changing image of a face that transforms into their own. This suggests that the mirror neuron system has a set of circuitry that maps out "self." This fits into the overall framework of mapping intention in which a match is made between self-map and map of other (Decety & Jackson, 2004; Frith, 2002; Gallese, Keysels, & Rizzolatti, 2004; Ohnishi, Moriguchi, Mori, Hirakata, Imabayashi, et al., 2004). In the case of mindfulness and the resonance circuitry, we are proposing that the awareness of intention maps out the observed self with the observer. It is this matching of these two maps—self as emerging and self as internally mapped, that is the locus of the attunement of "two" entities with each other. It is here where we see the resonance of two aspects of self and the creation of internal attunement.

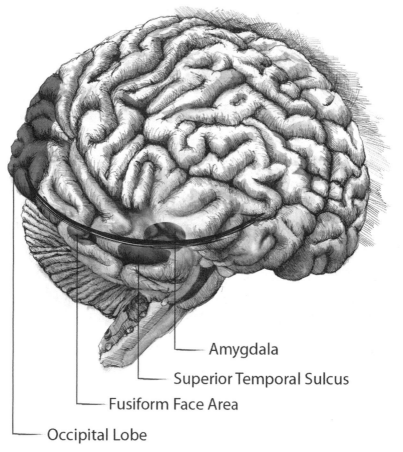

Amygdala

Superior Temporal Sulcus

Fusiform Face Area

Occipital Lobe

Figure 8.2 Face processing network. (Cozolino, 2006; reprinted with permission.)

A LOAD OFF HER MIND

During the silent retreat I met a 56-year-old woman who had recently undergone surgical removal of a benign tumor that had likely been growing for decades beneath her forehead. This meningioma, a plum-sized tumor on the lining of her brain, had grown slowly enough to push aside her brain without her being aware that something was not right. Nancy had spent years trying to find inner peace, which remained largely elusive despite a rich and varied intellectual and emotional life. Her meditation practice led to a greater degree of tranquility and important insights, but it wasn't until she had the tumor removed that she experienced a profound shift in her ability to experience the spaciousness of her mind. Her meditation became more fruitful, and her sense of attunement to her own inner world seemed to readily blossom.

After I suggested to her that the removal of the tumor actually may have enabled her to regain the integration that allowed who she could really be to emerge more fully, she said, "You've helped me understand something mysterious: I've become more myself than ever. Nancy is more Nancy."

Here's what this inspiring individual stated after attending our Mind and Moment meeting (Waring, personal communication, February 2006; see also Appendix I):

> I've had the serendipitous opportunity to share with Dan that I've had a five centimeter meningioma removed from my medial frontal lobe and had a full forehead reconstruction. The tumor and the hyperostosis it caused were mashing my brain. After the initial recovery from the surgery, I began to experience enormous spaciousness, exuberance, profound joy, and deep intellectual hunger. And Dan, in his wisdom, explained to me that the tumor had been sitting on those functions he has illuminated for us in his wonderful talk about the prefrontal cortex. I've been a meditator for 20 years. There has been a lot of striving and self-judgment in my practice. But since having this load off my mind, I'm better able to practice with a more balanced and self accepting effort. I've always been eager to further develop 'intrapersonal attunement,' to use Dan's language. Now it seems to be occurring naturally.

Nancy offers a single case history (Waring, in preparation) that suggests that our capacity to enter mindful states is influenced by pressure on the brain, if not specific pressure on the medial prefrontal region. Her relief from this tumor and the ensuing "reveling in what is" without effort is another hint pointing in the direction of this midde prefrontal region's involvement in mindful awareness.

NEURAL CORRELATES OF SELF
AND CONSCIOUSNESS

Our sense of self is shifted as we experience mindful awareness. This sense of coherence can be explored by examining ways in which the activity of the brain has been associated with dimensions of the self.

The brain continually maps out the deep layers of its own activity. A "neural map" is a cluster of neural firings, or a neural net profile of activation, that represents the "thing" it is mapping. Antonio Damasio (1999) outlined at least three levels of maps of the self. At the basic level, we have "first-order maps" that are the way the deeper brainstem structures have ongoing firing patterns of life-affirming processes, like breath and heart rhythms: the proto-self. We have little awareness of them, but they correlate neurologically with our basic, bare experience, moment by moment.

Next we have "second-order maps" in which the proto-self at time 1 is contrasted to proto-self at time 2. This Damasio called the "core self" and embeds the event that may have changed the proto-self across time within the field of attention. This is called core consciousness and exists in the here and now.

Finally we have a "third-order map," which functions to map the changes in the core self over time. As acceleration is to velocity, the autobiographical self is to the core self. An autobiographical self includes a connection of past, present, and future, akin to the mental time travel that Endel Tulving proposed as being part of autonoetic consciousness, or self-knowing awareness (Tulving, 1993). We bring into a focus the representations from the past as they relate to the future and overlay on our present experience.

We can propose that mindful awareness is open to all layers of self, all forms of consciousness. In this receptive state, we can become filled with the feeling of an autobiographical self but see its function as an activity of the mind. We can also sense the here-and-now immediacy of sensory experience, the derivatives of our proto-self's dance with the world. In fact all of the streams of awareness filling the river of consciousness are welcome within the open hub of mindfulness. It would be easy to say that mindfulness is like the core consciousness, existing in the here-and-now, and perhaps this would be a good place to start. But stopping there does not embrace the sense that mindfulness embeds an integrated multilayered dimension to awareness beyond just sensing in the moment and mapping the changes in the proto-self as the core self does. If the here-and-now embraces the cognitive flow of there and then and what-if's, then that may be our core experience of all those informational flows. The mindful state is as much imbued with meta-awareness as it is with awareness of what is. I guess we might say that mindfulness has never met a cognition it didn't like.

In addition to this important openness of mindfulness, there is also the perspective of mindfulness that is created with attention to intention. As we become aware of our intentions, the mind creates a representation of that intentional state that is not just a feeling, but it is sensed as an activity of the mind itself.

Let us imagine how the core self is changed by sensing its own intentions. Here we see that a resonant quality is created in which proto-self (time 1), event (sensing one's own intention with clarity and acceptance), and proto-self (time 2, matching and anticipating proto-self 1 as it is embedding its own state through the SIMA process). The core sense here is one of profound coherence: There is clarity of connection, a clear matching in the second-order map of the two proto-selves, and the observation of their own intention. This is the reverberant fullness of the core self within mindful awareness.

With a COAL state, this observation of intention is a shared intentional state, similar to what Gallese (2006) has termed "intentional attunement" for interpersonal relationships and the essence of our intrapersonal attunement.

We can apply Damasio's framework here to state that the map of these changes in the proto-self in response to the event of observing its own intention leads to the mapping of observing and emerging, observed and emerged, as coherently coordinated. This is the coherent resonance of mindful states.

PRIMING AND THE PRESENT

The SIMA process becomes important here in describing how the core self maps itself onto itself in mindful awareness. As we have seen with the focus on the breath, the core self senses its own intention and then the SIMA process of the resonance circuitry readies the core self for what will happen in the immediate next. This is not planning, or escaping the present to become preoccupied with the future, or the past; this is the inherent neural property of priming.

Priming reveals how the brain is an anticipation machine, always readying itself for the next moment. It appears that this is a fundamental property of neural circuits—it is how as parallel distributed processors they learn from experience. In contrast, planning is a prefrontal invention in which representations of past experiences are abstracted into concepts that allow us to mull over what happened and think through what we would like to do in the future. This is anatomically, neurologically, and subjectively quite different from the priming sense of "next."

Sensory implications of motor action (SIMA) enable the perceptual circuits to sense our intentions, engage anticipatory priming that readies us for the next moment, and then continually monitors changes in the system to continue the priming for the immediate next moment. This is, in brain terms, "now." There is no getting closer to now than this. And when we combine the power of intentional attunement to create a system of reverberant activations, we have the origins of our neural synchrony.

Chapter Nine

REFLECTIVE COHERENCE:
Neural Integration and
Middle Prefrontal Function

Attending to intentions may involve the mind *attuning* to its own state. Just as mindfulness permits us to sense the mind's activities for what they are through discernment, intention becomes yet another activity of the mind—one that is more complex, perhaps, but of the realm of mental life as well. As we have seen, awareness of intention may hold a special function beyond just being another dimension of noticing the seventh sense sector of the rim, mindsight's view of the mind itself. Awareness of one's own intention may be the very route to a special form of internal attunement, a secure self-relationship that promotes neural integration.

As we discussed in depth in the previous chapter, this internal attunement may be mediated by the social resonance circuits of the brain, including the mirror system and related areas that map self as observed and an observing self. This attunement creates a state of internal resonance. We propose here that the repeated activation of such attuned states results in neuroplastic changes with the structural outcome of neural integration.

With secure attachment between child and parent one also sees the attunement to the internal state—but in this case of another person. As we have seen, there appears to be something quite special when the mind attunes to a mind's internal workings, especially to the deep intention beneath behavior. When parents only attend to overt action, they miss that chance to attune to their child's mind, to the feelings and intentions that drive behavior. Children thrive on the benefit of having parents who focus on their internal worlds. In both mindful intrapersonal and interpersonal attunement, one mind attunes to the affective and intentional states of a mind and everyone benefits.

FINDING CONVERGENCE

In both mindful awareness practices and secure attachment there appear to be outcome measures consistent with the independently gathered functions of the middle prefrontal cortex.

Tucker, Luu, and Derryberry (2005) offered important insights into some of the relevant dimensions of brain function.

> The capacity to integrate conscious attention with emotional experience may be fundamental to empathic experience. Although we can now analyze the neural networks and circuits that are required, these neural mechanisms do not appear to become functional without appropriate developmental experience. (p. 707)

We can propose that the "experience" needed in childhood via attachment with parents can be paralleled to some degree in the internal attunement of mindful practice. As noted in Chapter 6, the authors cited work that supports the view of not only "brain activations that appear to mirror the experience of the other, but midline frontal activity (posterior cingulate, anterior cingulate, and frontal pole) that appears to reflect self-regulatory mechanisms integral to shifting self-other perspectives. These corticolimbic networks overlap in an important way with the attentional control networks of the brain" (Tucker, Luu, & Derryberry, 2005, p. 707; Rueda et al., 2005).

Here we see that the processes of developing skills of attention and attunement would have mutually reinforcing outcomes: adaptive self-regulation.

Prefrontal circuits are thought to play a central role in many dimensions of monitoring and then coordinating the activity of widely distributed areas of the brain and body-proper. It is these same regions that regulate attention, and are a fundamental part of the social circuitry of the brain. In fact, a wide array of research suggests that these self-regulatory prefrontal regions, especially the middle prefrontal areas, are dependent for their development upon proper experiences with caregivers. In other words, relational experiences promote the development of self-regulation in the brain. If mindfulness is considered as a secure relationship with the self, we can then make the link that this form of internal attunement would also promote the healthy activation and subsequent growth of these same social and self-regulatory prefrontal regions.

Seven functions of the middle prefrontal region are associated with both forms of attunement: body regulation, attuned communication, emotional balance, response flexibility, empathy, self-knowing awareness, and fear modulation. Though not studied yet in the field of attachment, mindful practice also appears to develop the two other middle prefrontal functions of intuition and morality (Kabat-Zinn, 2003b; Ackerman et al., 2005).

This mindfulness-attunement hypothesis suggests that attuning the mind to its own mental processes is the essential feature of mindful awareness practices. The social neural circuits involved in this attunement would include the middle prefrontal regions, insula, superior temporal cortex, and the mirror neuron system. These regions comprise the resonance circuits and enable one mind to resonate with the internal state of another and are hypothesized here to be at the heart of the experience of attuning one's mind to its own internal processes.

This proposal would predict activation of these regions and ultimately the strengthening of the synaptic connections in them as well. Sara Lazar's findings of increased thickness in the middle prefrontal and insular regions are consistent with this prediction. Further, her findings and those of other researchers support the view of activation in the resonance circuit areas (superior temporal and middle prefrontal cortices) in mindful awareness of the breath as we discussed in the last chapter (Brefczynski–Lewis, 2006; Lazar, 2006; Short, 2006).

SCIENTIFIC CAUTION

These are associational convergences that point our view in a certain direction. Further studies are needed to validate this proposal that the resonance circuits in particular, and the social circuitry of the brain in general, are involved in mindful awareness (see Appendix III, Resonance Circuits). But in science we need to formulate clear hypotheses that can then be rigorously tested. To create such hypotheses, we must use our imagination and build on the data and notice the implications of existing findings and the new ways in which we may be able to articulate the nature of reality. In pushing science forward, it is helpful to integrate wide areas so that new questions can be proposed and the studies created to answer them can be designed and their predictions proven or disproven. Such is the process of science that enables us to ask questions that can be ultimately answered. I will highlight some basic and testable aspects of this hypothesis that perhaps will be useful in order to carry out the necessary studies to verify or disprove its validity.

With the proposal of a relationship between attunement and mindfulness, we can explore the first dimension of our hypothesis: that attunement internally and attunement interpersonally will share common neural correlations. The first prediction would be involvement of the middle areas of the prefrontal cortex (orbitofrontal, medial and ventral prefrontal, anterior cingulate) along with the associated insular cortex, superior temporal cortex, and the mirror neuron system. Emerging data to support this view for interpersonal resonance now exist in the literature (Carr et al., 2003; Gallese, 2006). Our proposal extends the idea of interpersonal attunement into the realm of the hypothesized notion of intrapersonal attunement. This is a dimension of the proposal that can be explored, refuted, or confirmed with future empirical research.

For clinical practice, we need to blend the knowledge of "objective" science with the "subjective" dimension of human reality. Scientists are always learning new things, and we can prepare our minds to be ready to understand subjectivity in new ways as our scientific and personal insights are woven together.

With these acknowledgments in mind, we will continue our adventure into the deep dimensions of experience as we dive further into the potential ways in which mindfulness may involve attunement and neural functioning. To explore the nature of this intrapersonal attunement, we will now expand this hypothesis and delve into the possible neural correlates of this social facet of the mindful brain.

SENSING COHERENCE

What would the subjective sensation of self-attunement actually feel like and what might it "look like" in the brain itself? These forms of attunement each likely involve the creation of a state of highly complex functioning in the brain that emerges as a state of coherence. For the brain such a state would have the quality of neural synchrony, the harmonious firing of extended neural groups when they become linked in a state of neural integration.

For a mind, we have described the state of attunement as having the qualities that spell the word *coherence* itself: connected, open, harmonious, engaged, receptive, emergent, noetic, compassionate, and empathic. Attunement creates coherence in the mind. Supportive evidence comes on the mind side with descriptions of first-person accounts of a state of well-being, and the sense of "harmony" that emerges with mindful awareness practices.

When long-term meditators' electrical activity was measured during meditative states on objectless or nonreferential compas-

sion, different from mindfulness, high degrees of oscillatory frequency were revealed as gamma waves, suggesting high levels of
neural synchrony during that practice as reported by Antoine Lutz
and colleagues (2004). Interestingly, the premotor area was also
activated in these subjects, which now we can propose might be
related to the mirror neuron properties of those regions. The high
degrees of neural oscillation in general are thought to reflect the
postsynaptic activation of neurons, especially in the cortex. Oscillatory neural synchrony is the outcome when coordinated interactions occur among widely distributed regions. Such coordinated
activity can happen at various levels, from the size domain of small
groupings to large, and the distance domain from short range to
large scale. Though this study does not examine mindfulness, it
does offer an important glimpse into the neural correlates of compassion which reflect an integrated state.

Lutz, Dunne, and Davidson (in press) have suggested that when
neurons engage in such coordination it enhances the strength of
their connectivity, reinforcing their mutually shared functions at
that moment, and establishes the "salience" of their present activity compared to other neural groupings.

Short-range integration is thought to occur within localized
networks interconnected by single synapses that enable close, rapid
(a few milliseconds) firing among related neurons. Such short-
range integration would occur within modality related cortical
columns and help us to understand how perceptions are "bound"
together. We can also imagine how the dissolution of top-down
processing might occur with disruptions at this level of short-
range synchrony, offering a view into how mindfulness might dis-
rupt the secondary push of invariant representational influences.

Large-scale integration involves neural groupings that are further apart and connected to each other through multiple synapses
that thus require longer conduction times. An example of these
slower (10 milliseconds or more) integrative loops would be link-

ing areas of the cortex via the thalamic gating we have spoken of earlier. This is how neural integration enables consciousness.

Lutz, Dunne, and Davidson (in press) eloquently stated the intricacies of larger forms of integration and oscillation this way:

> These pathways correspond to the large-scale connections that link different levels of the network in different brain regions to the same assembly. The underlying mechanism of long-range synchrony is still poorly understood. Long-range synchronization is hypothesized to be a mechanism for the transient formation of a coherent macro-assembly that selects and binds multimodal networks, such as assemblies between occipital and frontal lobes, or across hemispheres, which are separated by dozens of milliseconds in transmission time. The phenomenon of large-range synchrony has received considerable attention in neuroscience since it could provide new insights about the emergent principles to link the neuronal and the mental levels of description.

When we think of the power of mindful awareness to alter our deep sense of the self and our perceptions of the world around us, we might be well advised to look at these levels of short-range and large-scale assemblies. We have seen above that small-scale assemblies might be disrupted to dissolve the immediate impact of the invariant representations pushing down from the higher layers of the cortex. More large-scale shifts in perspective that come along with ipseity may be achieved by way of these large-scale assemblies of neurons and the interruption in their integration as we discussed in Chapter 7. Having the insights into the transient and relative nature of our personal identity, getting the sense of ipseity beneath our historical adaptations and habits of mind, may be achieved via these large-scale integrative shifts that may occur with reflection.

Reflection, as we have defined it, involves at least three functional aspects: receptivity, self-observation, and reflexivity. Each of these distinct but mutually reinforcing aspects of the reflective heart of mindful awareness can be proposed to be capable of altering large- and small-scale integrative assemblies in the brain to shift the very nature of our conscious experience.

It would be unlikely that we would see the small-scale shifts that might be altering the secondary intrusions on primary sensation with a functional scanner or electrical assay of brain activity. The activity would likely be too small and focally located to actually detect. But disrupting the usual forms of personal identity within awareness may involve large-scale assembly alterations on a larger and more diffuse level that perhaps could be detected with careful computer assisted electrical measurements of whole system integration. These may be the levels at which top-down influences might be assessed and noted, as they are dismantled within mindful awareness.

A process of long-distance synchrony has been described by Engel, Fries, and Singer (2001). In their conclusion they suggest the possibility that "top-down processing is reflected in large-scale coherence across areas or subsystems, and that such patterns of large-scale integration can covary with specific predictions about forthcoming stimuli" (p. 715). Could the SIMA process of predicting the sensory implications of motor actions that we are proposing for mindfulness be one way in which this reflective form of awareness induces coherence and long-distance synchrony? Such coordinated functioning involves a form of phase synchrony that is present with large-scale, long-distance, macroassemblies of widely distributed regions. Perhaps this mechanism of inducing neural integration correlates with the state of mental coherence in mindfulness.

More sophisticated forms of analysis of these large-scale integrative states will likely help clarify what the "neural signature" for the functional states of mindful awareness might actually be. As Aftanas and Golocheikine (2002) stated, "the results point to the idea that dynamically changing inner experiences during meditation are better indexed by a combination of linear and non-linear EEG variables, giving additional insight into the integrative functioning of the CNS (Central Nervous System) with respect to altered states of consciousness" (p. 146).

These integrative assemblies create our underlying sense of awareness, moment by moment. Understanding the subjective nature of these states of neural integration can help us focus our journey into the mindful brain.

DEFINING INTEGRATION

This aspect of our proposal regarding neural integration could also be explored empirically by examining the ways in which the brain creates states of integration in mindful awareness practices. This would be a state measure, a transient function occurring at the time of practice. Sophisticated linear and nonlinear electrical measures may be needed to assess the subtle shifts in integration as traits of the individual.

Another testable dimension of the hypothesis is that these states of integrative function would become traits as revealed in long-term changes not only in function over time, but in neural structure. The proposal is that the state of neural coordination and balance created by intrapersonal attunement ultimately catalyzes the growth of integrative fibers in the brain. In turn these integrative neural connections would then support more ease of activating states of neural synchrony in the future.

With integration at the heart of the neural plastic changes, we would want to predict where one might find these integrative neural connections in structural images of the brain. A vast array of "interneurons" can function within the small-range integrative processes of closely aligned neurons (Soltesz, 2006). For the larger-scale integration, we would want to examine the fibers that reach out to widely distributed assemblies of neural groups, including the possible role of spindle cells in the prefrontal regions that enable rapid neural transmission (Frith, 2001; Nimchinsky, Gilissen, Allman, Perl, Erwin, & Hof, 1999).

When it comes to this large-scale neural integration, a number of regions are high on the list. One of these is the middle prefrontal cortex, connecting the body proper, brainstem, limbic regions, and cortex into a functional whole that also takes in the social signals from other brains/bodies. That is quite a list of disparate domains linked together into a functional whole, the definition of integration.

In addition, one might also want to consider other integrative circuits which link widely separated areas to each other, such as the dorsolateral (side) part of the prefrontal cortex, the hippocampus and corpus callosum, and the cerebellum. Each of these regions sends long projections out to distant areas, linking them structurally together and permitting them to play a role in creating functional integration.

A fascinating finding is that within the study of neuroplasticity (Benes, 1994; van Praag, Kempermann, & Gage, 2000), the neurons that grow in the process of neurogenesis appear to be those that are integrative, and they have also been found to be important in child development (Siegel, 1999). Martin Teicher (2002) came to similar conclusions when he reviewed the findings that child abuse and neglect lead to damage of the integrative neurons in the brain and that positive relationships are needed to allow them to grow.

INTEGRATIVE WELL-BEING

From a mathematical perspective, drawn from complexity theory, an integrated state enables the most flexible, adaptive, and stable states to be created within a dynamical, complex system. Extending these ideas into the realm of subjective experience, we can see that this model provides a view into the nature of well-being, helping us define mental health as flowing like a river flanked on one side by the bank of rigidity, on the other by chaos (see Siegel, 1999, 2001b, 2006). This view actually offers a useful vision of the nature of the symptoms listed in the *Diagnostic and Statistical Manual of Psychiatric Disorders*—they can be seen as examples of chaos, rigidity, or both (American Psychiatric Association, 2000). For example, with PTSD, one individual may exhibit chaotic states of flashbacks and emotional lability as well as rigid states of avoidance and numbness. Bipolar disorder reveals chaotic states in mania and rigidity with depression.

We have described the mental flow that emerges with integration as being flexible, adaptive, coherent, energized, and stable (FACES). This model then helps us see how mindful awareness, through the promotion of integration in the brain, may be directly harnessing our innate capacity for coherence and well-being.

Internal attunement promotes neural integration which enables mental coherence. But how does integration actually function in the brain itself? Why is it good to have the linkage of these assemblies of differentiated clusters of neurons? As discussed in Chapter 2, the overall idea is that neural integration entails coordination and balance in the functioning of the brain. This integrative functioning can also be tested in various ways, such as by examining the balance and coordination of the autonomic nervous system through studies of heart rate variability alterations in mindful and nonmindful states of awareness.

The described correlates of neural integration are coherence of mind and empathy in relationships. In these ways, neural integration, mental coherence, and empathic relationships can be seen as three aspects of the one reality of well-being. We do not need to attempt to reduce any one of these into some form of the other. Neural, subjective, and interpersonal together form valid dimensions of reality that cannot be simplified into the other.

INTEGRATION AND INTERPERSONAL RELATIONSHIPS

A related aspect of the proposal that could be tested is that attunement would lead to the development of the integrative functions within interpersonal relationships themselves. Intrapersonal attunement and neural integration will be associated with

enhanced interpersonal attunement. Each dimension will reinforce the other.

Anecdotal reports suggest that mindfulness meditation enhances
the capacity for individuals to detect the meaning of facial expressions without verbal clues. If this were true, why would this be the
case? One possibility is that the interoceptive focus of mindful practice develops this capacity to "look inward" which is the tool by
which we sense our inner world and detect the expressions of others. The resonance circuitry is actively involved in such nonverbal
perception, and has even be shown to be involved in responding to
our own facial expressions (Uddin et al., 2004). It can be proposed,
then, that interoception and mirror properties may work hand in
hand to develop this increased sensitivity to others' signals. With
such a developed skill, we could explain the reported finding that
interpersonal relationships are enhanced with mindful awareness
practices (see Appendix III, Relationships and Mindfulness).

Whether it is in our daily lives, clinical work, teaching, or scientific research, we can gain entry into this triad of well-being
through any window of opportunity that then can promote coherence of mind, empathy of relationships, and neural integration.
In other words, we could focus on promoting empathy in communication and we might find enhanced neural integration and coherence. We might focus on mindful awareness and promote coherence and neural integration, which then makes empathy more
likely to develop.

Mindfulness practices involve the attention on loving kindness,
on feeling the intention to care for the well-being of the self and
others. Here we see a fascinating convergence of mindful intrapersonal attunement with imaged interpersonal attunement. What
docs such mindful imagery do in the brain? This raises another
testable aspect: Are resonance circuits activated during mindful breath
awareness and in loving kindness aspects of meditation practice?

Studies of mental imagery have now clearly revealed that the
act of perceptual imaging not only activates those regions of the

brain involved in the carrying out of the imagined action, but also produces long-term structural growth in those very areas. For example, when a monkey is taught to use a rake with his right hand, the area of the brain devoted to right hand perception is more greatly increased than when he is taught the same action without the use of a rake (Obayashi et al., 2001).

The relevance to our proposal is that if we focus on attuning to our own minds or to the mind of another, we may be harnessing perceptual skills, embedded in neural circuitry strengthening, that then enable more robust intra- and interattunement to be attained. Mindfulness and empathy go hand-in-hand. This reveals why loving kindness is a fundamental part of mindfulness practice—both involve internal attunement.

If attunement produces integration in the brain, then interpersonal attunement (in secure relationships, or imagined in loving kindness directed toward others) and intrapersonal attunement (with loving kindness directed at the self as well as with mindfulness in which one attunes to one's own states of being, including intentions, bodily sensations and feelings) will reinforce each other and produce more neural integration. These could be the neural dimensions linking the ways in which mindful awareness promotes both relational and internal well-being as it creates states of integration.

ATTACHMENT AND NARRATIVE

Our discussion of integration and coherence of mind can be expanded by examining the framework of how our identity is shaped by memory and narrative that emerges from the study of attachment. In prior works (Siegel, 1999; 2001b; Siegel & Hartzell, 2003) I have offered an extensive review of the four general patterns of narrative organization that emerge with certain experiences within our lives as forms of adaptation to ways in which we were parented. As we grow, we respond to the attunement, or lack thereof, that is offered to us with either openness or with various forms of restricted cohesive frames of mind (Hesse, 1999; Main, 2000; Phelps, Belsky, & Crnic, 1997; Sroufe et al., 2005). Recent studies reveal that our attachment patterns directly influence our capacity to suppress negative thoughts as correlated with different patterns on functional brain scans (Gillath, Bunge, Shaver, Wendelken, & Mikulincer, 2005). Overall these studies confirm the notion that our adaptations to experiences early in life seem to impact our affective style, our narrative themes, and the ways in which we approach or withdraw from others in interpersonal relationships.

In mindful awareness we have the opportunity to get beneath these layers of adaptation and enhance the possibility of change. Our innate constitution—our temperament—will also impact our sense of identity. In this way, attachment patterns and constitution both contribute to our "personality." Here we will briefly explore the science of attachment and what we know from research about how the narrative structures emerging from attachment histories shape how we move forward in life.

If our parents were emotionally unavailable, we will tend to pull away from needing them, avoid dependence, and develop a narrative that minimizes our reliance upon others. This is called an *avoidant* childhood attachment and an adult's *dismissing* state of mind with respect to attachment, or just a dismissive stance. The internal world of such an individual tends to be disconnected from others and from their own emotional and bodily life. Here we would sense that the person's hub did not have ready access to the rim points of the sixth sense of the body, to aspects of the seventh sense of emotion, or to the eighth sense of relationships, with self or with others. The narrative has a tightly wound cohesion that excludes relationships and emotions from being considered important now or in the past. This narrative organization is often marked by the insistence that the individual cannot recall memories of family experience in any detail. Here mindful awareness is limited because significant avoidance of rim elements prohibits the person from attaining the receptivity, self-observation, and reflexivity that are fundamental to reflection. The offspring of these individuals are not offered attuned connections, and the cross-generational passage of these experientially related patterns is repeated.

If our caregivers were inconsistently attuned to us, with frequent instrusions of their own state into our own, then we will develop a core self experience of uncertainty. The child's attachment relationship in this case is called *ambivalent/anxious*, and the state of mind of the adult is termed *preoccupied*. The narrative here is one of instrusions of elements of the past into the present such that the person has a sense of confusion, especially when it comes to relational issues. We can picture in this situation that the hub of the mind becomes flooded with exogenous rim points that overwhelm the person's sense of being present with what is, as they are overcome with what *was* and what he or she wishes *would be*. Unfortunately, the children of such an individual are exposed to these internal instrusions because they interfere with the parent's capacity to be mindful while interacting with the child. These intrusive mental events within the parent lead to the inconsistent attunement with the child and, again, we see the pattern of attachment passed on to the next generation.

A third attachment pattern occurs in which the parent is the source of terrified or terrifying behaviors that induce in the child a state of fear without resolution. The child's brain experiences the simultaneous activation of one set of circuits to go away from the source of terror; the other set of circuits creates the impulse to move toward the attachment figure for protection and soothing. The problem in this situation, of course, is that the attachment figure is the source of terror. There is nothing "mixed" about this message: It is the child's conflictual state that leads him or her to have *disorganized* attachment. This childhood state ultimately gives rise to a form of fragmented self called *dissociation*, in which there is an interruption in the continuity of consciousness and a dis-association of usually connected elements, such as sights and sounds and implicit and explicit memory. The adult's narrative reveals *unresolved* trauma or grief—two treatable conditions. Unfortunately, without intervention, the ways in which unresolved parental states lead to frightening behaviors that create terror in the child continue the impact across the generations.

The important issue about these findings is that parents can alter their adult attachment stance. Each of these three forms of attachment "insecurity" is an example of a non-coherent state of mind that gives rise to these classic narrative patterns. I have proposed that these narrative findings likely reflect a state of impaired neural integration (1999). In *dismissing* individuals, the blockage of access to right hemisphere processes may lead to the left's providing a story that lacks the emotional imagery-based autobiographical richness from the right. In *preoccupied* states, an intrusion of excess right hemisphere episodic memory comes from the "leftover garbage" of a nontraumatic but nonattuned childhood set of experiences. In the case of *unresolved* states, the brain seems prone to severe disintegration in which the prefrontal cortex may shut down its integrating functions under minor stressors, which lead to an intense, sudden, and frequent "low-road" of response that is limbically driven and terrifying for the child. In this state, many of the nine middle prefrontal functions we've discussed may become temporarily suspended. While we are all prone to such states, those parents with unresolved trauma and grief may be especially vulnerable to rapidly, frequently, and intensely entering them, and they may have less resilience to recover quickly and then engage in the repair needed to reconnect with the child (Siegel, 1999; Siegel & Hartzell, 2003).

The great news is that parents who come to "make sense" of their lives can actually alter their attachment status and raise children who thrive (Siegel & Hartzell, 2003). The outcome is called an "earned" security, in which parents come to experience a coherent mind and narrative. Such coherence is created with neural integration. In this case the narrative is able to embed the positive and negative aspects of autobiographical memory into a story that acknowledges the impact of the past on the experiences of the present. In many ways, the evaluation of this research data derived from the Adult Attachment Interview (AAI) is akin to an assessment of the reflective aspects of mindfulness.

The AAI is a research interview that assesses the "coherence" of the narrative of parents (Main, 2000; Siegel, 1999). When parents have "made sense" of how their past has impacted their present, they became free to establish secure relationships with their children and others. Peter Fonagy and Mary Target (1997) have proposed a "reflective function" with which parents focus on the mind as being an important part of secure attachment. This function may parallel the noting and describing facet of mindul awareness. In some difficult or traumatizing attachment relationships, such reflective functions may be impaired in their development. These impairments may be repaired with a resultant "earned" security of attachment (Siegel & Hartzell, 2003).

With either continuous or earned security in an adult, the result is that the parent is able to engage in attuned communication with the child. When there are ruptures in that communication, as invariably happen in all of our relationships, the parent is "mindful" enough to make a repair. Such repair is at the heart of the child's secure attachment.

Trained as an attachment researcher, it was natural for me to place mindfulness as a central tenet in a scientifically informed approach to parenting. Now, immersing myself in the formal study of "mindful awareness," I can see that the attunement between child and parent mirrors that of the internal attunement we have been proposing for mindfulness.

It would be an interesting research project to explore this basic proposal that secure attachment actually promotes not only neural integration, but mindfulness traits. The interpersonal attunement of secure attachment would then lead to the neural integration of a mindful brain. Individuals who would have achieved such integration, whether reaching such secure states through parenting during the early years or later on earning security through self-reflection or positive, transformative attachment relationships as teens or adults, would be seen to have mindfulness as a trait of the self. We would thus see that even self-understanding—the "making-sense" process of creating a coherent narrative fundamental to secure adult attachment—could be viewed as an aspect of internal attunement that is fundamental to a mindful way of being.

An attuned system is one in which two components begin to resonate with each other. For two people, attunement is based on the resonance of each person's state. As such attunement exists in attachment relationships, neural integration is promoted in the child as stimulated by the parent's own integrated, mindful state. Within self-reflection and internal attunement, we come to resonate with our own state of being. Before long, the influence of the clear and open receptivity to direct experience creates internal resonance, an entrainment of lived and observing states with each other.

To achieve this fluidity of connection, we need to have a sense of openness to what is. As we've discussed, the neuroception that creates a sense of safety may enable us to enter that receptive state. In attachment, we need to be open to our child, feeling that safety in ourselves and creating that sense of "love without fear" in our child. In mindfulness, we need to be open to ourselves in order to create that COAL state of receptivity. Our observing self needs to be open to our "self-as-living." With the attention to intention we then develop an integrated state of coherence.

With the cohesive states of insecure attachment, the mind is "holding on" to old patterns in an outdated effort to just survive. This inflexible cohesiveness puts the person at risk of chaotic or rigid states. With the movement toward coherence, the system of the person becomes more flexible. Here we see that the narrative research of attachment can help us envision how adaptations to past experiences, embedded in memory and in our life stories, can restrict us in their cohesive stronghold.

COHERENCE AND COHESION

Coherence and cohesion are very different. To get a feeling for this difference, imagine this mathematical idea: A *cohesive* state is created as a set of equations that rigidly defines the in- and out-group status of any variable that it is assessing (Thagard, 2002). Here the circle drawn to define boundaries of the set is clear and distinct: You are either in or out, identity defined, certainty established.

In contrast, *coherence* can be imaged as an equation that embeds the variables under consideration into the numerical sequences of the equation itself. As each new variable is encountered, it actually alters the equation and changes the shape of the "self" that defines the in- and the out-group membership characteristics. The shape of the boundaries is continually emerging. Here we see that coherence embeds flexibility at its core.

In our working definition of well-being, we've put *f*lexibility as the starting point of the FACES path, along with *a*daptability, *c*oherence, *e*nergy, and *s*tability (FACES). Mindful awareness promotes coherence of mind. By reflecting on the nature of cohesive states of personal identity, the rigid adaptations can be noted and altered, giving rise to more flexibility and coherence.

Achieving emotional freedom and loosening the stronghold of personal identity involve being mindful of memory. In this situation, a cohesive and non-coherent state of mind has the feeling of choking, of restriction, of tightly wound boundaries that are unyielding and impermeable to the emerging experience of the mind's own development. Such a stagnant system lacks the feeling of harmony associated with coherence: States of rigidity or intermittent explosions of chaos dominate the temporal landscape.

In the integrated FACES flow of the river of well-being, the mind travels in a harmonious path bounded on either side by rigidity and chaos. Here we can see that mindfulness creates non-reactivity by placing the mind on this coherent flow. With the three elements in the *triangle of well-being*—neural integration, a coherent mind, and empathic relationships—our lives can move in the direction of a harmonious flow. We are in "emotional well-being" in such an integrated state. This is reflective coherence.

Mindfulness evokes a reverberant dynamic interaction among these three dimensions of well-being—neural, mind, and relational. Our social resonance circuitry is well-suited to participate in this triangle of well-being, linking together the mapping of intention with neural integration and the ways in which we attune to each other, and to ourselves.

Mindfulness permits tranquility even in the face of trauma or restricted memory processes that constrain the harmony and coherence of the system of the self. This is a crucial aspect of the discernment that mindfulness allows: We can learn to create new patterns of emotional regulation as we come to approach, not withdraw. From that stable, inner place of calm, the surface processes of chaos and rigidity, of dysregulation and defensive exclusion of lived experience, can now be melted away as they are recognized as "just" habits of mind, equanimity can be created, and true transformation can begin.

The secret is in opening your mind and feeling memory fully. Many people may see mindfulness as just "being in the present" and elect to ignore the nature of memory and identity. But our lived moments are enslaved by memory, and avoiding its structures keeps us locked in cohesive states that lack the vitality of an open, coherent flow.

Beneath the veil of self–identity that clouds clear vision rests a spaciousness of mind present in each of us. Mindful awareness makes that clarity more than a possibility, but a directly experienced reality.

Chapter Ten

FLEXIBILITY OF FEELING:
Affective Style and an Approach Mindset

The facets of mindfulness in which we are nonreactive and in which we describe and label our sensations, feelings, and thoughts can best be examined by exploring the ways in which we attain flexibility in our feelings and create a mindset of approach rather than withdrawal.

In the research literature the impact of mindfulness on emotional regulation has been explored in the work of Richard Davidson and colleagues in great neural detail. Davidson (2000) has offered a perspective on "affective style" as a way in which mindfulness training can alter neural function and enable us to become nonreactive. "Affective style refers to consistent individual differences in emotional reactivity and regulation. . . . It is a phrase that is meant to capture a broad array of processes that either singly or in combination modulate an individual's response to emotional challenges, dispositional mood, and affect-relevant cognitive processes" (p. 1196).

NONREACTIVITY

In the common notion of mindfulness as involving the focus of attention on the present moment, on purpose, and nonjudgmentally, we do not see the dimension of nonreactivity. Some consider the capacity for equanimity, or the evenness of reaction under stress, a sense of composure and level-headedness, to be an outcome of mindful awareness practices. Baer and colleagues' (2006) synthesis of surveys of mindfulness revealed that nonreactivity emerged as a useful independent facet. This means that with the idea of mindfulness as having many essential dimensions, this form of research considered nonreactivity as a core feature, not just an outcome.

The reality is that "outcome" and "process" are strange ideas when it comes to exploring the nature of mindfulness. The process is the outcome: Being here, just this, this moment, this breath, is mindfulness, is being mindful. When we begin to tease these elements apart, we can lose the whole forest as we dissect the trees.

If we maintain a larger vision and embrace the process reality of mindfulness as a being, not a doing to accomplish something, then we can explore these individual facets. The benefit of seeing the individual facets is that it makes it possible to integrate the experience of mindful awareness and the neural circuitry upon which "mindfulness rides." Recall that we say that "the mind rides along the neural firing patterns in the brain" to reinforce the bidirectional nature of mind and brain. The brain's activities contribute to our mental lives. The mind can also be seen to use the brain to create itself. With these ideas in mind, let us see how nonreactivity may emerge with mindfulness.

Within the brain we have seen that automatic responses, such as thinking or feeling, can be generated without awareness. This coordination in part may be carried out via the anterior cingulate cortex (ACC) which has a significant role in emotion activation and modulation. The ACC has divisions responsible for both bodily input and affective response as well as for the allocation of attentional resources that govern the direction of our stream of thought (Fellows & Farah, 2005). The anterior cingulate has been shown to be consistently activated during mindful awareness practice (Cahn & Polich, 2006) revealing the close linkage between our regulation of attention, thinking, bodily states, and feelings. When we bring neural firings into the focus of our attention, at a minimum we are engaging the side part (DLPFC) of the prefrontal cortex to link to whatever other areas are activated. If the subcortical limbic areas are firing, we may experience the arousal of affect, an emotional reaction. If this neural activation enters awareness we call it a "feeling," or our subjective experience of emotion.

WHAT IS EMOTION AND HOW DO WE REGULATE IT?

But how does the brain regulate its emotional responses? The first concept we need to state directly is that "emotion" is a complex entity and an equally intricate subject of study. Emotion includes a process whereby goal-directed behaviors are organized and enacted, appraisal of the meaning of events is created, information processing ("cognition") is shaped, perception biased, and affective arousal activated. Emotion also directly involves how we interact with each other in the present, and how we are impacted by activations from memory. In other words, what we call "emotion" is a dynamic and central function that *integrates* behavior, meaning, thinking, perceiving, feeling, relating, and remembering.

When we speak of "emotion regulation" we are referring to the monitoring and modulating of this wide array of functions, from feelings to communication. When we speak of nonreactivity as a facet of mindfulness, in many ways we are addressing this broad vision of emotion regulation (Adele & Feldman, 2004).

At the most basic level, we create nonreactivity by developing the circuits in our brain that enable the lower affect-generating circuits to be regulated by the higher modulating ones. This balance between emotion arousal and its regulation is often concep-

tualized as the relationship between the subcortical limbic amygdala
and the prefrontal cortex (Goleman, 1996). Mindful awareness may
directly influence nonreactivity by altering the connections between prefrontal cortex and limbic zones (see Figure 2.7).

In the brain, the prefrontal cortex has direct linkages to the
lower limbic areas. These linkages enable the prefrontal area to
both assess the state of arousal in these subcortical regions as well
as to modulate their firing. We have discussed how "integration"
in the brain involves coordination and balance. Here we see that
the integrative prefrontal areas can coordinate and balance limbic
firing so that life can have meaning and emotional richness, but
not excessive firing, where life becomes chaotic, or too little, where
life becomes dulled and depressing. In fact in teaching meditation,
parallel concepts are addressed as excitement and dullness.

TRAINING EMOTIONAL BALANCE

Lutz, Dunne, and Davidson (in press) described the issue this
way:

> Tension between stability and clarity is expressed in the two main
> flaws that hinder a meditation, namely 'dullness' and 'excitement.'
> When dullness first arises, the focus on the object will be retained;
> but as dullness progresses, the clarity of the object becomes pro-
> gressively hindered, and a sensation of drowsiness overtakes the
> meditator. If dullness continues, the dimness of the object will
> cause the meditator to lose focus on it, or in the case of gross dull-
> ness, the meditator will simply fall fast asleep. In contrast, when ex-
> citement occurs, the clarity of the object will often increase, but
> the intensity of the mental state perturbs the meditation such that
> distractions easily arise and focus on the object is lost. The ideal
> meditative state—one beyond the novice stage—is a state in which
> neither dullness nor excitement occurs; in short, stability and clar-
> ity are perfectly balanced . . . The subtle degree of dullness or ex-
> citement that they encounter is corrected by equally subtle adjust-

ments to the clarity (for dullness) or the stability (for excitement) of the meditation state until both stability and clarity reach their maximal, balanced state."

This description reveals that even for early practices of meditation, the focus is on the balance of states of arousal. At their extreme, these states represent chaos (for excitement) and rigidity (for dullness). Achieving nonreactivity in large measure can be seen as way of pausing before externally responding and then attaining a coordination and balance of the neural circuits involved in the "accelerator and brakes" function of the brain. Those two aspects of the autonomic nervous system, the sympathetic and parasympathetic branches, respectively, function so as to activate or inhibit the system. The regulation of the two branches of this system resides in the middle aspects of the prefrontal cortex.

The prefrontal regions in both the middle and the side also play a role in what I have called "response flexibility"—the way that we pause before action and consider the various options that are most appropriate before we respond.

In these two ways we can see that "nonreactivity" is likely to involve both internal affective and autonomic balance and interactive flexibility. These, and other dimensions of our internal homeostasis, are achieved through the integrative (coordinating, balancing) functions of the prefrontal cortex. It is these regions that we can propose are likely active during mindful practice and grow and strengthen their connections as a consequence.

AFFECTIVE STYLE AND RESILIENCE

Richard Davidson (2000) addressed some of the central issues about affect regulation when he stated that

> One of the key components of *affective style* is the capacity to regulate negative emotion and specifically to decrease the duration of

negative affect once it arises. The connections between the PFC
and amygdala play an important role in this regulatory process. . . .
We have defined *resilience* as the maintenance of high levels of positive affect and well-being in the face of adversity. It is not that resilient individuals never experience negative affect, but rather that
the negative affect does not persist. (pp. 1207, 1198)

Nonreactivity reveals a central aspect of resilience. How could
mindful awareness nurture the development of such resilience? In
animals—(monkeys in the work of Stephen Suomi (1997) and rats
in the work of Michael Meaney (2001))—we see that the ways in
which a young animal is nurtured by its mother directly affects
the development of behavioral flexibility and social function. In
Meaney's work, for example, alterations in the number of receptors in various regions, including the emotion-reactive amygdala
and deeper brainstem structures, and in the regulating prefrontal
areas, suggested that high licking-grooming mothers produced
positive changes in their offsprings' brains. Meaney was able to
show, in fact, that these grooming behaviors led to the activation
of genes in specific ways that led in turn to the protein production that produced the receptor changes in particular regions of
the brain itself. Cross-fostering studies established that it was not
the genetics of the mother, but her behavior that determined the
genetic expression and neural outcome. The essential issue is that
these "attuned," caretaking interactions induced the neuroplastic
changes that produced resilience in the offspring.

Sroufe, Egeland, Carlson, and Collins (2005) have performed
extensive research on human beings to examine how the attuned
communication within attachment between child and parent leads
to the development of resilience in the offspring. Those children
raised in stressful homes who do exhibit resilience have invariably
been found to have an attuned relationship that has been interpreted by these researchers as the source of the development of
their resilience. Allan Schore (2003a, 2003b) explored the possible

neural correlates of attachment findings and has proposed that at-tuned communication leads to the growth of the prefrontal regions, especially in the midline areas (most notably the orbito-frontal region). My own work has focused on the ways in which the process of neural integration, mediated in part by prefrontal structures, but also including more large-scale dimensions such as the two halves of the cortex and interpersonal communication, promotes coherence of mind, empathy in relationships, and overall resilience in our lives (1999, 2006).

These findings suggest the following. Resilience can be learned through experience. Affective style is not fixed in cement by genes or by early experience, but can be seen as a skill that with training can be moved in the direction of well-being. What we know about the relationship between caregiver and offspring is that attentiveness and care lead to the development of resilience. (See Appendix III, Developmental Issues).

I am suggesting that we view mindfulness as a form of "attention and care" focused on oneself. This is how we can see mindfulness as a form of intrapersonal attunement that also promotes resilience. In the previous two chapters we have explored in greater depth the details of this attunement within mindfulness and how it may promote the growth of integrative fibers in the middle prefrontal areas. Here we will address the facet of nonreactivity and what we know about mindfulness and the development of affective style.

APPROACH AND WITHDRAWAL

A major construct in both psychological and neurobiological literature is on the distinction between approach and withdrawal tendencies in our minds, our behaviors, and our brains. Approach drives us toward a thought, engages us in an interaction, and appears to preferentially involve activation of the anterior parts of the left hemisphere. Withdrawal pulls us away from something, disengaging us from an interaction, and revealing dominance in right sided activation, especially the anterior regions.

Heather Urry and colleagues (2004) have offered a view of these two states as being a neural window into well-being.

> Although this earlier work focused on the role of affect in explaining the right-left distinction, recent work indicates that stable individual differences in relative activation over the prefrontal regions are not actually indicative of hedonic tone (positive or negative) per se, but instead are related to the propensity to display stable approach-oriented (left hemisphere) or withdrawal-oriented (right hemisphere) behavioral tendencies in the face of appropriate sources of stimulation. (p. 368)

They go on to propose that engaging in goal-relevant events is a necessary dimension for achieving well-being. In their study they make a distinction between eudaimonic and hedonic forms of well-being. Eudaimonia is more about a sense of equanimity than about the sensory pleasure focus of hedonia. A eudaimonic form of well-being embraces the psychological qualities of autonomy, mastery of the environment, positive relationships, personal growth, self-acceptance, and meaning and purpose in life. Hedonic well-being in contrast focuses on life satisfaction, frequent pleasant emotions, and infrequent unpleasant emotions.

Using these two constructs, Urry and colleague's study was able to disentangle the left prefrontal activation as being important as a form of approach mindset rather than just a source of positive affect. In their discussion they pointed out that:

> The association between frontal asymmetry and affect reflects a lateralized role for the PFC in the instantiation of approach and withdrawal motivational tendencies that are part and parcel of affective responses. The left PFC is active in response to appetitive stimuli that evoke the experience of positive affect because these stimuli induce a fundamental tendency to approach the source of stimulation. (p. 370)

With baseline higher left dominance, such individuals would thus be motivated to move toward the events in their lives that could create meaning and pleasure in their way of living. This may contribute to higher levels of well-being. "Moreover, hemispheric-specific analyses demonstrated that left prefrontal activation was associated with eudaimonic but not hedonic well-being after that variance associated with PA (dispositional positive affect) was removed" (p. 370). In other words, approach tendencies correlate with eudaimonia: We can move toward distressful events with equanimity.

As we move into integrating this work with other dimensions of our discussion of mindfulness, it is helpful to note the following statement from Urry et al.'s study:

> It is unclear to us why our findings were limited to the frontocentral leads. This region is more posterior than the frontal regions that have revealed significant associations with affective-style measures in many studies in the past. . . . At least one study has suggested that activity in this region may reflect supplementary motor area activation . . . which raises the possibility that approach-related behavioral tendencies are associated in part with tonic activation in the supplementary motor region. (p. 371)

In Chapter 8 we discussed the possible role of mirror neurons in mindfulness which would be consistent with this finding in that this supplementary motor area (SMA) is filled with mirror properties (Decety & Grezes, 1999). Could it be that in this research paradigm where individuals were "just" resting with eyes closed (were they focusing on their breath?), that they could be activating an approach state and attuning with themselves?

BASELINE STATES

Neuroscientists have described a baseline state that involves the activity of certain neural circuits, as revealed when subjects rest with their eyes closed. Gusnard and Raichle (2001) have explored the nature of a default mode or baseline as involving specific circuitry. These researchers (Raichle, MacLeod, Snyder, Powers, Gusnard, & Shulman, 2001; Gusnard, Akbudak, Shulman, & Raichle, 2001) have found that though the brain at rest consumes about 20% of the oxygen used by the body, it only accounts for 2% of bodily weight. This oxygen consumption is not distributed evenly, but involves areas that include a frontal region and a posterior region. The posterior part may be important for assembling information about the world at large, and possibly aspects of the self. The frontal regions include aspects of the middle part of the prefrontal region, including the orbitofrontal and medial prefrontal areas. Gusnard and Raichle noted:

> The orbital network is composed of cytoarchitectonically discrete areas that receive a range of sensory information from the body and the external environment. This information is relayed to the ventral medial prefrontal cortex through a complex set of interconnections. Areas within the ventral medial prefrontal cortex are also heavily connected to the limbic structures, such as the amygdala, ventral striatum, hypothalamus, mid-brain periaqueductal grey region and brainstem autonomic nuclei. Such anatomical relationships indicate that these medial areas might mediate the integration of the visceromotor aspects of emotion with information gathered from the internal and external environments. (p. 692)

Further, the authors note that these middle prefrontal (OFC, VMPFC) areas "might contribute to the integration of emotional and cognitive processes by incorporating emotional biasing signals or markers into decision-making processes." Recall that another midline structure, the anterior cingulate cortex (ACC), also has been shown to integrate these processes as well (Bush, Luu, & Posner, 2000).

Another related midline region active at baseline is the dorsal aspect of the medial prefrontal cortex (DMPFC). The mental functions associated with this region involve the monitoring of one's own mental state and reporting these internal states to others, intentional speech, self-generated thoughts, and emotions. Another set of activities associated with the DMPFC include attributing mental states to others. Frith and Frith (1999) have postulated that this dorsal medial prefrontal region is crucial for the mental representation of self.

These interactive ventral and dorsal medial prefrontal areas have intricate relationships with each other as revealed in the following ideas from Bird and colleagues (Bird, Castelli, Malik, Frith, & Hussain, 2004):

> The role ascribed to the medial frontal cortex is in top–down control over processing taking place in other parts of the mentalizing circuit (Frith & Frith, 2003). It is quite possible that, in adults who have developed normally, such top–down control is unnecessary to perform the kinds of tasks used in this study and is only necessary for rapidly modulating processing in complex, novel social situations. (p. 925)

In these studies, the baseline activity decreased under task conditions that did not require social circuitry activation. What this implies is that in general the imaging of mental processes, mindsight, involves an intricate interplay of circuits that become engaged with effortful and intentional activities in response to new social and psychologically relevant situations.

SHIFT TO THE LEFT

The issue of the default mode, or baseline activity of the brain, complicates research interpretations because when individuals are given a task, the specific focus on the external task is thought to actually decrease the activity of these more globally focused mentally directed circuits. If a scientist sees no shift, does that mean that the activity is actually continuing to engage these areas? If there is a decrease, does it mean those areas are just becoming more efficient when given a task to complete, even if it is mind oriented?

For these reasons, we must be patient and respectful about the challenges of careful brain imaging research and how to interpret results. The finding that mindfulness meditation is associated with anterior cingulate activation is a good beginning (Cahn & Polich, 2006) and the preliminary findings of orbitofrontal and superior temporal activation with breath awareness present some exciting hints (Lazar, personal communication, June 2006).

Even regarding the variety of meditation forms within the Buddhist tradition, Lutz, Dunne and Davidson (in press) have stated:

> The neuroelectric signatures of these various meditative techniques (Focus Attention, Zazen, Vipasyana meditation) have not yet been firmly established. Our current understanding suggests that the selection or the exclusion from attention of particular contents (sensory, motor, internal tasks) is correlated with the activation or inhibition of specific brain areas as indexed by specific changes in selective brain oscillatory patterns.

Though we may not know yet the exact signature, we do know one important general profile: Mindfulness meditation appears to produce a left shift in frontal activation.

Independent fields have studied laterality and revealed that the right hemisphere seemed to encode for uncomfortable, negatively charged affect (Davidson, 2004). In studies of children, infants raised by severely depressed mothers had a shift to dominance on the right which persisted into their young childhoods and reflected the similar right-sided dominance in frontal activity in their mothers (Dawson, Frey, Panagiotides, Yamada, Hessl, & Osterling, 1999).

Another possibly relevant set of studies involves examining those children with extreme shyness, a temperament trait associated with withdrawal from novelty and heightened right-sided activation in new situations. Jerome Kagan found that the way parents treated children could determine the developmental outcome for shy kids (1994). Those parents who were attuned to the temperamental needs of their children and were able to provide a secure base and connection, while at the same time helping them move out into the world, to lovingly support them in trying new things, had children who outgrew this behavioral tendency to withdraw. Even though they might continue to have increased neural signatures of fear, they could adapt and maintain a resilient stance and approach challenges. Those children not so fortunate maintained their anxiety and uncertainty. The relevant point here is that developing the affective style of approach can be a learned skill that develops with experience, in this case in the setting of a child's attachment relationship with the parents.

As we have discussed, Richard Davidson and colleagues have found a shift in the baseline of long-term meditators toward left anterior activation, and in newly engaged practitioners the degree of left shift was correlated with enhancement of immune function following an eight-week mindfulness based stress reduction (MBSR) training program (Davidson et al., 2003; Davidson & Kabat-Zinn, 2004).

Brain electrical activity was measured before and after the training program and immune activity in response to an influenza vaccine was assayed. The magnitude of increase in the left shift was proportional to the degree of immune response.

It is helpful to delineate how this study was conducted. Before and after a training that included mindfulness meditation (MBSR), the subjects were given the task of writing down both negative and positive events in their lives. Electrical activity was measured at baseline and just after this task. In the trained subjects, as compared to controls, the left sided frontal activation following the task was more in both the positive and negative condition.

The authors suggest that with more than eight weeks of training, the baseline shift may also have been found—as is the case for studies of long-time meditators. In those nonprospective studies (see Davidson et al., 2003, for a review) we cannot know if the meditation led to the shift, or if the shift led them to meditate.

The power of the MBSR prospective study is that these subjects were divided into two groups that included a control subset, and none of the participants had prior meditation training.

But why would writing down a negative event in your life activate the so-called "positive affect" left hemisphere? The issue of approach-avoidance is crucial here. As Davidson's and as Urry's articles suggest, the concept may be best thought of as approach (left) over withdrawal (right). With this view in mind, it appears that being given the skill of mindfulness one is more likely to approach even negative events with an approach mindset. This approach response enables the individual to move toward even uncomfortable experiences, rather than withdraw. That is a straightforward description of resilience. Approach can be far more adaptive and enable you to move through life with more equanimity; and equanimity in turn can enable you to feel better about your self and your sense of agency in the world.

AFFECTIVE STYLE AND MINDFULNESS

Taken together these findings suggest that the approach mode/ left shift may become activated during mindfulness meditation and ultimately may be a part of the transition from state to trait that is associated with the various forms of physiological, psychological, and interpersonal well-being that have been reported for mindful awareness practices. As we come to approach our internal world with curiosity, openness, acceptance, and love (COAL), we learn the steps of approach—to literally welcome all visitors in the field of awareness. The hub of our mind is wide open and receptive to whatever comes from any point on the rim. The actual training of mindfulness in various practices, including meditation of the sitting and walking sort we focused on in that silent retreat, directly hones the ability to focus attention and then to open the mind.

As the contents of the mind become the object of attention, it is soon clear that their mental nature, the fundamental comings and goings of our thoughts, feelings, images, and sensations, are something we can observe from a spacious inner place of stability and clarity. This is not the same as relaxation; this is a place of equanimity that lends itself not to spacing out, but to expanding the space within. Affective style appears to be capable of being shifted by mindful awareness practices toward resilience. Literally, this means that the tendency we may have to pull away from distressful feelings is replaced by an open spaciousness in our minds to move toward a challenge, to go forward and engage in the internal and external world. With this approach mindset, our feelings can become more flexible. The hub of the wheel of awareness can welcome anything from the rim—uncomfortable feelings and fear, memories or stories, social challenges or moments of isolation, with an approach of openness and equanimity. With resilient affective styles our feelings are more flexible. We achieve the mindfulness facet of nonreactivity in the form of equanimity as we come to approach our internal world with acceptance rather than to dread and avoid it, or to hate and attack it. A resilient way of being includes the capacity to rebound from negative states, not to eliminate them completely from our lives. We are all human, and the idea is a flexibility of feelings, not an exclusion of the full spectrum of our humanity.

MENTAL NOTATION: DESCRIBING AND LABELING WITH WORDS

One facet that may support emotional balance is the capacity to use words to describe our feelings. An important aspect of creating flexibility in our feeling, of shifting our affective style toward approach and resilience, can also be seen in the ways we make mental notations about our internal world. Though verbal activation may not correlate in the brain with those specific areas involved in the "left-shift" (Richard Davidson, personal communication, August 2006), mindfulness itself has this fundamental noting process. This facet of mindfulness is called "describing/labeling with words."

In the field of child development, we use the term *self-talk* to describe the ways in which children develop an internal dialogue. When this self-talk is about the contents of the mind itself, we call this "mentalese" or language that enables us to describe and label the mental nature of our inner worlds. Some children develop this well; others do not. For various reasons, some related to temperament and others related to experiences within families (Siegel & Hartzell, 2003), we each develop our own unique capacity for internal dialogue about the mind.

I use the term *reflective dialogues* to denote the ways in which we have conversations with our children about the nature of their minds. It may be that the experience of such conversations with children becomes internalized as the capacity to describe our internal states as we grow (Siegel, 1999; Vygotsky 1934/1986). This ability reflects the domain of mindsight in which we come to see the world in mental terms, focusing on our own inner world and the mental life of others.

Research of various sorts in psychology and in neuroscience has revealed the important finding that people who use words to describe their internal states, such as their emotions and what they perceive, are more flexible and capable of regulating their emotions in a more adaptive manner (Ochsner, Bunge, Gross, & Gabrieli, 2002). Mindfulness as a construct is associated with the facets of both nonreactivity and describe/label with words, and this is totally consistent with the independent research from these fields. But how does describing something make us better able to maintain equanimity in the face of stress? Why would labeling a nonverbal internal dimension of the mind with a word actually be a good thing?

Mental notation appears to require a left-sided approach with going toward an internal state and naming it. But then the modulation of the emotional arousal itself may involve right-sided activation.

What researchers at UCLA have observed in brain scans is that the act of labeling the type of intense emotion you see in a picture keeps limbic firing more in balance than observation without description (Hariri, Bookheimer, & Mazziotta, 2000). This may sound too amazing to be true. But to give you a feeling for this, here is a part of the summary of Hariri et al.'s study:

> Matching angry or frightened expressions was associated with increased regional cerebral blood flow (rCBF) in the left and right amygdala, the brain's primary fear centers. Labeling these same expressions was associated with a diminished rCBF response in the amygdalae. This decrease correlated with a simultaneous increase in rCBF in the right prefrontal cortex, a neocortical region implicated in regulating emotional responses. These results provide evidence for a network in which higher regions attenuate emotional responses at the most fundamental levels in the brain and suggest a neural basis for modulating emotional experience through interpretation and labeling. (p. 43)

A related study by Creswell, Way, Eisenberger and Lieberman (submitted) found that individuals with higher degrees of mindfulness traits had more active prefrontal activation than those without those traits during a procedure in which they named the emotion they saw on a photo of a face. The right ventrolateral cortex and medial prefrontal cortex were each activated during the labeling task. This prefrontal activation was accompanied by diminishment in amygdala activation in response to faces and was a process not found to this significant degree in those without mindfulness traits. As discussed in more detail in Appendix III on middle prefrontal functions and development, this suggests that mindfulness skills may promote more effective affect regulation.

INTEGRATING LEFT AND RIGHT

Notice in these findings that at the moment of the affective arousal and amygdala activation, the right prefrontal area became more active. Here we see the intricacies of data in science: Left hemisphere activation would be required for use of language (recall, the left specializes in the four L's: linguistics, logic, linearity, and literal meaning). But emotion modulation seems to be a specialty of the right hemisphere in these and other authors' views; see Schore (2003a) for a summary of this perspective.

In particular, research on fear extinction and affect regulation has revealed that the middle (ventromedial and ventrolateral) aspect of the prefrontal cortex sends projections directly to the amygdala that release the inhibitory transmitter GABA. Yet our working memory involves the side (dorsolateral) area of the prefrontal cortex which does not have direct synaptic connections to the amygdala. Taken together, we can state that to make a mental notation one must consciously harness left hemisphere linguistic processes within awareness (dorsolateral prefrontal regions) that then must link to the more direct middle prefrontal regulatory circuits (especially the ventral regions) on the right.

Such bilateral (cross-hemisphere) integration would help us see where the coordination of processes, left and right, would result in a more flexible, adaptive, coherent, energized, and stable state (FACES). This FACES state emerges when we create integration. Mental notation, using words to describe and label our internal experiences, is a wonderful example of the kind of intentional integration that creates coherence in our lives.

But how does left-sided word creation shape right-sided emotion modulation? We don't yet know the answer. One possibility is that the two regions of the brain activated are homologous areas. These matched left-right zones seem to function such that activation in one leads to inhibition in the other. Such a homology left and right makes interpretation of neurological lesion studies challenging. A left-sided lesion, for example, might either diminish function on the left or increase function in the homologous right side when the usual inhibition is now gone.

Interestingly, left-sided language areas are thought to be related to our capacity to use mirror neurons in the creation of speech patterns. Though not yet formally studied or proposed, we can use free-ranging imagination to envision the possibility that our left-sided language mirror areas might be homologous with the right-sided emotional-resonance areas. If this were the case, then perhaps language use in the left might dampen emotional arousal in the right, via a homology coordination mediated via the ventromedial and ventrolateral prefrontal areas, which may carry out such regulatory and integrative functions. Recall that integration consists of coordination and balance. The intricacies of how such proposed integrative self-regulation might occur in the process of labeling our feelings will need to await further research.

Whatever the actual neural mechanism, the practical point is that in both neuroscience studies summarized here, and in the subjective experience of mindfulness as detailed in research, we find that nonreactivity and emotional balance go hand-in-hand with the facet of labeling and describing internal states. They are differing mechanisms, separate facets of mindfulness, but one clearly supports the existence of the other.

These experiences of mental notation teach us the skill of labeling to help balance our minds, not constrain them with top-down prisons. We learn that what before felt like an unchangeable and distressful feeling can now be observed and noted and we can come back to equilibrium more readily. This is the essence of a resilient affective style.

Chapter Eleven

REFLECTIVE THINKING:
Imagery and the Cognitive Style of Mindful Learning

When I was in medical school I found the first two years both exhilarating and disturbing. I love science and found that part interesting, even though shifting from a study of life in biology to disease and death was often an existential roller-coaster of anguish and despair. But when the time came to see patients, I fell in love with the individuals I was able to get to know. The opportunity to connect with people from all walks of life and to help them unravel the nature of their struggles and explore the intricacies of their lives was deeply moving. But when the time came to present the stories I had gathered from the patients to my professors, everything changed.

I was told repeatedly not to discuss the patients' feelings, as this was "not what doctors do." I was urged to focus on the physical exam and not on what was going on in the person's life. In ways I couldn't articulate then, I was being conditioned to ignore the minds both of my patients and myself. As a young and eager student, I tried in many ways to follow my teachers' directives to not feel. But soon I found myself feeling empty, without a sense of meaning in the present, and losing touch with my ideals from the past. This was not what I had thought becoming a physician would be. There seemed to be no way to find a path into a future that made sense.

I dropped out of school hoping to find a new profession, fantasizing about many careers—in dance or salmon fishing, carpentry or counseling. I had the applications for graduate school in education and psychology, and was testing the waters in various pursuits. I explored these options on a trip across the continent, ultimately returning to my home town to be with friends, to help my grandmother with my dying grandfather, and to reflect on where I was going.

During that time off, or really time "in," a friend's neighbor heard of my transition and handed me a just released book called, *Drawing on the Right Side of the Brain* by Betty Edwards (1979). I had never been skilled in painting or drawing, but something about that book attracted me and I immersed myself in the experience and found a whole new way of sensing the world. Whether or not this immersion in direct seeing is right or left, up or down, this "right mode" of perceiving the world was quite a different way of experiencing reality from what I had been doing as a part of science in college and medical school. It also was extremely different from the disconnected and indifferent state I had entered during the conditioning by my professors to not feel. Now I was feeling in ways that were alive and fully present.

Years later I'd discover the field of mindfulness and gain new insights into what that year had allowed me to experience. In her book, *On Becoming an Artist*, Ellen Langer (2005) not only makes a case for the psychological and physical benefits of mindful creativity, but her research shows how to use a new creative task (painting, photography, music—even gardening or cooking) to help create a personal renaissance that seems akin to what my time tuning in to myself during that year off felt like. Langer believes that we should strive to be mindful as much as possible, using creative means to navigate roadblocks and attain this flexible state. She suggests that the challenge of being mindless is that we are not aware of being in that state so we can't "fix it," or in essence know to find a way to emerge from automatic pilot. Finally, toward the end of my second year of school, before I left, that automatic pilot had come to feel so numb that I just couldn't go on any further. Perhaps others feel a dullness in their day-to-day, routine lives that can also serve as a wake-up call to such a passive existence.

The "creativity" of being away from others' prescribed activities and plans liberated me to find a new way of experiencing the world, life, and my own mind. Once I began to feel the numbness, it became clear that I needed to take a break from the ways in which the educational system we found ourselves in at that time seemed to be disregarding the importance of our subjective lives, the essence of who we each were as patients, students, and teachers. It was in this separation from the planned path that my journey seemed to bring me to a creative entry into my own inner world that had been ignored for so long. In so many ways, finding a direction toward a future of possibility for me required that I pause and take time to find my own mind first.

Before I left medical school I recall feeling that there must be another way to treat patients than to just see them as capsules of disease. After that time away and exploring these new avenues of knowing my inner world and seeing the outer world, I decided to return to school. I was filled with a sense of openness to the experience, and an awareness that the medical school socialization process would push us to go "on automatic" and just mindlessly learn to diagnose, dispense, and disperse. Somehow the shift in perspective during that year of what may have been a mindful exploration seemed to have given me the strength and the presence of mind to remain more grounded. I seemed to at least have the intention to be attuned to my own and my patients' inner world.

Years later as I was preparing this exploration of mindfulness, I came across the writings of an old classmate. Ronald Epstein (1999) wrote a powerful piece on the importance of mindfulness in the clinician. That contribution suggested that professionals need to engage in "mindful practice" in order to bring themselves more fully, with reflective presence, to the clinical relationship. More recently, Epstein (2001) wrote a bit about school life when we were there:

> Musical practice has had a different influence. Because I trained first as a musician, then later as a physician I was surprised in my otherwise excellent medical education by a striking lack of attention to the self of the practitioner. In contrast, in music study, which can be as theoretically and technically complex as any medical specialty, the self of the performer is an object of constant study and reflection. (p. 64)

I remember enjoying listening to Ron play the harpsichord with some close friends and feeling the fullness of their presence as they immersed themselves in the music, and connected with each other in the piece.

Why couldn't the same be true with the "nonartistic" professions? Where had the art gone in the art of medicine? When I left in the middle of school I sought dance and drawing as a way of being immersed as a "self" in life. Unknowingly I was seeking a way to be present and connected. Too often our professional lives train us to be selfless processors of information, disconnected from ourselves and the work itself, to be mindless. But this form of educational annihilation would become an area of study just across the river from where Ron and I were experiencing this "striking lack of attention to the self." Ellen Langer would soon be conducting research on how to bring the self and the mind back into education. Fortunately, the medical school has changed as well.

MINDFUL LEARNING

Within the fields of education and psychology, Ellen Langer has been pursuing the idea that learning can be approached in a fundamentally different way from how it has commonly been practiced (Langer, 1989, 1997). Her study of mindful learning offers us a view of "mindfulness" that has elements that appear on the surface both similar and distinct from the thousands of years of the practice of mindful awareness. In Langer's own words (1997): "When we are mindful, we implicitly or explicitly (1) view a situation from several perspectives, (2) see information presented in the situation as novel, (3) attend to the context in which we are perceiving the information, and eventually (4) create new categories through which this information may be understood." (p. 111). These features of multiple perspectives, novelty, context, and new categories are the essence of mindful learning.

Langer has proposed that if we approach situations in life with an open mind we will learn better, enjoy more, and live longer. She cites a wide array of research to support these compelling findings, noting that people ranging from those in nursing homes to college students respond with better memory and more enjoyment when educational presentations are made with *conditional* statements. Instead of presenting information in absolute ways, such as with statements like "the nation is" or "these contracts always require," the teacher offers phrases like "the nation may be" or "often contracts may require." The use of terms such as *might, can be, could be, might entail, may on occasion, could involve, may have,* and *could have been,* rather than the absolutes of *is, are,* and *were* create the specific conditional priming of mindful learning. These conditional statements, offered in direct oral or written material, seem to induce a cognitively mindful state that evokes the active engagement of the student's own mind. This is mindful learning.

If this sounds subtle, consider this: When our minds lock onto something as being absolute, it enters our memory stores in a very different form from the way it would were we to be tentative about the contexts and conditions in which what we just learned might apply. We can propose that turning to the brain may help expand our insights into why this would be true. Our efficient neural association machine creates memory systems that can take a "fact" and create a rapidly accessible node of neural firing patterns that form a building block in the scaffold of our "semantic" knowledge of the world. But with a conditional statement, that neural nodal point must have far more intricately established connections for it to meet the criteria for inclusion into the scaffold of knowledge: We need to be able to link the "may" and "at times" conditions to all the moments of possibility in which that point may or may not apply. These enhanced neural connections can be proposed to be one possible mechanism by which the conditional presentation of mindful learning engages a more complex set of neural associations, making it accessible in the future for retrieval in more flexible and adaptive ways. The key issue is that any process by which the mind of the student must engage a conditional set of learning will be more powerful as a form of education. It will engage the mind more, likely one part of the reason why such practices are associated with more enjoyment and more longevity.

INTEGRATING RIGHT AND LEFT MODES

As I have come to learn about mindful learning, I cannot help thinking about my own time away from medical school in which I became immersed in that "right mode" of perceiving. We explored the differences of right and left modes of cognitive processing in Chapter 2, noting that millions of years of development as vertebrates have led to significant differences in the modes of handling perception and information processing in the two sides of the brain. This is just a biological reality of our nervous systems. Often right and left work together, but their contributions to the whole, science suggests, are quite distinct. Here we will continue to use the term *mode* to refer to this general predominance of one layer of neural processing's contribution to the integrated whole (see also Appendix III, Laterality). The right mode is able to handle context-dependent thinking, seeing the "big picture" and embracing ambiguity. The left mode is more expert in specifics, clearly defined words, and their concrete applications, active strategies for problem defining and solving. The left mode is goal-directed, analyzing the details, and seeking a solution. Mindful learning, as Langer has defined it, can be seen to draw on the additional processing of the right mode. This is not an exclusion of factual knowledge (a left mode specialty) and problem solving, which are so often a focus of conventional education, but can be seen as the addition of the more process-oriented, large-picture "contextualizing" of the right mode's perspective.

Mindful learning involves concepts such as intelligent ignorance, flexible thinking, the avoidance of premature cognitive commitments, and creative uncertainty. These can each be seen as the addition of the right mode of processing onto the usually dominant left mode's attempt to create intelligent sureness, clearly defined routes of analysis, categorical clarity, and a sense of certainty and predictability. The feeling of these terms is that we can approach work as teachers with an active effort to bring the full self, left and right mode, into the learning.

This important expansion of how we see the frame of mind of the learner is additionally promoted by the mindful learning approach that encourages students to create their own perspectives and to explicitly realize the contribution of their own mindset on the learning process itself. One of the approaches to mindful learning directly lets people know that the outcome of their experience (a class, a trip to the hospital) will be shaped in part by their own attitude. Rather than just suffering by feeling that one has no impact on the process, such instructions give people the freedom to be mindfully engaged and have a sense of agency.

When we bring a sense of self into the process of learning, we can also state that we are inviting the right mode to participate in the experience. This is the title of a paper in a major neurology journal, "Right Cerebral Hemisphere Dominance for a Sense of Corporeal and Emotional Self" (Devinsky, 2000). Many authors now see that so much of our autobiographical memory and deep senses of even a social and reflective self entail aspects of our right mode of processing. Our whole self is an integration of left and right; and this is just the point. If educational processes, in schools, colleges, and graduate and professional programs like medical school, leave out one mode or the other, the integration needed for balanced learning will be absent.

Mindful learning invites the whole person to participate in the learning process. The invitation is to engage fully both left and right modes of processing so that, I believe, integration is encouraged. It is for this neural reason of full involvement of the student, we can propose, that mindful engagement may support such a different experience of learning. As I write this I am saying to myself, which "mindful" do I really mean? And this is exactly the point we will explore next.

WHY CARE ABOUT SIMILARITIES AND DIFFERENCES?

Are there really similarities between mindful learning and mindful awareness? Langer (1989) has dealt directly with this issue:

> While there are many similarities, the differences in the historical and cultural background from which they are derived, and the more elaborate methods, including meditation, through which a mindful state is achieved in the Eastern traditions should make us cautious about drawing comparisons that are too tidy. (pp. 77–78)

Why even care that these two uses of the word *mindfulness* might relate to similar or to different processes? The first reason is that both pursuits of mindfulness can help people, and if finding similarities in their processes can make the scientifically established benefits of their applications more readily available, more people will be helped. That's reason enough to move forward with such a comparison. But a second reason is this: The differing dimensions of each of these forms of mindfulness may be seen as complementary, so that combining efforts into a broad understanding of "mindfulness" may help us have a deeper insight into our lives than the sum of the parts. In other words, finding connections between these two "mindfulnesses," if there are some, might be rather powerful. A third reason is that in practice, educational, clinical, and personal efforts to enhance our lives may require fairly different "windows of opportunity" to actually offer people in those contexts access to a new way to experience awareness.

COGNITIVE AND AFFECTIVE "STYLES"

The idea of cognitive mindfulness emerged from the worlds of social psychology and education. In that world, Robert J. Sternberg (2000) suggested that Langer's mindful learning can be best conceptualized as a "cognitive style" rather than a cognitive ability, form of intelligence, or personality trait.

Sternberg's view of mindful leaning as a cognitive style relates to the notion that,

> styles are preferred ways of using one's cognitive abilities. . . . That is, they represent not abilities per se, but how people like to employ their abilities in their daily lives. Styles can be of different kinds: thinking styles, learning styles, teaching styles, cognitive styles. . . . These styles, like mindfulness, involve a preferred way of viewing the world in general and specific problems in particular. (p. 138)

Sternberg noted that there are descriptions of various cognitive styles, but mindfulness does not overlap with these and it offers an important addition to describing such a preferred way of processing information. It should be noted that Langer herself sees mindful learning as more than just cognition, as mindful distinctions involve the whole person (Langer, 2005). Langer's mindful learning, as she understands it, "relates not only to education, but to all aspects of life." It was her "purpose to correct the formal learning, be it in school, business learning, or sports, where the teaching actually fosters mindlessness" (Langer, personal communication, 2006).

In contrast, mindful awareness emerged from contemplative practices from around the world over thousands of years. Richard Davidson, in exploring the world of mindfulness that has rigorously developed from a Buddhist tradition, has examined the "affective style" that seems to be directly shaped by mindful meditation. As we explore the inseparable nature of affect and cognition, of feeling and thought, we may find that the layers of resilience and well-being in one form actually may overlap with the initial findings of the other.

Mindful awareness focuses us in the present and does not address learning and memory directly. Mindful learning, on the other hand, studies how the way we focus in the present (on novelty, distinction, and the consideration of differing points of view) directly shapes the pleasure and efficacy of learning. Although developed historically and learned in practice from extremely different sets of experiences, these two "styles" of affect and cognition may be more closely aligned than initially meets the eye.

ESSENTIAL FEATURES

Mindful learning is defined as having the components of openness to novelty; alertness to distinction; sensitivity to different contexts; implicit, if not explicit, awareness of multiple perspectives; and orientation in the present. These dimensions can be highlighted with the terms *open to novelty*, *alertness to distinction*, *context sensitivity*, *multiple perspectives*, and *present orientation*. When people are taught with conditional phrases, for example, they learn better in that they must be alert to distinction, pick up on novel aspects of the material, and remain focused in the present. This conditional approach to teaching evokes mindful learning and greatly enhances memory retention and pleasure in the process of education. As we've seen, embracing uncertainty heightens alertness to novelty and distinctions.

Mindfulness has been operationalized for research purposes to have four or five facets (Baer et al., 2006), which we have been exploring: (1) nonreactivity to inner experience; (2) observing/noticing/attending to sensations, perceptions, thoughts, feelings; (3) acting with awareness/(not) on automatic pilot/concentration/nondistraction; (4) describing/labeling with words; (5) nonjudgmental of experience. These can be summarized with the words: *nonreact*, *observe*, *actaware*, *describe*, and *nonjudge*. In college-aged nonmeditators, as we have discussed, observation may have not been as robust an independent facet, but for completeness we will include it here in our analysis.

Taken one by one, we can see that some of these elements overlap whereas others seem quite distinct.

Nonreactivity does not seem to have an obvious correlate on the surface with aspects of mindful learning. It would be interesting to carry out a study to see if the liberation people experience by not being constrained by inner lability might actually encourage many of the cognitive dimensions to occur, in that the individual would feel a sense of equanimity that would enable an openness to novelty; for example, to be engaged with a sense of approach rather than withdrawal. Such a state of nonreactive balance would then lead to the "left prefrontal shift" moving toward new situations. In such an open state, we could imagine the person's awareness of distinction and capacity to consider other frames of reference would also be encouraged. Each of these would support being oriented in the present because there would be no affective state to lead to withdrawal. Being available to whatever arises would be the reflective mindful state supporting the mindful learning. Indeed, Langer (2005) has shown that individuals who see things from multiple perspectives are less reactive. Similarly, she demonstrated that people who make fewer social comparisons are less likely to blame and experience envy, and appear more satisfied.

Observing internal mental activities also does not correlate conceptually with the four cognitive dimensions, but might actually support their realization. We could imagine that someone with a well-developed observing function would in fact be able to shed automatic constructs and create the openness to novelty and other features that reflect being oriented to the present. Here we see that the capacity for internal knowing that comes with self-observation might support cognitive mindfulness—but it may not be in reverse. In other words, being in a mindful environment that supported conditional and self-referential education may not on the surface seem to directly lead to the broader internal sense of being aware of one's own internal mental activities. It turns out that mindful learning has indeed been found to enhance awareness of internal mental processes (Langer, 2005). Conditional presentations and a focus on the state of the learner may evoke self-observational circuits that could explain this finding.

Acting with awareness has a great deal of overlap with all of the dimensions of cognitive mindfulness. This facet in many ways seems almost identical to the notion of not being on automatic pilot that is at the heart of being a mindful learner. Actaware then seems to be a shared facet of mindfulness in both forms.

The facet of *describing/labeling with words* the internal activities of the mind does not relate on the surface to the cognitive features. However, in many ways the essence of having a person engage the "self" in the experience at the heart of mindful learning involves a self-aware function that we could imagine would be reflected in an overlap in these two. The invocation of learners as active participants in learning, encouraging them to consider that their frame of mind, their "mindset," as Chanowitz and Langer (1981) and Dweck (2006) would call it, plays a crucial role in the learning experience, and directly involves a form of self-awareness. This invitation to consider the role of one's self may build on self-observational capacities, as we discussed earlier. Clearly the actual training of mindful awareness through meditation directly develops the skill of labeling one's internal world. It would be interesting to see if mindful learning also supported that same development of the ability to label one's internal world.

The largest difference between these two approaches seems on the surface to be the facet of being *nonjudgmental*. Within mindful awareness, top-down influences, as we have seen, begin to be jettisoned as their influences are observed, noted as activities of the mind, and then disengaged. This is an active process of letting go of old habits of thought. It is in certain ways a letting go of premature "hardening of the categories" (Cozolino, 2002) and "cognitive commitments" (Chanowitz & Langer, 1981). On the surface the view that mindful learning involves an active effort to create new categories might make these two forms seem contradictions of each other.

But on a deeper level, one we will explore next, this dissolution of old constraints I believe is actually a shared and central dimension of both forms of mindfulness. I would suggest that if we carried out a study of mindfulness meditators, they would meet the criteria for a tendency to be highly adept mindful learners. We would find as students they would support involvement of conditional and self-referential states that evoked the many aspects of mindful learning. As teachers, we can imagine, they would naturally create the helpful dimensions of learning that make it more effective and enjoyable in these cognitively mindful ways. I think even my own teaching since experientially diving into mindful awareness has become more cognitively mindful.

If we approach this analysis of similarities and differences from the other direction, what would emerge? If we examined the mindful learning aspects of openness to novelty, alertness to distinction, context sensitivity, multiple perspectives, and present orientation, would these match with the five facets of mindfulness?

Being *open to novelty* is the exact experience of mindful awareness. The ordinary somehow seems to become extraordinary as each moment becomes unique unto itself. It is interesting to note that the right mode seems to specialize in awareness of novelty, actually driving the individual with a sensitive and reactive right hemisphere to withdraw from novelty. Being "open" to novelty would require that we be able to left-shift into approaching these new conditions rather than running from them, or trying to not sense when they are present, as in denying their existence in closed mindedness.

Alertness to distinction between differing contexts is also activated during mindful awareness. But arousal of the system's state of awareness of the moment in mindful awareness does not seem to encourage using that noticing of distinction explicitly to create new word-based categories and classifications to describe the differences. This is a distinction to which we must be alert as a core difference between the two: This is the difference between just noting and letting go in mindful awareness versus being alert to distinction and organizing new categories of classification in mindful learning.

With *context sensitivity* we engage the big picture and realize that the setting in which an event is occurring changes the frame from which we can understand it. This sense is a right mode specialty that seems engaged in mindful awareness as well. We come to see the interdependent nature of reality, the interconnectedness of things and events across time. Much of life becomes verbs rather than nouns: events are happenings, not just unmoving facts. In conditional learning the student is encouraged to sense this verb-like quality of knowledge much as the present participles became the verb forms of labeling the internal world that kept the mind spacious. Instead of noting a "thought" as such, calling it "thinking" helped open the mind rather than rigidifying the thought.

Seeing mental activities as dynamic, fluid entities filled with uncertainty is shared by both forms of mindfulness.

Embracing *multiple perspectives* has the quality of a metacognitive skill. In the study of how we come to think about thinking, there are acquired capacities called representational "diversity" and "change" that enable individuals to sense that each of us may have a different perspective, and that even the viewpoint we have at one time may change in the future. In this metacognitive view we can then see perspective as not only a changing frame of reference but also one that needs to be considered in viewing the situationally embedded meaning of knowledge. Mindful awareness has at its essence metacognitive development. We become aware of awareness, can think about thinking, attend to intention. Awareness of multiple perspectives may then share a portion of this metacognitive framework for how to be aware in life.

All of these dimensions of mindful learning are supported by a *present orientation* on the level of information processing and self-relevance in learning. This orientation to the present feels like a completely consistent frame of being aware of the present moment with the more rigorously developed mindful awareness that emerges with training in a mindful awareness practice. And here is the central idea of this entire analysis. Though mindful awareness may be trained with deep practice, and mindful learning may be evoked rapidly in a teaching setting, these two approaches may be mutually compatible and reinforcing. The development of one may support the other in fascinating and practical ways.

"SIDEWAYS LEARNING" AND "ORTHOGONAL REALITY"

Ellen Langer considers mindful learning as not a top-down or bottom-up approach, but a "sideways" stance to learning (1997). Mindful conditions set the scene for learners to be conditional in how they take in information. This context dependence makes uncertainty a friend. In fact, it is this creative uncertainty that appears to strengthen the learning and even make the experience of learning more enjoyable.

Jon Kabat-Zinn (2003b) has suggested that we see mindfulness as an "orthogonal" reality. We need to let go of our engrained ways of seeking goals and objectives, letting the process be the essence of being, not doing. This orthogonal perspective engages our awareness in a new way, shedding the secondary enslavements of plans and contingencies, evaluations and outcomes. As we have seen, too, mindful awareness is much more than just letting go of top-down and just being with bottom-up: Mindful awareness has the essential aspect of meta-awareness and attention to intention that makes this a powerful dimension of being in the present moment.

When we deeply sense what Langer and Kabat-Zinn are proposing, we can become aware of a great deal that they share. Naturally there are profound differences in how one moves in each world. In MBSR, the deep learning of mindful practice in sitting and walking meditation and yoga exercises is experiential and sensory. In mindful learning it appears that the focus is on engaging with the outside world, not so much in achieving a test score or skill, but in becoming a part of a learning experience in which novelty and uncertainty engages the mind to create new categories of learning. These are significant differences clearly in practice and focus. But the similarities of both being process oriented and engaging a context-sensitive present focus of attention seems compelling.

In both forms of mindfulness, the self is at the center of experience. In mindful learning, it is the engagement of the self that is seen as central to the measures of impact: improved retention, enhanced pleasure, better health. The self in mindful awareness has a very different quality. As the immersion in mindfulness unfolds, a bare awareness of the *ipseity* of one's experience emerges—the sense of a grounded self beneath the layers of constructed identity. From this core place, the hub of the mind's wheel of awareness, it becomes possible to sense the activities of the mind as the transient brainwaves on the rim that arise moment by moment.

I am not sure how the deeper sense of self is overtly experienced in classes taught with mindful learning at their base. But I imagine people do not reach toward ipseity, at least on a level of conscious reflection. On the other hand, learning in a way that dissolves false certainty is a parallel process to ipseity. As we release our brain's natural tendency to lock onto clear and unchanging definitions, of the world in the case of facts and of our selves in terms of personal identity, we embrace the fluid reality of the world and ourselves. The focus being external, there may be just a hint of a conscious sense of ipseity as mindful learning wakes people up from the prior bombardment of mindless learning. On a deeper, perhaps nonconscious level, though, this hint toward a more flexible and adaptive state of mind may offer us an important view into the overlap of positive findings in both forms of mindfulness.

DISSOLVING TOP-DOWN MINDSETS

In Chapter 7 we spoke about the ways that mindful awareness may create the conditions necessary to jettison judgments and suspend the influence of top-down processing. The long practice of mindfulness meditation reveals that it requires sustained effort to achieve this deep capacity for entering a more nonjudgmental state. Such a receptive state helps alleviate suffering and to enhance well-being.

In mindful learning, the process also involves a way to dissolve previously entrenched mindsets that are both nonproductive and destructive. Langer points out that mindlessness can lead to trivial or tragic outcomes, with a range of effects including damage to one's self-image, unintended cruelty to others, loss of control, and stunted potential. As an example of the latter she points to the findings in which when people believe that they are not intelligent, they will act accordingly. Such a view is shared by the intriguing work of Carol Dweck (2006), who also demonstrates that the way we believe we can, or cannot, influence our own pathway (intelligence, personality, health) has a huge impact on outcome. If we have the mindset that our "self" is an outcome of fate, we will not put effort into altering the results. If on the other hand we believe these traits are acquired, shaped by effort, then we can exert our focus of attention and build the skill necessary for intelligence, or happiness. This notion that processes such as happiness are actually learnable skills is shared by contemplative mindfulness practitioners (Ricard, 2003). In these forms of mindful learning, the individual is engaged to take an active part in learning and in decoupling automatic constraints, such as beliefs about aging, failing memory, and intelligence that shackle us in a prison we often cannot see.

In both forms of mindfulness, the individual is encouraged to see with more clarity and vitality. Learning becomes alive as we see the unfolding of experiences as new in each new context. This is a view shared deeply by both perspectives. In many ways both forms are an an excellent example of how mindfulness can help us see the world through "new lenses."

Langer (1997) presented this finding for us: "When shown a sentence with a word repeated in it, people almost always miss the extra word." (Take a look at the last sentence of the prior paragraph and see what you see.) Langer went on:

> When a small group of people with head injuries was shown such a sentence, all of them caught the double word, *an,* in the example. Why is this so? We can only hypothesize that those who have lost some of their familiar abilities are no longer able to take the world for granted. (Experienced meditators also found the double word with no problem.) (p. 138)

When I read that paragraph I naturally thought of all that we have been discussing about seeing the world without the secondary influences that enslave our perceptions. Mindfulness meditation can help us dissolve those influences. Head trauma can also induce a state where sensory input is seen with fresh eyes. In these ways, both cognitive and reflective forms of mindfulness may help us dissolve the top-down influences of invariant representations.

With the conditional presentations of mindful learning, we can propose ways in which the right mode of processing might become activated to engage the incoming data in ways that are distinct from a dominant left mode of semantic, factual encoding. Research in memory reveals (Schacter, 1996; Gazzaniga, 2000) that the left hemisphere appears to specialize in factual memory, whereas the right utilizes imagery, emotion, and references to the self, such as in laying down emotionally rich autobiographical memory. We can propose that mindful learning activates right mode memory processes that are governed by the principles we have described earlier of uncertainty, context dependence, and self-integration. In this manner, right mode activation in mindful learning might be the specific way in which the brain may carry out the alterations in large-scale assemblies of neurons that we have proposed would be the general manner in which top-down enslavements could be disengaged. The learning that would occur with such novel neural conditions would likely be much broader and with more retention, consistent with the learning assessment that Langer (1997) has found.

EMBRACING UNCERTAINTY

Both forms of mindfulness honor uncertainty. This shared respect is more than just on the surface, it is embedded in the deep structures of both approaches to mindfulness. Cognitive uncertainty naturally has a different feel from reflective uncertainty in which all of our internal presumptions are up for grabs. Long periods of silence to get to know and to attune to our own minds without structure enables us to experience uncertainty first hand. In this mindful awareness, the mind truly becomes a guest house in which all visitors, as uncertain as the guest list might be, are invited in and welcomed at the table.

In mindful learning, uncertainty is the opening of categorizations from prior constraints. This, too, can feel somewhat disorienting. In fact, when professionals may have become accustomed to traditional approaches of nonconditional teaching, an educational focus on the experience of the student, rather than the outcome of learning or the results of some test of achievement, may feel uncomfortable. I imagine that the effort to offer mindful learning in standard curricula is filled with a feeling of doubt and uncertainty, which is then approached with a top-down movement to see these suggestions through conventional lenses. That's just a guess, it might be true, but it might not be, and perhaps we need to mindfully reflect on that.

CONTROL VERSUS AGENCY

This brings us to another crucial issue. Langer (1989, 1997) used the term *control* repeatedly in her writings. "Mindful awareness of different options gives us greater control. This feeling of greater control, in turn, encourages us to be more mindful. Rather than being a chore, mindfulness engages us in a continuing momentum" (1989, pp. 201–202). Control, per se, is something reflective mindfulness is not about. Here is a seemingly huge and insurmountable conflict. To be in a state of mindful awareness means giving up "control."

My sense of this issue is that Langer's use of "control" actually signifies the feeling of agency, of one being the center of intention and will. After all, acknowledging the ever-changing contexts of the world is giving up "control," yet attaining a sense of membership in the dynamic world of things. We become an agent of intention, not a controller of perspectives. In this sense, it feels that in fact these two forms of mindfulness share a centrality of intention. While we could approach the use of the term *control* in a nonmindful way, if we see the context, distinction, and perspective of the use of this word, we may be able to come up with a new category in which to place it. With this mindful approach, agency becomes a common theme that may, in fluid fact, be shared by these two forms of mindfulness. This is an area worthy of further exploration.

REFLECTIVE THINKING

What do we know about how the mind lets go of certainty? The work of psychologist Stephen Kosslyn (2005) on a process he called "reflective thinking" may shed helpful insights into the nature of how we dissolve top-down influences in both mindful learning and in mindful awareness practices.

As we discussed earlier, the brain responds to experience with the firing of neural net profiles of activation. These clusters of firing patterns embed information, a neural symbol of something that "stands for" something other than itself. When we see a tree, for example, our brains create a neural net profile of activation that symbolizes the tree; there is no tree in our heads. Our first five senses respond with firing as we see, smell, touch, and, if we want, taste and hear the tree. Sensation then serves as the primary data, the bottom-up input of firing, which will be soon processed further in the brain.

The brain responds to sensory input with perceptual processing, encoding those primary neural firing patterns into layers of subsequent neural translations. Kosslyn has illuminated the nature of the perceptual images that emerge, enabling us to see how the brain creates perception. These early perceptual neural symbols create mental representations that we call "images," which are not limited to the visual modality. Instead, images include all modes of processing—short of descriptive concepts or word-based labels.

When we move from the earlier image representation to the later conceptual and linguistic based categories, we have now moved to the level of description. Kosslyn's proposal is that as information processors, we take in sensation, create images, and then deposit those images into long-term memory. To be maximally efficient, we then categorize and classify image representations into a descriptive form that allows us to rapidly gain access to the vast, and potentially overwhelming data stored in long term memory. Descriptions are constructed summations of numerous images encoded over time.

Reflective thinking is information processing that manipulates images, not descriptions. This is in contrast to what we can call conceptual or linguistic descriptive thinking. Image-based information processing helps deposit experience into long term storage and then is processed for more rapid access into descriptive categories. Rather than considering every situation worthy of creating context-dependent images to encode the specifics of their features, descriptive thinking takes over to make information processing more efficient.

In many ways, Kosslyn's use of the term *reflective thinking* opened up a new gateway for describing what we have been discussing as the dissolution of top-down influences in mindful awareness, and now mindful learning.

Kosslyn suggested that "reflective thinking occurs when what is stored in long-term memory (LTM) is not sufficient to allow one to accomplish a task directly, and thus one must use working memory to derive new information on the basis of what one knows" (p. 851). In mindful learning we can propose that the condition-dependent phrases and references to self-mindsets initiate reflective thinking. This would mean that instead of just utilizing automatic classifications, the individual would be engaging in imagery-based processing.

The concept of reflective thinking may apply to our discussion of both forms of mindfulness in that top-down, autopilot driven states of mind are disengaged. Reflective thinking engagement in mindful awareness and learning would enable a more fluid state to be achieved as the stream of thoughts flow through consciousness and are not locked in to any one particular prior classification.

Kosslyn (2005) summarized that,

> reflective thinking occurs when automatic processing is either not sufficient or fast enough to perform a task; reflective thinking involves working memory; and working memory relies on representations that underlie conscious awareness: mental images. These ideas imply that reflective thinking is important to the extent that the world is not predictable, and that new and unexpected events occur. During reflective thinking we pause to examine the consequences of various actions or events, and such processing helps us make novel decisions. (p. 854)

Put simply, reflective thinking engages mental images rather than linguistically based categories and previously constructed conceptual classifications.

PUTTING CLASSIFICATION ON HOLD

In mindful awareness we mentally note the fluid nature of mental activities and enter a state of reflection we have characterized by receptivity, self-observation, and reflexivity. This mindful reflection in many ways enables us to disengage from the top-down influences of prior classifications and conclusions of the mind.

In mindful learning, the presentation of conditional phrases and mindset perspectives also invites the learner, implicitly and explicitly, to consider context and perspective in engaging the unique aspects of information in an open fashion. This, too, is fundamentally an engagement of the mind to reflect on the novel aspects of knowledge. The learning is more extensively integrated with the self and the fuller sense of the dynamic, uncertain, and fluid aspects of the real world.

In reflective thinking, a process defined by its focus on images rather than descriptive representations, we also see this dismantling of classifications. Kosslyn (2005) noted

> People tend to recode perceptual information as descriptions after they access such information, and thus with age and experience they come to have increasingly larger sets of descriptive information in LTM. These representations allow us to respond automatically, without needing to engage in reflective thinking. This is a good thing, in that to have to reflect about each and every decision posed by circumstance would be exhausting. But it is also a bad thing, in that we may often fail to notice something new or to reconsider our habitual responses. (p. 860)

This is parallel to the proposed enhancement of orienting to novelty of reflective mindfulness and the sensitivity to distinction in mindful learning. Here we can sense the exciting convergence of mindful awareness, mindful learning, and reflective thinking as sharing similar mechanisms of declassification.

SENSING NOVELTY

Sensing novelty is also a common feature of these three dimensions of being aware. The brain has a natural drive to detect patterns. As an associational organ, it clusters those patterns into mental models that automatically classify the world into generalized schema that help us to rapidly sort through the huge amount of data in present sensation and in memory. Part of the way that the brain achieves this is through looking for the invariant features of stimuli, such as the shape of a cat, and then creating a category for that feline creature. "Cat" becomes the mental model for all whiskered, purring, independent small animals chased by dogs, another category of animal. Invariant representations can then enslave our primary sensory inputs to conform to this previously established classification scheme (Hawkins & Blakeslee, 2004). Instead of life feeling vibrant and novel, it can, if overly done, become dulled and routine.

At the extreme, our brain can rapidly seek these invariant features, called "constraints," and classify everything rapidly into one grouping or another. The result can restrict the quality of life, and the flexibility of learning. Kosslyn (2005) suggested that

> Processing information stored in LTM is exceedingly unintelligent: such processing requires only that activating one representation in turn activates or inhibits (as specified by the nature of the association) other representations to different degrees. Input activates specific representations, and if there are enough cues, only a single stored representation of a concept may be consistent with all the activated representations at once. (p. 854)

Thus we can come to premature hardening of the categories, shutting down learning, and seeing these through old lenses. Engaging in reflective thinking not only lets us see things in a new way, literally, but it helps reorganize long term memory itself and alters the ways in which we can gain access to those now loosened classifications. Reflective thinking also helps reprogram LTM and affect the circumstances when reflective thinking will be used in the future. By entering "new information in LTM, reflective thinking provides new grist for the constraint satisfaction mill: it provides additional cues that can be used to retrieve specific memories" (pp. 855–856).

In a practical way, sensing novelty may require that we turn toward images, not word-based categories. This movement toward imagery may feel vaguely familiar to you at this point. We have presented the notion that the right brain mode is imagery based.

We discussed how our prelinguistic world in development was dominated by right hemisphere activation and growth in the first few years of life. And we experienced how diving into direct experience in mindful awareness brought us face-to-face with the preworded world.

Kosslyn (2005) suggested that in his view,

> young children do not have as much stored information that allows them to respond automatically, and thus will need to reflect more often. It is tempting to speculate that it is this phenomenon, of reflecting about what adults consider ordinary, that produces the 'childlike freshness' of the young child, who can delight in what we adults find common-place and can be annoyingly persistent in asking 'why?' (p. 856)

Mindful awareness and mindful learning may be an important return to reflection in thinking, in feeling, in being in our lives.

THE HUB

Mindful awareness expands the reflective hub of our minds in which we can receive into awareness any aspect of the rim, from input from the outer world to the inner workings of our body and mind. In mindful learning, the student is engaged in a taking-in process that requires that the self be present as the active recipient, not just the passive receptacle. This participant-observer function likely engages the brain in a different manner from passive learning. Much like the difference between automatic versus actively engaged reading, the learner's own mind brings curiosity to the event. These are the "why's" of the wise child, the reflection that brings us beneath the words to the deeper and unclassified meaning in experience. The embedding of neural firing patterns in this more reflectively engaged process is likely fuller and lends itself to more extensive interlinked representations of self and alternate possibility.

In mindful learning the engagement of "may" and "your attitude matters" likely activates circuits of self-observation and conflict resolution that may also involve the reflective hub of our
wheel of awareness. In the mind we may feel the sentiments of
"I need to be here to hear this one—and what if it isn't that way
but it's another way." These circuits at a minimum include those
prefrontal regions we have been exploring for reflective mindfulness: the middle aspects and the side portion of the prefrontal
cortex. The side (DLPFC) would be more engaged for working
memory. The middle areas would be activated with conflict resolution and the linkage of affect with cognition involving the anterior cingulate and orbitofrontal cortex. Activation of the medial
prefrontal areas would also occur with awareness of one's own
mind. Taking in multiple perspectives may involve other medial
areas for metacognitive processing. These mindsight circuits would
participate not only in the encoding of these conditional/self-ac-
tivating teaching tools, but they would be actively engaged in their
registration through the hippocampus into more self-integrated
memory involving the right hemisphere in conjuction with the
left's factual encoding. Autobiographical storage will have more
retrieval strength as the study of our life stories reveal.

As we encourage image-based explorations beneath descriptive
categories, we are directly engaging in reflective thinking. Promoting reflection in this educational way will pull in the neural
circuits of self that make life more memorable, more meaningful,
and more fulfilling.

MINDFUL INTEGRATION

We can view our discussion of reflective thinking, mindful
learning, and mindful awareness as having quite deep overlapping
principles that may share similar neural correlations. The active
dissolution of top-down invariant representations can be seen as a

neural process that dismantles cortical enslavement of incoming informational streams. Instead of being constrained by this prior learning, mindfulness involves a sense of freshness and fullness. By "enhancing the odd ball," reflective thinking and both forms of mindfulness may actually be seen to expand our sense of subjective time. This would be achieved by increasing the density of bits of information that are now seen with "beginner's eyes" and taken in afresh, because each moment is its own context.

We can imagine that mindful awareness might inhibit the usual brain mechanisms that classify experience and directly shape the quality of our "freshness" in awareness as discussed in Chapter 6. Openness to novelty is a defining characteristic of mindful learning. The inherent features of conditional learning create a natural emphasis on sensing the unique aspects of situations as they arise. And in reflective thinking, the movement to imagery disengages the descriptive categories of information processing.

These shared mechanisms may underscore a way in which we can come to integrate the two very divergent ways in which these forms of mindfulness are evoked and draw also on this independent perspective of reflective thinking. Mindful learning seems to enable internal knowledge structures to become loosened, as each perspective is respected and embraced, each condition considered equally possible. With mindful awareness developed through a turning inward, the focus begins with an attunement to one's own internal landscape. The deep ways in which we become aware of our own changes in perspective, and the conditions of transience of the moment-to-moment unfolding of life, bring with them a deep sense of acceptance of the bare essentials of our minds.

Nothing is taken for granted in mindfulness. The moment is a condition, a perspective, a novel point in time that is embraced within that particular focus of our attention. In mindful learning, the aim of our attention is primarily on the outer world—but the self is a full participant. With mindful awareness, what begins as an inward attention evolves into a mind wide open, ready to receive the fullness of inner and outer events as they arise.

Research projects could explore ways in which the inward focus might lend itself, for example, to readily teaching the outward focused mindful learning in a classroom setting. Do mindfulness meditators as teachers more readily utilize in their teaching mindful learning techniques? Do students engaged in mindful learning have easier access to their internal worlds so they can reveal facets of that form of mindfulness more readily in their lives? Can we establish brain imaging studies that might reveal middle prefrontal activation during mindful learning, as has been demonstrated for mindfulness meditation? And what might the other regions of the resonance circuitry's role be in mindful learning, in which one's attention to the intention of the question may be a part of how to interpret the queries posed in such a self-connecting way?

Integrating these ideas, mindfully, with the possible overlap with reflective thinking, would help us explore the role of neural representations in a mindful state. Do we have a way of assessing the activation of imagery rather than that of classification? Can we learn how to help people more intentionally move from descriptive categories into reflective images? If we can understand these deeper layers of processing, we could link reflective thinking, mindful learning, and mindful awareness in ways that might be quite useful in creatively, and more effectively, applying these avenues toward freedom from mindlessness that could then help a broader group of people. These and many more questions could be the focus of an integrative program directed at understanding the many reflective mechanisms and dimensions of mindfulness.

It would also be exciting to see ways in which we could make these life-affirming, health-promoting approaches accessible to the many who could benefit. Working together, ancient wisdom, clinical practice, neural insights, and inspired teaching may go hand-in-hand to enhance the lives of this and future generations.

PART IV

REFLECTIONS ON
THE MINDFUL BRAIN

Chapter Twelve

EDUCATING THE MIND:
The Fourth "R" and The Wisdom of Reflection

An important place to begin to address the practical implications of the mindful brain is in our approach to education. So much of school experience focuses on the acquisition of important skills and knowledge regarding the outer world. We learn to read, to write, to calculate numbers. Perhaps this approach stems from our educational system's emphasis on a curriculum of content, rather than one that focuses on the process of cultivating the mind itself. Yet we can see that personal well-being and prosocial behavior require that we nurture the capacity for self-understanding and empathy in youth, qualities that emerge from learning to be reflective. This life-enhancing facility of the mind develops as a skill that promotes flexibility and resilience, within ourselves and within our relationships with others. The basic ingredients of well-being and compassionate social living are, in fact, teachable. Reflection is the common pathway by which our brains support such abilities, our relationships come to thrive in them, and our minds can achieve a state of internal attunement and sense of harmony.

THE FOURTH "R" OF EDUCATION

At the heart of mindfulness is the teachable capacity for reflection. This learnable skill is just a breath away from being readily

available as the fourth "R" of basic education to children throughout their development. We once saw reading and writing and
'rithmetic as luxuries for a selective few, but now these skills are
considered the three basic R's of education. Wouldn't it make
sense to teach children about the mind itself and make reflection
become a fundamental part of basic education?

Education is a key component to a child's development. The
relationships that teachers have with their students and the experiences they provide for them directly shape the neural circuitry
of the next generation. Teachers in this way can be seen as the
"neurosculptors" of our future.

When children leave home during the toddler years to enter
daycare, or as three- and four-year-olds to attend preschool, they
begin a long journey of relationships with teachers. These important connections can profoundly shape a child's sense of self, belief in his or her own talents, and willingness to try to succeed in
the face of challenge. Important findings show that the beliefs of
the teacher in the child's capacity to learn directly shape the realization of the child's learning. Indeed, a child's belief in his or her
own capacity to improve intelligence with genuine effort can
make all the difference between just settling for mediocrity or
pushing for excellence and achieveing potential (Dweck, 2006).

What would happen if teachers were also aware of the scientific finding that how a person reflects internally will shape how
he treats both himself and others? If teachers became aware that
attuning to the self—being mindful—can alter the brain's ability to create flexibility and self-observation, empathy, and morality, wouldn't it be worth the time to teach such reflective skills
first to teachers and then, in age-appropriate ways, to the students
themselves?

We know how to teach reading. We have strategies for how to
teach writing skills. We actively engage in a progressive program
to teach mathematics. Teachers have all of these skills themselves

as individuals; imparting them to students comes naturally. Each of these three basic R's focuses the mind on the external world: others' thoughts in books, essays and reports often about what we've seen on the outside, or conceptual ideas and skills about numerical procedures. These are all important. But—as was the case in my own experience not only in primary and secondary school, but in college and medical school as well—a focus on the self, and in particular on the mind, is often absent from those thousands of hours we spend in the classroom.

Of the many downsides of self-absenteeism or mindlessness, one is that we miss the opportunity to develop mindsight, our capacity to sense the mind in ourselves, and in others. Without this skill, our own internal life is a blur, and the minds of others are often missing from our sense of the world. This absence of a focus on mindsight in education is bolstered by technology-driven media that bombard children with stimuli devoid of elements that promote self-understanding or compassion. Absent self, missing mind, empty empathy.

Reflection is the skill that embeds self-knowing and empathy in the curriculum. Various lines of research suggest that training a child in social and emotional skills promotes resilience and may harness the neural circuitry of executive function (Greenberg, submitted). Here we see the important overlap of social, emotional, cognitive, and attentional mechanisms—each reinforcing one another. As we've seen, the prefrontal areas of the brain may mediate each of these dimensions of our mental life.

In neural terms, the fourth "R" of reflection would essentially be an education that develops the prefrontal cortex. This is our "cortex humanitas," the neural hub of our humanity. In addition to reflection being a part of our prefrontal heritage, this integrative region also supports relationships and resilience, perhaps giving us a fifth and sixth "R" of basic education. We have a fairly clear idea about how to promote prefrontal growth when we consider the role of attunement in neuroplasticity: Interpersonal attunement in adult-child relationships promotes the development of prefrontal functions. The proposed teaching of mindful awareness would harness these same processes that emerge with prefrontal neural integration and promote a reflective mind, an adaptive, resilient brain, and empathic relationships.

REFLECTIVE SKILL-BUILDING

How do we teach reflective skills?

Reflection, as we have come to define it, has at least three dimensions: receptivity, self-observation, and reflexivity. Each of these elements can be a focus of school-based exercises that nurture the prefrontal region's capacity to be open, self-aware, and meta-aware—the awareness of awareness.

Teachers can promote these three dimensions through a number of approaches tailored to the age of their students and the setting of their teaching. Ultimately these reflective skills harness our prefrontal capacity for executive attention, prosocial behavior, empathy, and self-regulation.

The overall insights from brain science suggest that how we focus our attention activates certain neural circuits. With neural activation, the potential is created to enhance the connections in those regions which can help transform a temporary state into a more long term trait of that individual. The experiences we provide as teachers focus students' attention, activate their brains, and create the possibility of harnessing neural plasticity in those specific areas. Coupled with emotional engagement, a sense of novelty, and optimal attentional arousal, teaching with reflection can utilize these prime conditions for building new connections in the brain.

Our study of the mirror properties in the brain suggests that how we arrive as teachers ourselves with this sense of engagement, emergence, and focus will directly activate those states in the student. An initial approach to consider as an educator is how you experience these processes. To develop reflection and internal attunement in our students, we need ourselves to be familiar, personally, with the way of being that is mindful awareness.

Much of what may occur in families, classrooms, and within psychotherapy that promotes mindfulness in the developing person (child, student, patient) has to do with the presence of the parent/teacher/therapist. *Presence* is the state of mind that comes with all the dimensions of reflection; the quality of our availability to receive whatever the other brings to us, to sense our own participation in the interaction, and to be aware of our own awareness. We are open to bear witness, to connect, to attune to our students' internal states. This is professional presence that entails us being personally present.

The attunement of the teacher with students creates the grounding for them to become mindful. We see ourselves in the eyes of the other, and when that reflection is attuned, we have an authentic sense of ourselves. When the other has presence, when his or her reflective skills permit mindful awareness, then in that moment we are seen with authenticity and directness.

And so, being mindfully present yourself is an important start. Once you embrace the intention to be open and in the present, there are specific ways in which people of all ages can be encouraged to reflect.

Susan Kaiser Greenland (2006a) has organized a program (InnerKids.org; see also Appendix I for other resources) in which preschool- and elementary-age children are introduced to simple exercises that help build mindful reflection. As a member of her Board of Advisors, I had the opportunity to observe the program first hand and see the powerful impact of the teaching on the children. The students have an hour session each week for twelve consecutive weeks during the school year in which they are engaged in fun, age-appropriate, and playful group "games" designed as a form of mindful awareness practice to help them become more aware of their own internal processes. As with other mindful awareness practices (MAPs), these exercises likely build the complex triad of reflection in which becoming open, self-observant, and aware of awareness are the fundamental skills.

Examples of these group experiences include the children playing instruments and listening to the others while they wait their turn; placing their hands near someone else but not touching; presenting an idea in their mind about an animal they'd like to include in a song while they listen to others offering their own ideas; and having "floor time" in which they sense the upward and downward movement of a plush monkey as they lie flat on the floor and try to put their monkey to sleep with the gentle rocking of their abdomen. Each of these simple exercises helps develop the child's awareness of now, their sensations of impulses and capacity to hold them in check, and their awareness of their sixth sense of the body, including awareness of the breath.

In her pilot project in four different school sites, Kaiser–Greenland found—after reviewing data from the self-reports of older (9–12 years) children and teacher questionnaires from all the children and then applying statistical analyses to the results—significant improvements in several areas (Kaiser-Greenland, 2006b). Though self-reports for children are considered less reliable statistically, these reports showed that the school children themselves noted improvements on being more aware of their behaviors. The more dependable, third-person data revealed that the teachers reported that the children in the program had significant improvements in a few characteristics in the domains of (not) "getting into trouble," "able to see others' views," (not) "easily frustrated," (does) "adapt easily," and (does) "engage with others." Clearly these are impressive results that need to be replicated in a more extensive controlled study in the future. What's the big deal about this set of simple exercises? Isn't this just school as usual? These playful group "games" offer skill-building experiences to enhance reflection. They open the mind's receptivity to feelings in the body, input from peers, sensations of the mind; create an environment of active self-observation; and promote reflexivity, as attunement with the breath generates that resonant state of awareness of intention and of awareness itself.

As we say in our Mindful Awareness Research Center at UCLA, "Simple solutions to complex problems." The solution is that such reflection promotes deeper capacities for self-regulation, empathy, and compassion: a flexible and friendly mind.

Observing these games directly gave me the feeling that Kaiser-Greenland and her teachers are promoting neural activity in the very regions we need them to grow in order to promote reflection, empathic relationships, and emotional resilience: the middle prefrontal areas that enable the nine functions we've discussed to emerge. Recall that these functions include body regulation, attuned communication, emotional balance, flexibility, empathy, insight, fear modulation, intuition, and morality. (See Chapter 2 and Appendix III, Middle Prefrontal Function). I can imagine the insula bringing data up into the midline cortical regions as the wisdom of the body is given respect in this school experience. The body's processing of information through neural networks surrounding the heart and intestines is an important source of non-verbal insight. With a focus on their own and others' internal worlds, the middle prefrontal regions will also be activated and their connections reinforced. If children can be nurtured in the development of these important circuits of wisdom, we'd create the possibility for a transformation in the next generation.

While we'll need to await detailed brain studies to confirm these proposed correlates and neuroplastic changes, Mark Greenberg's work (submitted) on a parallel form of social and emotional skill training suggests that executive functions carried out by these regions are in fact improved with school-based programs similar in certain ways to Kaiser-Greenland's (see Appendix I).

The overarching idea is that what teachers provide can directly develop life-enhancing skills: Life can become more flexible, meaningful, and connecting. Children can develop reflective capacities through skill training that have a long-lasting influence on the promotion of well-being. With reflection, students are offered a neural capacity to socially, emotionally, and academically approach life with resilience. What a gift for healthy development.

MINDFUL AWARENESS PRACTICES: MAPS

"The faculty of voluntarily bringing back a wandering attention, over and over again, is the very root of judgment, character, and will. . . . An education which should improve this faculty would be the education par excellence. But it is easier to define this ideal than to give practical directions for bringing it about" (James, 1890/1981, p. 401).

This often quoted statement from the scholar and psychological visionary of the last century reminds us that education can direct our attention to developing faculties of the mind, not just facts in memory. It turns out that William James, though he was respectful of contemplative practice, was apparently unaware then that many cultures had actually developed thousands of years of practice of just such an education: mindful awareness practices.

We've seen in Chapters 3 and 4 that direct experience in the processes of mindfulness meditation derived from the Vipassana Buddhist tradition of "clear seeing" enabled this fundamental step of "voluntarily bringing back a wandering attention, over and over again." In many ways, this process is the core element of how reflective skills are nurtured. Other cultures, too, and even different branches of Buddhism, offer their own approaches to mindfulness.

In his excellent text on attention and the development of the mind, Allan Wallace (2006) stated:

> The modern psychological account of mindfulness, which is explicitly based on the descriptions of mindfulness presented in the modern Vipassana (contemplative insight) tradition of Theravada Buddhism, differs significantly from the Indo-Tibetan Buddhist version. The modern Vipassana approach views mindfulness as nondiscriminating, moment-to-moment "bare awareness"; the Indo-Tibetan tradition, however, characterizes mindfulness as bearing in mind the object of attention, the state of not forgetting, not being distracted, and not floating. (p. 60)

Here we see that our secular adaptations of the insights from contemplative traditions, in this case from specific forms of Buddhist practice and thought, need to "mindfully" embrace the variations in approach. The issue here is to use the broadest notion of what it means to be intentionally aware of what is happening, as it is happening, be it sensory processes in the present, or reviewing memories from the past or plans for the future. As we've seen in our discussions of the facets of the mindful brain, the act of being aware of awareness and paying attention to intention characterize a broad notion of mindfulness. Within mindful learning we further sense the centrality of embracing uncertainty as we flexibly approach our awareness of the present moment. In all of these ways we can sense that the mindful brain is a universal component of our human heritage, not merely the province of one practice or perspective.

At the UCLA Mindful Awareness Research Center (see Appendix I), we have been compiling ways in which what we call mindful awareness practices (MAPs) can be cultivated. MAPs refer to a class of approaches or exercises (e.g., meditation, yoga, tai chi, qigong, and others) designed to cultivate mindful awareness, increase attention and emotion regulation, reduce stress, and foster a sense of well-being and compassion. Mindful awareness itself can also be incorporated into and cultivated by other activities including art, music, dance, writing, psychotherapy, touch (e.g., massage, acupuncture), and sports.

Tai Chi

For example, tai chi chuan is an ancient practice (Roth, 1999) that embodies a deep philosophical tradition with a dynamic form of mindful movement. In the actual practice, one learns a sequence of steps and bodily motions that require the practitioner to remain focused on the movements as they are happening. The intentionality of the steps and the internal state of being aware of one's awareness of the body reinforce the fundamental mindful nature of this graceful practice. In its fullest form, the deep conceptual ideas of Taoism and the non-conceptual ways of knowing are woven together with the self-observation of one's dynamic practice and the sensory fullness of the balanced movements. In this way, the full practice of tai chi involves all four streams of awareness: sensation, observation, conception, and knowing. But even in the simpler approach of mindful movement, benefits to this simple and elegant practice have been known for generations. As mentioned in the first chapter, Michael Irwin (2005) has found a correlation between improvements in immune function and the practice of tai chi in his pilot study of a modified form of tai chi when taught to a group of elderly individuals.

Yoga

Another MAP, perhaps more readily accepted by children and adolescents because of its adaptable steps that can be modified for different age groups, is the practice of yoga. While many forms of yoga practice exist, the overall approach is similarly one of focused attention on one's own awareness of the body, breath, stillness, and motion. This mindful practice combines the aspects of reflexivity—awareness of awareness—with self-observation that engages awareness of the body. These somatic sensations anchor the practitioner in the present and enable the wandering attention to be repeatedly brought back to the body or the breath. In the practice of yoga, balance becomes a readily experienced measure of a wandering attention, faltering with distraction and centering when one returns to mindful awareness. Formal studies of the use of yoga, and other MAPs in young children, are in their infancy but their use in adults, as we've discussed, appears to support their positive impacts on a sense of well-being (Brown & Gerbarg, 2005a, 2005b).

In mindful learning, discussed in detail in the last chapter, the use of conditional statements and the involvement of the student, at least in the studies of adults, have positive impacts on enjoyment and efficacy of learning. Here the teacher can seemingly activate a flexible state of mind in which sensitivity to novelty and the distinctions that emerge from new contexts become a part of the learning experience. In all of these MAPs, we need to have controlled studies of their efficacy in children and adolescents to establish their short- and long-term impacts on a range of outcomes, from emotional well-being to prosocial behaviors as well as their impacts on physiology and long-term medical health.

The work of the PATHs and CASEL programs (Greenberg, Weissberg, O'Brien, Zins, Fredericks, Resnick, & Elias, 2003; see also Appendix I) reveals research established approaches to support school-based programs that nurture resilience and promote social and emotional learning. Though these programs may not directly teach "mindfulness" as a designated skill, their educational programs overlap to a great degree with the general idea of MAPs as promoting emotional intelligence and prosocial behavior as they enhance self-awareness and self-regulation.

I serve on the leadership council of the Garrison Institute's initiative for awareness and concentration in learning (see Appendix I). The "Garrison Institute report on contemplation and education:

A survey of programs using contemplative techniques in K–12 educational settings: A mapping report" offers a useful overview of practices presently taking place across the United States that aim to promote contemplation in education. The Report offers this statement (Garrison Institute Report, 2005):

> With regard to methodology, contemplative programs for K–12th-grade students have much in common. In general, they incorporate mindfulness and other contemplative techniques to train and refine attention, promote emotional balance, and, by extension, help students develop the capacity for self-regulation. However, programs define the terms *attention*, *mindfulness*, and *contemplation* inconsistently, and often imprecisely. At the programmatic level, a theoretical framework for defining *attention* appears to be absent; so too is a well-accepted definition of *mindfulness*.
>
> Despite methodological and pedagogical differences, contemplative programs share a common set of outcomes consistent with those of mainstream education. The main short-term or immediate outcomes include enhancing students' learning and academic performance, improving the school's social climate, as well as promoting emotional balance and prosocial behaviors. These programs also share common long-term or ultimate outcomes including the development of noble qualities such as peacefulness, internal calm, compassion, empathy, forgiveness, patience, generosity, and love. (p. 4)

Overall the Garrison Report offers us an important overview of what approaches are now being initiated in our schools. The report urges us to combine our efforts in attempting to create programs that work, and share that knowledge with each other. In a meeting sponsored by the Garrison Institute and led by Mark Greenberg, a range of scientists gathered to focus on how executive attentional mechanisms develop and what school interventions might be implemented to support such preventative measures in the educational setting. It became clear at that meeting that grounding our efforts to help children requires an understanding of new insights into how the brain develops in response to experiences that we as adults offer to the growing child. Teaching reflection may be useful in the schools, but we need to understand how the developmental stage of a child will make the ways we implement such teaching quite different across developmental stages. Knowing about the brain's development can help guide us in understanding how to create and implement effective programs to promote reflection in the school setting.

TEACHING WITH THE BRAIN IN MIND

In teaching reflective skills, we need to understand that reflection in children may take on a different form than the more complex manifestations in adulthood, where the cortex—especially the prefrontal cortex—is far more intricate. Reflective thinking may be more dominant and accessible in children who naturally utilize imagery, enabling them to see with "fresh eyes" the novelty in the world. The need to dissolve top-down constraints may not be the focus of reflection in the case of children, as it often is with adults. Instead, approaches that give them more awareness of their internal worlds, such as simple breath-awareness exercises, can offer them a base of self-attunement that can continue forward with them as a form of reflective coherence as they grow. Circuitry which becomes established and reinforced is more likely to be available in the future. Neurons that fire together, wire together, and survive together (Post & Weiss, 1997).

This basic principle of brain development lets us know that experience can shape the circuitry of resilience. For example, studies of children and their caregivers reveal that relationships before and during adolescence serve as a major form of resilience as the child enters the tumultuous teen years (Sroufe et al., 2005). Other research suggests that the parents' capacity to reflect on the nature of their own internal life, and the internal world of the child, is a major predictor of the child's security of attachment, which, in turn, predicts a form of resilience and positive development (Fonagy & Target, 1997; Sroufe et al., 2005).

Recall that after birth there is a rapid, genetically-driven growth in synaptic connections during the first three years of life. The connections between the two hemispheres will begin to grow at this time and continue their integrative development well into adulthood (Gazzaniga, 2000). The growth of the connecting corpus callosum will link the right hemisphere, dominant during those early years of life in its growth and activity, with the left, which becomes more active during the preschool years. In preschool the saying "learn to put words to your feelings" reflects this emerging capacity to link the verbal left with the nonverbal and more spontaneously emotional right hemisphere.

During elementary school, synapses are forming rapidly in response to new experiences as children are open to new knowledge and skills, including the learning of foreign languages and musical facilities. The elementary years are a period of assimilation of knowledge and skills as the child's brain soaks in experience like a sponge in school and home life. Knowledge is assembled rapidly but with effort, as the child does not have the complex cortical architecture to rapidly enter new representations within long-term memory. Reflective thinking may be dominant during this period as experiences are sorted in "imagery" form into new categories in the emerging scaffold of knowledge that shapes long-term memory storage.

After the elementary school years, the young child enters the preadolescent period marked by new brain changes (Casey et al., 2005; Blakemore & Choudhury, 2006). The rapid growth of synapses that characterized the first three years of life returns again during this pre-pubertal phase, and cognitive functions may actually become less efficient as this excess in connectivity may decrease the speed of information processing.

As adolescence begins, the second genetically programmed growth of synapses is followed by a long decade of brain remodeling that involves the programmed destruction of neurons and their connections that are not being used. This parcellation process in which connections are pruned is thought to be a "use-it-or-lose-it" neural reshaping that is exacerbated by stress. Such a period of brain change is also marked by vulnerability, as underlying neural deficits, unrealized before adolescence, may become exposed during the pruning process.

Many of the changes in adolescent executive function and social cognition may be due to this cortical restructuring, especially in the prefrontal areas (Blakemore & Choudhury, 2006). During this period there may be instability in the nine prefrontal functions we discussed (see Chapter 2, p. 43 and Appendix III, Middle Prefrontal Functions), including emotional balance, insight, and empathy. The "low road" of functioning, with a temporary disabling of the prefrontal integrative functions, may be more likely to occur during this period. If we offer children before they reach puberty the sense of connection and the social and emotional skills of reflection—experiences that bolster important executive prefrontal circuits—the path in adolescence may be improved.

These findings of resilience and brain development support the idea that teaching reflective skills to children makes sense. We can propose that learning such skills in youth may help grow integrative neural fibers that will offer resilience during the challenging years of social and neural change inherent in the adolescent period, which, research reveals, seems to last into the mid-twenties (Giedd, 2004; Sowell, Peterson, Thompson, Welcome, Henkenius, & Toga, 2003).

My own personal experience, being a child psychiatrist and parent, is that such reflection can also be supported by direct teaching about the brain itself. When people—children, teens, or adults—learn about the correlations between brain function and structure, neural development and the impact of experience, and how their mental lives unfold, a kind of discernment develops in which people come to see their own minds in a new light. The activity of the mind becomes something that can be seen on the rim from the hub of their wheel of awareness as they can envision how the mind uses parts of the brain to create itself (see Chapter 6, p. 121). The brain's emerging structure also directly impacts how the mind itself will function, as in the lability of emotion during the remodeling of the prefrontal cortex in adolescence.

Knowing that the middle prefrontal functions enable emotional balance can help each of us understand how its temporary dysfunction (when we "flip our lids") can lead to frightening behaviors in others, and in ourselves. Reflecting on this neural correlate enables us to understand experience, not to explain it away. Rather than rationalizing excuses for inappropriate behavior, such neural insights seem to actually help us to have more compassion and discernment, for ourselves and for others.

In this way, we can add an education about the brain itself to our tool kit for helping develop mindfulness. The more we can come to "clear seeing" about the nature of our mental reality, the more reflective coherence and empathic relationships we can promote for each other.

Why shouldn't kids—and adults—learn to flexibly experience their own minds? Being able to reflect on our own inner world is a basic part of our skill set and knowledge base that promotes well-being and a meaningful life. Even with the adolescent changes in prefrontal function that alter cognition during and after this period of rapid change, laying down the tracts of reflection with mindful awareness practices may be a wise educational investment in thoughtful prevention throughout the lifespan to support physiological, mental, and relational well-being.

When children are reflective, they have the tools to not only experience mindful awareness in the moment, but they are being given the gift of prefrontal reinforcements for challenging times in the future. Youth with well-developed reflective skills and a mindful brain can be prepared to be more flexible in new contexts, and they can also engage in interpersonal relationships, which, in turn, will be more rewarding and support their sense of well-being and flexibility as they grow.

BEING PRESENT AS A TEACHER

The lessons of the mindful brain suggest that our presence as a person will inform how we attune to ourselves and to others. It is this capacity for reflection that some researchers are coming to sense may be the true attribute of wisdom (Staudinger, 1996, 2003; Staudinger, Singer, & Bluck 2001; Staudinger & Pasupathi, 2003). As teachers we are in a unique position to offer to our students not just our capacity to impart knowledge and skills, but our essence as people. In this connection we can inspire our students' desire to learn more. As William Butler Yeats said, "Education is not the filling of a pail, but the lighting of a fire." When we bring our full selves, our authentic passion for the mysteries of life and the power of connections, we can inspire our students to rewire their brains.

Mindful learning also teaches us to offer material in such a way as to evoke a sense of context and meaning to the conditional nature of the information. This presentation directly activates the self of the learner, likely interlacing the new material in a much wider scaffold of neural connectivity than absolute knowledge. We need to embrace uncertainty ourselves to be able to impart this mindful learning to our students (Langer, 1997; Napoli, 2004; Ritchart & Perkins, 2000; Thornton & McEntee, 1993).

With the position that we are all lifelong learners, such a stance is not only liberating, but it invites the student to join us in the experience of learning, not just the memorization of falsely certain "facts." Learning becomes a verb, and the scaffold it creates is then a dynamic, living entity beyond just a static set of names and places, facts and figures (Zajonc, 2006).

In addition, we can create an awareness in our students that their minds matter. Who they are, their state of mind, the meaning of the material to them—each of these makes a difference in how they'll learn. These features encourage the student to reflect on the nature of their relationship with the learning that will make the experience more enjoyable and more effective. Such an approach likely evokes the middle prefrontal circuits involved in our personal and social selves, reinforcing the enjoyment and impact of the experience of learning and making access to that knowledge more readily achieved.

When we focus specifically on emotional and social skills, we directly help to "inspire to rewire" their brains, engaging their middle prefrontal regions so that they will develop in these important dimensions of their lives. School can be much more than a place of facts if we as teachers make it so. Teachers need to be aware of their intentions and mindful of their roles, so that they can make the experience of learning as meaningful and as engaging as possible. In return, they, too, will feel inspired and engaged in the passion of the work.

With reflective skills, children, adolescents, and adults can engage the passion and pleasure of mindfulness to connect with themselves and with others as they move through classrooms and school halls, and down all the paths of their lives.

Reflection as the fourth "R" can be a basic part of education and life, as simple and accessible as breathing.

Chapter Thirteen

REFLECTION IN CLINICAL PRACTICE:
Being Present and Cultivating the Hub

The implications of our journey into the mindful brain point to the importance of our own reflective presence as professionals. Whether we are teachers or clinicians, the ways that we help others grow will be directly shaped by our own mindful presence. Engaging in "mindful practice" (Epstein, 1999) in the healing professions creates in us a state of reflection and emotional availability that are at the heart of effective clinical work.

Mindful awareness can become a fundamental part of the mental health effort of psychotherapy to improve people's lives and reduce mental suffering in both direct and indirect ways (Germer, Siegel, & Fulton, 2005; Epstein, 1995; Johanson & Kurtz 1991). Some approaches use formal mindfulness meditation techniques, such as MBSR (Kabat-Zinn, 1990) and MBCT (Segal, Williams, & Teasdale, 2002), while others use applications of mindfulness skills such as with ACT (Hayes, 2004) and DBT (Linehan, 1993). In these approaches, the availability and empathy of the therapist that emerge with the therapist's own mindful presence may be a common source of healing in psychotherapy across the various "schools" and specific orientations. These may be considered the "indirect" effects of a mindful therapist on the patient's experience. Such indirect impacts may be seen to emerge from the empathic availability of the clinician to be mindfully present for whatever arises in the shared attentional field of the therapy experi-ence. But teaching mindfulness itself, within formal meditation or other skill-building exercises, can directly offer patients useful capac-ities that can transform their relationship with themselves, reduce suffering from symptoms, and create a new approach to life itself.

Direct applications of mindfulness skills teach people how to become more reflective. The overall idea of these approaches, as we discussed in Chapter 12, is that the various facets of mindful awareness are cultivated. Such practices enable individuals to jetti-son judgment and develop more flexible feelings toward what be-fore may have been mental events they tried to avoid, or towards which they had intense averse reactions. Becoming nonreactive and developing equanimity in the face of stressors supports the view of mindfulness directly shaping the self-regulatory functions of the brain by promoting reflection of the mind.

BUILDING REFLECTION: CULTIVATING THE HUB

Mindfulness is a teachable skill, as shown in Chapter 12. In many ways, this learning parallels the idea of mindsight, or our capacity to see the mind in ourselves and in others. Developing the circuits of mindsight, as with mindful awareness, can be done through re-flective dialogues and skill building.

Reflective dialogues are the ways in which we, as participants in a conversation, focus our mutual attention on the nature of the mind itself. As we use words to illuminate the mind, the linguistic representations develop our capacity for mindsight (Siegel, 1999; Siegel, in press). Describing and labeling these mental events with words is a facet of mindfulness that reflective dialogues can di-rectly foster. As we've seen, the capacity to label seems to balance the arousal of the limbic amygdala and the right hemisphere with the activity of the left to create a more flexible, integrated state.

As reflective dialogue becomes internalized, the individual can develop a new source of insight into his or her own mind. Life is transformed when mindsight is developed: Being able to "be" with whatever arises is greatly helped by being able to "see" what it is that is arising. Sometimes words can be of great help in setting the stage for seeing this dynamic and nonverbal world of the mind. These dialogues may be of central importance in helping children and other patients in therapy develop the reflective thinking needed to sense the mind itself. When offered with mindful learning principles in mind—with the state of the learner, the conditional nature of learning, and the sensitivity to contexts and distinctions as a part of the dialogue—then reflective conversations can create new states of mindful awareness.

But words by themselves are often not enough. Conceptually-based words should be supplemented by our other streams of awareness: sensation, observation, and knowing.

Teaching mindfulness involves developing the skill of direct sensory experience and the observational focus on the nonverbal world. If we imagine the four streams of awareness, we can sense how therapy may utilize mindful reflections. The stream of sensation becomes an important grounding point in which to wake up the mind, often drowning beneath waves of anxiety or depression, fear or numbing, which as "symptoms" have taken over the hub of the mind. Learning to dive into sensation can be frightening, especially for those who've experienced trauma and are avoiding being aware of the body. Here we see that the balance of all of the streams in actual clinical practice becomes essential. Observation is crucial to enable people to decouple automatic mental processes, such as flashbacks or intrusive memories, as well as habits of mind, such as derogatory internal voices or emotional reactivity. Additionally, the conceptual understanding of the nature of these processes, and their neural correlates, can help dis-engage the mind's stormy activity. Within nonverbal sharing, interpersonally and internally, a deeper sense of a nonconceptual knowing about healing and well-being often illuminate a sense of the innate drive toward a more integrated state of mental health. This can often be experienced as a sense of direction, a "glimmer of hope," or an image of healing. These nonconceptual knowings are often hard to articulate with words and sometimes are felt as "insights" that emerge, as we discussed in Chapter 3, or as shifts in perspective or a new frame of mind, rather than an outright, word-based thought that can be easily shared.

Psychotherapeutic approaches that utilize mindfulness offer well-developed nonverbal exercises that enable the individual to dip into direct sensation beneath the veil of words that may often conceal the mind's pain. This sensory immersion enables the individual to disengage from the top-down enslavements at the root of suffering. Imagery and body observation, intentional movement exercises, and sensing emotion and enhancing awareness of the present immersion in direct experience are all techniques that help build the skills of mindfulness. For example, in MBSR, a focus on the sensations of eating a single raisin over many minutes enhances the individual's sensitivity to the sensory stream of awareness. Likewise, the body scan enables the mind to open its receptivity to the subtle sensations from throughout the soma that are so often excluded from our day-to-day living (Kabat-Zinn, 1990; see also Appendix I for audiotapes of these exercises).

The benefits of mindfulness may also be attained outside of therapy itself. MAPs such as mindfulness meditation (Kornfield, 1993; Kabat-Zinn, 1990), yoga (Brown & Gerberg, 2005a, 2005b), qigong (Jones, 2001; Chen, 2004), and tai chi chuan (Wall, 2005; Irwin, 2005) all share a deep focus on one's own intention and are coupled with the awareness of awareness. For some patients, suggesting enrollment in classes that teach these MAPs may be an important adjunct to work in the therapeutic sessions.

I have also found that teaching people to focus on the wheel of awareness in their own minds has been extremely useful. I see this, literally, as enabling patients to develop their middle prefrontal regions and insular cortex (Lazar et al., 2005). These skills help promote a sense of well-being and improve interpersonal relationships and physiological health that come from the wisdom of these ancient practices.

One example of an opportunity I've had to directly teach reflective skills is with a high school junior who had been having severe bouts of irritability and depression. A second opinion validated my concern that he might be revealing either a severe case of major depression or an emergence of the first stages of manic-depressive illness. Close to initiating medications, I had recently been immersed in these mindfulness retreats and thought of trying to teach him to meditate as an initial intervention. I have nothing against medication and use it when necessary. But, if safe and possible—assessing for dangers to self or others and keeping extremely close track of how symptoms respond to the treatment—why not try a nonpharmacological intervention first?

With his parents' permission, we began a focused treatment that consisted of teaching him mindfulness meditation skills and encouraging him to exercise aerobically six days a week. Aerobic exercise not only seems to help with depression directly, but it encourages neural plasticity. Exercise, novelty, emotional engagement, and optimal states of attentional arousal are each ingredients that promote neural plasticity. When we use specific techniques to activate certain brain circuits, we are refining which neural areas we are trying to engage and develop. One view of depression holds that it involves the shutting-down of neural growth, giving the depressed individual the sense that life is "dead" inside. Here the mind is sensing what the synapses are lacking. When we are closed down to new learning, vitality vanishes. A proposal about manic-depressive (bipolar) disorder suggests that the neural circuitry connecting the ventral lateral prefrontal cortex to the limbic amygdala is deficient (Blumberg, Kaufman, Marin, Charney, Krystal, & Peterson, 2004). Recall that this is part of the same circuitry uniquely harnessed in those with mindfulness as a trait (Creswell, Way, Eisenberger, Lieberman, submitted; see Appendix III, Development Issues).

In a single case such as this, despite my conviction as the therapist that this might work, one never knows what the essential elements were that led to improvement. Anecdotal case reports are helpful only if taken with their significant limitations in mind. But it turns out, now almost a year later, that his symptoms that virtually disappeared after the first four months of meditation and exercise have remained absent. Will this last? Studies of mindfulness-based cognitive therapy's impact on preventing relapse (Segal, Williams, & Teasdale, 2002) suggest, in fact, that symptoms likely will not return. The same is true for other mental health issues, such as obsessive compulsive disorder (Baxter et al., 1992; Schwartz & Begley, 2003). As people learn these skills of reflection and self-regulation, they become lifelong features of a newfound resilience. The important point is that even in the face of possible constitutional features of difficulties with mood, anxiety, or perhaps attention (Zylowska et al., submitted), individuals can often be helped with mindful awareness practices that offer crucial new skills.

I teach many of my patients about the brain and how it may correlate with what is going on in their mind and in their relationships. This capacity to envision the neurological dimension of the triangle of well-being (coherent mind, empathic relationships, and neural integration) helps create a distance and perspective that may be a useful part of the discernment that emerges in this learning. Seeing the brain as contributing to your obsessions, to your drug addiction, or to your depression and emotional instability can help you begin to take an active role in how your mind can intervene with the brain's functions.

Recall that the mind uses the brain to create itself, and so in certain situations we can ally ourselves with the mind to create more integrated functioning in the neural system itself. Disengaging automatic reactions makes a huge difference and is one example of the way in which we can actually improve the bodily reactions that we come to feel enslaved by. For example, a number of individuals who come to therapy for anxiety breathe primarily with their chests, something we do in a state of danger to prepare ourselves for flight or fight responses. After being taught how to become aware of their body and to then breathe with the abdomen, a basic technique of yoga, many individuals experience a great reduction in their anxiety. There are many steps, for example, to the treatment of obsessions and mood disturbances, that can specifically help to disengage from the automatic reinforcements that exacerbate an anxiety or dysphoria into a full-blown disorder. Ultimately, when we teach reflection, we are giving a lifelong gift of mindful self-regulation.

In addition to teaching patients about the brain's role in a certain pattern of mind or behavior, helping the individual to attain a state of reflective awareness is often also essential. To achieve this receptive, self-observant, and reflexive capacity, elements of the time-tested mindfulness meditation can be extremely useful. Recall that the word "meditation" simply means the cultivation of the mind, and so this is truly a skill-building exercise that helps develop a mental ability. In this case, that ability is one of reflection.

A wide array of applications of mindfulness in therapy exists. A certain exercise to entering a mindfully aware state as a starting point has become a part of what I teach as a skill to my patients and students. People sometimes make a recording of my voice during this short, 15-minute meditation exercise. There are many available recordings from others, including ones that are easily obtained from our Mindful Awareness Research Center web site (see Appendix I). This exercise is just one that I've come to use in practice and I gratefully acknowledge the many individuals whose wisdom and mindfulness have helped me to articulate this particular one. Please try it yourself and develop your own style that works for you and your own practice.

This is a simple exercise I use with patients, and the one I offered to the young man described earlier. Even those without depression have found this exercise a grounding place to start, one they practice each day for just few minutes, often in the morning.

A Reflective Exercise

It's helpful to be able to become aware of your own mind. That can be a very useful awareness to have. Yet not much happens in life that lets us come to know ourselves. So we are going to spend a couple of minutes now doing just that.

Let yourself get settled. It's good to sit with your back straight if you can, feet planted flat on the floor, legs uncrossed. If you need to lay flat on the floor that's okay, too. And with your eyes open first, try this. Try letting your attention go to the center of the room . . . and now just notice your attention as you let it go to the far wall . . . and now follow your attention as it comes back to the middle of the room . . . and then up close as if you're holding a book at reading-distance. Notice how your attention can go to very different places.

Now let your attention go inward. You might let your eyes go closed, and as they go closed get a sense inside of you of your body in space and where you're sitting in the room. And now let yourself become aware of the sounds around you. That sense of sound can fill your awareness. (Pause for some moments.)

Let your awareness now find the breath wherever you feel it most prominently—whether it's at the level of your nostrils, the air going in and out, the level of your chest as it goes up and down, or the level of your abdomen going inward and outward. Perhaps you'll even just notice your whole body breathing. Wherever it comes naturally: just let your awareness ride the wave of your in-breath, and then your out-breath. (Pause.)

When you come to notice, as often happens, that your mind may have wandered and become lost in a thought, a memory, a feeling, a worry, when you notice that, just gently take note of that inside and gently, lovingly, return your awareness toward the breath—wherever you feel it—and follow that wave of the in-breath and the out-breath. (Pause.)

As you follow your breath, I'm going to tell you an ancient story that's been passed through the generations.

The mind is like the ocean. And deep in the ocean, beneath the surface, it's calm and clear. And no matter what the surface conditions are, whether it's flat or choppy or even a full gale storm, deep in the ocean it's tranquil and serene. From the depth of the ocean you can look toward the surface and just notice the activity there, as in the mind, where from the depth of the mind you can look upward toward the waves, the brainwaves at the surface of your mind, where all that activity of mind, thoughts, feelings, sensations, and memories exist. You have the incredible opportunity to just observe those activities at the surface of your mind.

At times it may be helpful to let your attention go back to the breath, and follow the breath to ground you in this deep tranquil place. From this depth of your mind, it's possible to become aware of the activities of the mind and to discern that those are not the totality of who you are, that you are more than just your thoughts, more than just a feeling. You can have those thoughts and feelings and also be able to just notice them with the wisdom that they are not your identity. They are a part of your mind's experience. For some, naming the type of mental activity, like "feeling" or "thinking," "remembering" or "worrying," can help allow these activities of the mind to be noted as just mental events that can gently float away and out of awareness. (Pause.)

One more image I'll share with you in this inward time is one that you may find helpful. Perhaps you'll consider it something you want to use as well. You can think of the mind's structure as similar to a wheel of awareness, imagining the wheel of a bicycle where there is an outer rim and spokes that connect that rim to an inner hub. In your mind's wheel of awareness, anything that can come into your awareness would be one of the infinite points on the rim. One sector of the rim might include our five senses of touch, taste, smell, hearing, and sight, those senses that bring the outside world into our minds. Another sector of that rim of the wheel is the sense of the body, the feeling in our limbs, our facial muscles, and the feeling of the organs of our torso, our lungs, our heart, our intestines. All of the body brings its wisdom up into our minds and this bodily sense, this sixth sense if you will, adds another texture to what we can become aware of. Another set of points on the rim are what the mind creates directly, like thoughts and feelings, memories and perceptions, hopes and dreams, and this segment of the rim of our mind is also available fully to our awareness, what you can call our seventh sense: our capacity to see the mind itself, in ourselves and in the minds of others. We may also be able to feel "felt" within our eighth sense as we feel our attuned relationships resonate with others and ourselves.

We can choose if we want to pick one segment and send a spoke out to that point on the rim. We may choose to pay attention to the feeling in our bellies, and send a spoke there. Or we can choose to pay attention to a memory, and send a spoke to that area of our seventh sense to see that part of mind.

So these spokes represent focusing on a point on the rim. And the spokes emanate from the depth of our mind, which is the hub of the wheel of awareness. And as we focus on the breath, we can develop the spaciousness of that hub. As the hub expands, we develop the capacity to be receptive to whatever arises from the rim, to give ourselves in to the spaciousness, to the luminous quality of the hub that can receive any aspect of our experience, just as it is. Without preconceived ideas or grasping onto judgments, this mindful awareness, this receptive attention, brings us into a tranquil place where we can be aware and know all elements of our experience.

The hub of our minds, like the depth of the ocean of our minds, is a place of tranquility and inquiry, where we can explore the nature of the mind with equanimity, energy, and concentration. This hub of our minds is always available to us, right now. And it's from this hub that we enter a compassionate state of connection to ourselves, and feel compassion for others.

Let's focus on our breath for a few more moments, together. Opening that spacious hub of our minds to the beauty and wonder of what is. (Pause.)

When you are ready you can take a more voluntary and perhaps deeper breath if you wish and get ready to gently let your eyes open, sensing this depth of your mind, and we'll continue our dialogue together.

After this reflective skill-building exercise, people often describe feeling calm, serene, and clear. With simple practice, just a few minutes a day seems to make a big difference in people's lives. A number of patients in my practice have reported feeling less anxiety, a deeper sense of clarity, and improvements in depression. Interpersonally, couples have described that this practice has improved the nature of empathic communication, offering more access to attunement with each other, and that important sense of "feeling felt" by another.

Mindfulness meditation enhances the very circuits involved in insight and empathy. There is something about the resonance in interpersonal attunement and in intrapersonal attunement that seems to promote a deep sense of well-being. A young teenager in my practice had been quite upset about something in a session and then, after feeling understood by me, he said "Wow, I feel so much better now that I've told you about this—how does this happen in the brain?" The resonant state that's created with attunement is derived from integration and creates a coherent mind. In many ways, internal attunement creates that deep sense of feeling felt. With mindfulness, I believe, we come to feel felt in a genuine way by ourselves. This is internal attunement.

The experience of starting the day with mindful reflection with an exercise like this or the many others that are available (see Appendix I) makes a big difference, even if its just 5 minutes or 10 minutes a day. The reason for this great impact from such a small amount of time, I believe, is that intrapersonal attunement creates a highly integrated neural state that enables the trait of reflective coherence to last throughout the remainder of the day. What would happen if we promoted intrapersonal attunement—that luminous space of possibility for resonating—that then, as all the studies show and experience has demonstrated, promotes interpersonal resonance and compassion with each other? What a different world we'd have.

Chapter Fourteen

THE MINDFUL BRAIN
IN PSYCHOTHERAPY:
Promoting Neural Integration

As we discussed briefly in the Preface, interpersonal neurobiology is an integrative approach that draws on a wide array of ways of knowing to create a picture of human experience. This approach builds on many disciplines of science to propose how we might define the mind and its emergence in the moment, and its development across the lifespan. We've seen that the human mind can be defined as an embodied and relational process that regulates the flow of energy and information. The mind emerges as this flow occurs within and among people, and it develops as the genetically programmed maturation of the nervous system is shaped by ongoing experience.

Through this synthetic analysis emerges the perspective that mental well-being is created within the process of integration, the linkage of differentiated components of a system into a functional whole. In this view, drawn in part from complexity theory, we see that when a system's components become functionally linked—when they are integrated—they can be defined as having a FACES flow: flexible, adaptive, coherent, energized, and stable. Outside of that flow the person, family, community, or society may experience chaos or rigidity. In the flow, the experience is filled with coherence: connected, open, harmonious, engaged, receptive, emergent, noetic, compassionate, and empathic. These working definitions of the mind and of mental well-being have been useful in educating teachers and therapists to consider a possible view of a healthy mind.

Through our emerging understanding of the mindful brain we can build on these ideas to offer a framework for how an interpersonal neurobiology approach to therapy may be created.

AN INTERPERSONAL NEUROBIOLOGY ROLE IN UNDERSTANDING AND PROMOTING WELL-BEING

Personal transformation can be considered to involve the three legs of our triangle of well-being: coherent mind, empathic relationships, and neural integration. There is no need to simplify these three into a single aspect of reality as they're mutually reinforcing. Naturally, being all a part of the energy and information flow of well-being, we could say these are three aspects of one reality. But these "three aspects" have unique, irreducible qualities.

If integration enables a FACES flow, it is a logical next step to examine how integration within and among these domains is promoted. If we begin on the plane of the physical domain of reality, we can say we are seeking separate aspects of a system which can then be linked together. Before exploring this approach in detail, let's discuss some general principles.

It is important to remember that this is one therapist's experience, one approach to finding windows of opportunity to help people move toward well-being by promoting integration in their lives. I offer this view for your consideration, not as a statement of how to do some particular therapy, but as one way of being as a therapist. If you are a clinician yourself, or if you are in psychotherapy, I hope these ideas and the following stories of actual experiences are of help in illuminating possible avenues of change that will be useful in creating your own approach. In a mindful state we can see others' suggestions as a possible route, rather than as a roadmap delineating the only way to go. We each are different, our lives complex, and having a sense of possible directions may be more helpful than locking on to some idea of an absolute truth.

ATTUNEMENT

Shared attention initiates attunement. As we engage with others, we mutually focus our awareness on the elements of a person's mind that become the shared center of the hub of our minds. As this joining evolves, we begin to resonate with each other's states and become changed by our connection.

Attunement can be seen as the heart of therapeutic change. In the moment, such resonant states feel good as we feel "felt" by another, no longer alone but in connection. This is the heart of empathic relationships, as we sense a clear image of our mind in the mind of another. A simple acronym for remembering this feature is ISO, the *i*nternal *s*tate of the *o*ther, an awareness that you as the therapist have of your patient, and your patient has of you. Each person senses his or her mind clearly in the expressions of the other, experiencing that embodiment of one's own authentic mind inside another person. Here we see the notion of "embodied simulation" of the mirror neuron system (Gallese, 2003, 2006), in which our neural processes integrate what we perceive with our body's priming for action and emotion.

Another way in which we attune to the mind of another is by way of a *n*arrative *o*f *t*he *o*ther, or NOTO. By taking in the experiences of the patient, we create a story in our own minds of who he or she is. In small and large ways, we can reveal that we have a narrative of the other inside of us. If a patient comes back from a trip to San Francisco and I say upon his return, before he speaks, "How was your trip to the Golden Gate Bridge?", he will know that he exists inside of my head even when we are not with each other. On a larger scale, a NOTO is revealed in the ways in which the life experiences of a patient fill my mind and I can sense her struggles, see her journey in its route across time, and let her know in our discussions how that evolving story exists in my mind through the ways we connect around making sense of her life.

As patients feel our authentic concern and our capacity to embed them in us in the present within ISOs and across time with NOTOs, they come to feel felt by us and attuned with us. To achieve such direct connection, to integrate minds, it is crucial that the therapist have an open hub in which to mindfully receive whatever arises in the course of therapy. This attunement not only feels good in the moment, it likely alters the self-regulatory integrative fibers of the brain, especially in the middle aspects of the prefrontal cortex. Attunement interpersonally and the nurturing of attunement internally are the central processes of psychotherapy. Attunement of both forms is built upon integration.

SNAGGING THE BRAIN

In mindfulness we direct our attention to our intention. Where attention goes, neurons fire. And where neurons fire, they can rewire. This process can be summarized by the term SNAG, signifying the way we *s*timulate *n*euronal *a*ctivation and *g*rowth. In mindful awareness we are "snagging" our own brain by focusing attention on our own intentions in a way that stimulates our middle prefrontal regions and promotes integration. This prefrontal activation engages axonal fibers that extend out to link together various disparate regions: cortex, limbic areas, brainstem, body-proper, and even the social world of other brains. The growth of prefrontal fibers anatomically means that functionally, we will be promoting neural integration.

Internal attunement is proposed here to snag the brain to promote integration. Interpersonal attunement can be seen to catalyze similar neuronal activation and growth. Attunement then becomes a central focus of our understanding of how therapy can change the brain.

Let's recall the list of nine middle prefrontal functions correlated with activation of the associated areas of medial and ventral prefrontal, orbitofrontal, and anterior cingulate cortex: (1) body regulation, (2) attuned communication, (3) emotional balance, (4) response flexibility, (5) empathy, (6) self-knowing awareness, (7) fear modulation, (8) intuition, and (9) morality. How many of this list would you include on your desired results for your own or others' growth in life? From this perspective, we can examine how interpersonal attunement in attachment, internal attunement in mindfulness, middle prefrontal function, and effective psychotherapy might converge in their common mechanisms of action.

THE DOMAINS OF NEURAL INTEGRATION

We can propose that for any form of therapy to be effective we must "snag" the brain toward neural integration, promote coherence of mind, and inspire empathy in relationships. This is how therapy focuses on the triangle of well-being. The strategy we'll take to describe this dynamic and individualized process will be to delineate nine distinct domains of neural integration and how to promote each of these within our lives (Siegel, in press). These domains include those of (1) consciousness, (2) vertical, (3) horizontal, (4) memory, (5) narrative, (6) state, (7) temporal, (8) interpersonal, and (9) transpirational integration.

If we focus on the domains of integration within our neural systems, we can see the simultaneous creation of empathy with others and coherence within. The following vignettes of patients (identifying features have been removed from these stories), may help illustrate the use of this approach within psychotherapy, as we apply the principles of the mindful brain to clinical practice.

The Integration of Consciousness

Hi Dr. Siegel . . . just wanted to let you know that I am feeling a whole lot better . . . a bit more clarity on this issue, and a far better view of the rim . . . it is amazing—and a real insight as a therapist—that how even knowing and practicing all that I know and practice (i.e., watching my breathing, COAL, SOCK), my mind gets hijacked still by what happened so long ago . . . I feel much better now—that nice normal calm feeling—I think because I have been able to untwist this twisted stuff and can look at it without twisting myself inside out . . . I have not forgotten it once yet, and I am feeling like I probably won't lose complete sight of it any more . . . it's kind of like even when I forget, I remember that I forget, and that is sort of like not forgetting, really . . . I cannot wait to work more on these aspects of my self next week . . . thanks Dr. Siegel . . . I just am so grateful for your guidance . . . see you Wed . . . best, Mary

This is an email from Mary, a thirty-five-year-old psychotherapist with a painful history of abuse by a step-father during her childhood that led to significant difficulties with posttraumatic stress and dissociation. Because her childhood experiences were terrifying, a disorganized attachment pattern developed. She survived by dividing her sense of consciousness: some aspects of her mind acknowledged the events, another part of her mind was unaware of the abusive relationship.

In the course of therapy, coming to know the truth about her experiences within the frame of a close, connected relationship with her therapist—me—allowed her to experience these memories in a new way. The hub of my own mind needed to be receptive to whatever arose: I could feel aspects of the terror, could sense her fragmentation and helplessness, and would try to be present as best I could to "contain" these overwhelming sensations. When

memories are shared in this way, when there becomes room to feel
the sensations fully and then to have the reflective experience that
this knowledge can be borne, that it can be tolerated, then the
nature of the memories can actually transform. As we'll see more
in the upcoming section on memory integration, such an interpersonal sharing can widen the "window of tolerance" for knowing
about painful past events. This expansion is an enhancement of
self-regulation, the capacity to bear witness to one's own pain and
remain present as that implicit recollection is integrated into a
broader sense of the person's life. The key is for me as a therapist
to remain fully present for whatever arises—not passing judgment,
being right there, in the moment, following the shifts and stabilizing of different states, welcoming all into the therapy experience.

With such a mindful approach, Mary seemed to change as we
directed attention, together, on the various ways she had come to
adapt to her hostile family environment. As she went ahead in her
own therapy she found that direct teaching about mindfulness was
helpful in her daily life. I taught her the meditation that I offered
in the last chapter, and she found the hub to be a useful visual
metaphor for being able to know about elements of the past as
activities of her mind, not the totality of who she is. In many ways,
this mindful discernment feels like the cornerstone of therapy, not
just for Mary and other patients, but for us, as therapists, as well.
We sense our patients' pain, but we do not have to become that
pain. Having that modulating capacity to be open but not to "become" our patients is a fine line between being empathic, and developing secondary, or vicarious, traumatization. Perhaps it is a
theoretical set of "supervisory mirror neurons," broadly hypothesized by Iacoboni as a possible component of our prefrontal abilities that enable us to resonate but not "become" another, that we
build as therapists and that in general enable us as people to be
present but not to get lost in others' experience (Iacoboni &
Siegel, 2006). Mindfulness as a therapist, being attuned internally

so that we can know the distinctions between resonance and empathy, versus flooding and overidentification, seems an essential step in our work.

Integration of consciousness can be promoted by both direct and indirect means, as we have discussed. Our open presence as therapists alone is an invitation to have people experience more aspects of the rim of their mind. As we feel the mindful spaciousness to embrace whatever arises in the field of awareness, patients will sense an opening space, an encircling embrace, that can contain what before was unbearable knowledge, emotion, or memory. As we share attention, we initiate attunement. In this way, sharing attention with others is the beginning of a resonant state with two people. As we "share" attention with ourselves, as we develop the spaciousness of the hub of the mind to attend to our intentions, we align our reflecting and experiencing selves.

Direct applications also are helpful and include all of the mindful awareness practices that help focus attention on intention. Beginning with awareness of the breath, it is amazing how taking pause to reflect inward can initiate an opening of the hub that feels natural and yet profoundly moving. Returning awareness gently to the breath when attention has wandered strengthens the hub and initiates the reflexive capacity to become aware of awareness. With practice, sometimes for just 10 minutes a day, patients seem to develop a self-observational ability that then prepares them for the next step of opening their minds to enhanced receptivity.

In a session, receptive awareness can be catalyzed by simply suggesting that the patient become aware of not just the breath, but of whatever enters the field of awareness. As the patient notices whatever arises as it arises, he or she will be reinforcing the self-observational skills that can decouple automaticity—a vital "Yoda" skill in promoting the next layers of integration.

As Mary progressed in her therapy, she came to a resolution of the conflicts across her many states of adaptation to the severe trauma. She read an entry in her journal to me that expressed the ways in which mindfulness brought a sense of clarity to her healing:

> From the hub of my mind, I can view all the chaos, fear, terror, threats, brushes with death, wishes, and plans for death, pain, mind binds, all-mind knowing, all-mind not knowing, all-body knowing, all-body not knowing, states of adaptation that now reside happily and benignly on the rim . . . over there on the rim, I can view and know the states, but in the hub, I am not those states, I am only the knowledge of those states—how they came to be, how they saved me, and how they have now evolved into a story about what happened to me, about how crazy and disturbed my family was, and about how I survived it and am profoundly able to be present as I move forward in full awareness of and liberation from the prison that was my childhood . . . all those many years ago . . . finally making sense of it all.

Integration of consciousness permits us to find peace within the chaos as we develop the hub of our mind. In that spacious place of reflection, healing can begin as we come to deeply sense the fullness of our lives, from the past, in the present moment, which free us in the future. Such healing will be illustrated in many of the stories that follow.

The other domains of integration are listed on the following pages in a sequence, because this is a linear and logical format, but they might be better explored as a circle, with each of the following seven perhaps encircling the integration of consciousness. The ninth and last domain—transpirational integration—may indeed sometimes emerge following the integration of the first eight (Figure 14.1).

Vertical Integration

Sandra, a 67-year-old grandmother of five, feared going to the cardiologist, saying "Something is wrong with my heart and I

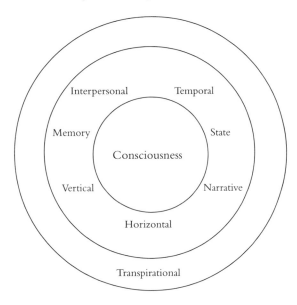

Figure 14.1 Domains of integration.

don't want to find out." During her fourth visit with me, Sandra had a panic attack when it came time for her to focus on her chest during a body scan, which we were doing as an introduction to a direct application of mindful practice in therapy. As she focused her mind on her chest, it was natural to think that she might fear losing her cherished relationships with her family. But what was ultimately revealed in therapy was the unresolved loss of her father when she was a young child, something she had never thought about, no narrative, "making-sense" process had occurred, no sharing of the loss with her brothers or sister, or her mother. Instead she had "cut herself off from the neck down" in order not to feel. In reality, we came to understand, she was terrified of becoming aware of her broken heart.

Staying with sensations enables the wisdom of the body to gain access to the mind. *Vertical integration* is one domain in which we can begin the important process of disentangling our unresolved losses and cohesive adaptive states that have cut us off, literally, from the vitality of being fully immersed in our senses. Creating coherence in our lives and making sense of our life story involve gaining access to the full spectrum of senses from our body.

Vertical integration is the way in which distributed circuits are brought into connection functionally with each other, from head to toe. Here we are focusing on how input from the body is brought up through the spinal cord and bloodstream into the brainstem, limbic areas, and cortex to form a vertically integrated circuit. You may wonder what this means or why this is necessary, given that the body is already "connected" to the brain. But it is possible to have neural activations outside of our conscious awareness. Bringing somatic input into the focus of our attention changes what we can do with this information: Consciousness permits choice and change.

A range of studies suggest that our bodily state directly shapes our affects which all interact to influence our reasoning and decision-making. Having averse reactions to our own bodily inputs—or trying to avoid awareness of them—leads to a restricted access of the hub to any points on the rim. In this situation, we cannot be mindful because our receptivity is hampered and we become inflexible. In such a nonintegrated state, the individual is susceptible to patterns of rigidity or outbursts of chaos, far from the FACES flow of well-being. In Sandra's case, she had developed a cohesive adaptation that shut off her bodily sensations and kept her rigidly confined to a life without much deep sense of meaning. Her panic attacks illustrated how this overly controlled cohesive state was prone to a rupture into chaos in the form of panic.

In psychotherapy, vertical integration can be the focus during a session by beginning with awareness of the body in which you suggest to your patient that he or she just notice the sensations that emerge. A total body scan would involve moving progressively from toe to head, enabling the feelings to fill the patient's awareness, and keeping the hub's spoke on the sixth sense area of the rim. Just sensing, "staying with" the sensations in awareness, "going with that" when a feeling arises, are all reflective pauses that help the mind focus on vertical integration. Notice that "just sensing" is distinct from "just noticing," as they likely involve the two differing streams of awareness: sensing and observing. In full integration, we encourage all of the streams of awareness to be brought into balance. In restrictive adaptations, sensing may be warded off and a disconnected form of observation may become, at best, a way a person is aware of the body: noticing it, but not directly sensing it.

As we've seen in Figures 4.3 and 6.1, the spoke that connects to an element of the rim, such as a point on the sixth sense of the body, can be viewed as involving any or all of the four streams that enable the "data" from the rim to enter the hub's awareness. Each of the streams is important, each having its role to play in mindful awareness. For Sandra, feeling the direct *sensations* was not possible at first without a terrifying reaction. We therefore focused first on the *concept* of the importance of the body in our discussions. Next, we gently moved into helping her with the ability to *observe* the body from a more distant perspective, such as noting the state of the whole body rather than directly feeling the sensations of her chest. *Knowing* is a stream that sometimes cannot be directly addressed with words, emerging more as an insight, coming perhaps as a shift in perspective or a deep, almost ineffable sense of clarity. In Sandra's case, it wasn't until we began with the stream of *sensation*, first on her feet and ankles, and then on her breathing, that she was ready to focus on her heart.

We have the ability to shift our awareness, to prevent the large-scale assemblies of incoming primary data from creating awareness of sensation. Vertical integration is the intentional focus of attention on bodily sensations. Does that sound too strategic to be included within the framework of mindfulness? My sense within therapy is that to dissolve top-down enslavements, like Sandra's avoidance of awareness of her body, we need to be mindful of the brain's automatic push to not attend to some aspect of the rim. Here we see that "stay with that" helps our patients, and ourselves, move against those secondary forces that keep us from attuning to ourselves. If we don't feel comfortable using the term *mindfulness* with strategic "snagging" like this, we might be better served by emphasizing *reflection*, with its tripartite components of receptivity, self-observation, and reflexivity.

With reflection, Sandra was soon examining her autobiographical history and finding a slow emergence of aspects of her father's death, and his life, that she had never known in this open, integrative way. At one point in the work she said that she was ready to "go back to my heart" and we attempted the full body scan again. At this point she could move her awareness to her chest without a panic reaction, though she had an outburst of tears and sadness. Images of her father emerged, and she was able to talk about her grief, and her longings for him. Her broken heart was what she had feared, and now she was able to face it directly in our work with her loss, together.

Our secondary adaptations can lock us in unresolved states of trauma or loss, feelings of anxiety, avoidance, and numbing. With vertical integration we reflect on bodily sensations and stay with them to enable their natural dynamic movement in the mind to take its course. This is the often astonishing aspect of this reflection: When we pause and stay within awareness of bodily sensation, the integration of a reflective mind seems to take care of itself.

Horizontal Integration

A 50-year-old attorney came to me at the request of his wife who thought he must have some form of "disorder of empathy." When Bill and Anne arrived together, she said that she was at the end of her rope. He responded that he didn't "know the ropes" she was talking about. Only Bill laughed. It became clear that Bill revealed insensitivity to Anne's feelings in their couples' sessions. But even more, Bill seemed to be unaware of even his own emotional life. In many ways, Bill's awareness seemed quite limited to the world of the physical and lacked an awareness of the subjective world of the mind that was the province of the right mode of awareness.

Our two hemispheres cannot speak to one another easily. The "L's" of the left—linear, logical, linguistic, literal thinking—cannot take in or connect directly to the holistic, imagery-based, nonverbal, emotional/social processing of the right. If people are not in a state of hemisphere attunement, it's easy to feel bereft, as Anne had been feeling for years. Humor is wonderful, but only when people can join, not feel excluded. What people don't realize is that our attachment history can create modes of adaptation, discussed in Chapter 9, which can be seen to prevent bilateral integration and leave one hemisphere dominant over the other. In this case, each of them seemed to be leaning to one side, only their lopsided styles did not match.

The work with Anne and Bill required that they each examine their own history and, in particular, try to understand how their adaptations had locked them into impaired horizontal integration within their own minds. Bill's "growth edge," the place for him to focus his work in therapy, was to become more aware of the nonverbal, whole body, emotional textures of the elements of the right mode on his rim of awareness. Anne's challenge was to find words to help describe and label her own internal world so that she could achieve more equanimity. This was clearly a strategic "snagging" of each of their brains within the context of the promotion of mindful awareness.

Anne and Bill each benefited from being taught basic reflective skills. My hope was that by developing the integrative middle prefrontal fibers, they would both find a way to expand their window of tolerance for feelings and reactions that before were automatically closed off. This was an expansion of the hub's capacity to be receptive to whatever arose on the rim. I spent time focusing with

Anne and Bill such that he became more aware of his imagery and sensory world, and she learned to distance herself enough to gain discernment over her reactions that in the past just swept her up into their compelling intensity.

As Anne and Bill achieved new levels of reflective awareness, they could stay present with each other to be able to say what they really experienced in that moment. The feeling of relief with that interpersonal attunement was palpable in the room. The natural unfolding seemed to involve, at first, an internal attunement with mindful practice and the readiness to attempt to try, again, to connect. Fortunately in this case, they were able to approach each other with kindness because they could see the deep commitment each had to do the inner work and make the interpersonal repair.

The example of Bill and Anne illustrates that there are many windows of opportunity through which to enter a system. With this initial work to help them relate to each other, we needed to dive deeply into the nature of the adaptations that had formed their personal identities. This unraveling of emotion, memory, narrative themes, and restricted ways of being enabled each of them to see that they were survivors seeking connection. Luckily they have found each other, now, in the authentic reception that they had longed for their whole lives.

In Bill's history, a cold and distant pair of parents created an emotionally isolated childhood. With the adaptations to that familial culture in which the mind was absent, Bill learned to see things through the lens of the left mode of processing. For Bill, the absence of emotional communication in his family deprived his right hemisphere from interactive nutrients and moved his development toward the left: logical and linear thinking bereft of a sense of his own internal world. As Decety and Chaminade (2003) affirm:

> Our ability to represent one's own thoughts and represent another's thoughts are intimately tied together and have similar origins within the brain ... Thus it makes sense that self-awareness, em-

pathy, identification with others, and, more generally, intersubjective processes, are largely dependent upon the right hemisphere resources, which are the first to develop. (p. 591)

The therapeutic goal for Bill was to have him integrate his dominant left mode with his relatively underdeveloped right mode of being. Exercises focusing on the nonverbal world, opening the hub of his mind to the previously inaccessible senses of his body, his mind, and his relationships, opened the door to a new form of freedom to experience his inner world, and to connect to Anne.

Horizontal integration includes the linkages of the two sides of the nervous system and connecting circuits at similar vertical levels of organization within the same hemisphere. In the bilateral dimension of this domain, for example, we link the logical, linguistic, linear, and literal output of the left side with the visuospatial imagery, nonverbal, holistic, emotional/visceral representations of the right. What emerges with this horizontal form of integration is a new way of knowing, a bilateral consciousness. Horizontal integration enables us to broaden our sense of ourselves, as often distinct layers of processing of perception and thought, feeling and action, are brought into alignment.

Within the hub of the mind, focusing on the feeling sense of these different modes of our minds can be quite helpful. As we've seen, labeling with words is not only a part of mindfulness, but it helps balance firing in the brain's response to distressing emotional expressions in others, and in ourselves. When we become aware that the right hemisphere specializes in imagery whereas the left is a wizard at words, we can see that imagery-based reflective thinking may activate a right mode dominance.

The right mode also has an integrated map of the body, and thus in the body scan and breath-focus of mindfulness practice we may be also evoking this right-sided function. The totality of mindfulness appears to involve a bilateral integration, enabling us not to get lost in these images or bodily senses but to open ourselves to soaking them in while also having a noticing and describing function as well. Some studies suggest that this more distant, witnessing function that notices and narrates our experience may be correlated with left mode functioning. In this way, both left and right play a part in mindful awareness. Integration, not favoring one side over another, appears to be the thrust of mindful awareness as well as of the emergence of well-being in psychotherapy.

Memory Integration

In *memory integration* we see that the early stages of encoding within implicit memory become assembled into the next layers of explicit memory. The feeling of this is one in which the implicit puzzle pieces of memory in the form of perceptions, feelings, bodily sensations, and behavioral impulses are woven together with our mental models to produce new clusters of explicit factual and episodic memory. Before their integration into explicit memory, implicit-only representations can feel as if they are just the "here-and-now" reality of our feelings, perceptions, and behavioral impulses. With memory integration, these explicit forms now have a sense, when recalled, that something is coming from the past.

These issues of memory became important when I began work with a 26-year-old business student, Elaine, who was experiencing severe anxiety near the end of her program at school. She had been offered a job at a new company and felt terrified that she would "fall flat" on her face if she accepted this challenging new position. When we met it felt as if she had no internal space in which to separate herself from the activities of her own mind, to discern that these were just mental events, not the totality of her being.

With these new insights into the nature of development and mindful awareness seen as a form of internal attunement, it seemed to me that her self-regulatory skills were not optimal to enable her to think clearly about this career decision. After an evaluation to rule out medical difficulties, such as endocrine or cardiac issues, and psychiatric conditions like mood, posttraumatic stress, or obsessive disorders which might be contributing to her panic, I suggested that it might be helpful for her to get to know her own mind a little better.

Using the reflective skill exercise presented in Chapter 13 (p. 284), I taught her about the basic capacity for mindful meditation in order to begin our work into the integration of consciousness. As we've seen, meditation simply means cultivating the mind. In my own view, I felt that helping Elaine develop the hub of her mind would likely begin to promote the growth of her prefrontal fibers. Elaine responded well to this direct application of mindfulness skills. I suggested she try "meditating" each morning for about 10 minutes. Patients sometimes worry about the amount of session time required. Regularity is important, so suggesting a short, daily meditation time for those not able to take on large time commitments is likely to spur more active involvement in the plan, especially for students enrolled in school. Elaine actually found the meditating so helpful that she would find moments after lunch at school to just sit quietly and focus on her breath. Here's an example of a brief instruction: When the attention to the breath wanders and you notice that, just gently bring your attention back to the breath. Focusing on the breath itself sets up an attuned state that stabilizes the mind and enables not only calming, but a sense of self-observation to emerge. The experience of repeatedly returning the focus of attention back to the breath builds awareness of awareness. This, as William James suggested, is the mind's "education par excellence."

When we moved in the session from simple breath awareness to the openness of receptivity, of being aware of whatever arises, I asked Elaine to tell me what came to her mind about her job. When she started mentioning issues of finance and logistics, things we had covered before without benefit, I suggested she just become aware of her body. She paused and then began to shake. She grasped her arm and said "Ouch! What is going on?" I suggested she just "go with that" and see where it took her. The pain moved up her arm and into her jaw. Of course, clinically, we need to worry about heart pain, but this was an outer experience, on her skin, not in her chest. She then grasped her jaw and started to cry. Soon Elaine was describing what was going on in her mind: She recalled having fallen off a tricycle when she was young and breaking her front teeth and her arm. As she stayed with the sensations (vertical integration), and articulated the images using words (horizontal integration), she came to examine the memory-sense of what before felt like a here-and-now experience and then, as the session progressed, emerged into a sense of recall of something from the past. This is memory integration.

The implicit bodily sensations of pain and the learned mental model of "if you try something new with excitement you'll fall flat on your face and break your teeth and arm" had been embedded as implicit-only representations in Elaine's head. With the excitement of finishing school and being offered a wonderful opportunity, this implicit configuration surfaced and paralyzed her with panic. Moving through the layers of consciousness, vertical, horizontal, and memory integration enabled her to free herself from this top-down prison of the past. Not only could she take on the new job, but her old fear of being excited about romantic relationships seemed to dissipate as well, as she developed discernment for these mental events that could be sensed for what they were: outdated lessons and remnants from the past.

Within mindful awareness, we can observe these elements of implicit memory that before may have swept us up into their sensory richness but now can be discerned to be elements of earlier experience. Such a dis-identification from implicit memory as being the totality of who we are can be the essential first layer in integrating memory toward its explicit form. This may be a fundamental step in the resolution of trauma that enables free-floating implicit elements that previously were intrusive in a person's life as fragments and flashbacks to be finally resolved as they become integrated into the larger autobiographical memory system.

Narrative Integration

For Anne and Bill, introduced in the section on horizontal integration, moving deeply into their individual life stories was a profoundly healing experience. In couples work, one of the benefits is to enable a collective hub to develop in which the rim elements of one person become received by the hub of the other. This "we wheel" of awareness seems to catalyze a joint mindfulness which is deeply connecting. Within their individual lives, Anne and Bill could sense the pain that the other had struggled with in adapting to the ways in which their basic needs for attunement were not met in their families of origin. Insecure attachment, in its various forms, is a result of how our need for connection is overlaid with adaptations to what we're missing.

When our caregivers don't see our minds, when they do not resonate with our internal worlds and show us in their own faces a reflection of who we actually are, then we shrivel into a chronic state of disconnection from clear awareness of the mind itself. Bill's adaptation to emotionally distant parents remained with him as an adult without his hub's access to much beyond his first five senses: He did not feel his body, know his mind, or sense his connections to others, or himself. This blindness to his own sixth, seventh, and eighth senses was evident in the ways he also was not open to those same dimensions in Anne. He was not receptive to her bodily signals, had no mindsight that would give him empathy for her internal world, and couldn't feel the absence of resonance between them. He had been right: He did indeed not "know the ropes" of this thing called relationships. The ropes that were missing were the integrative circuits of his brain. Bill didn't even understand the notion of attunement when I tried to describe this to him.

We could understand how Anne had thought that Bill had a disorder of empathy. But it appeared that Bill's impaired mindsight was not so much rooted in his genetic make-up, but rather was an adaptation to his experiential history of avoidant attachment. This is fortunately a trait of the individual that can be modified by experience—in this case, within therapy.

Anne's narrative was quite different. Instead of the lack of access to details of autobiographical memory and the insistence that "relationships didn't and don't matter" that characterized Bill's dismissing stance, Anne's story revealed a preoccupation with her left-over "garbage" from an intrusive and entangled relationship with her parents. Her father's alcoholism and her mother's anxieties after their divorce when she was 10 years old left Anne with a feeling of uncertainty about others. Her mother would rely on her, treating her like an adult who was to take care of not only her two younger siblings, but her mother as well. When Anne found the "self-sufficient" Bill, it was a dream come true. As is so often the case, we are attracted to people whose own patterns of adaptation complement ours; but then when we begin to grow toward integration and get more access to a primary self beneath those top-down narrative themes, we find that those surface traits in the other are the exact ones we cannot tolerate. Anne needed reliable connection, not disconnection. Her initial attraction to Bill's lack of intrusiveness was understandable given where she came from, but now it was making her distraught.

As we explored each of their narratives, the patterns of adaptations emerged as themes of their life stories. These are the personal identities we carry around with us that mindful awareness permits us to get beneath. Utilizing their emerging skills of reflection developed directly with mindfulness training as a focus in therapy, Bill and Anne could now access a primary self beneath those layers of secondary adaptation. This is the way in which narrative integration is more than just making up some story—it is a deep, bodily, and emotional process of sorting through the muck in which we've been stuck.

Narrative integration enables us to weave together the story of our life. This domain utilizes the unique aspect of our species as a storytelling animal. Our brains appear to have a left hemisphere drive to use our basic neural capacity to sort, sequence, and select neural maps to weave a story to explain the logical relationships of events in our lives. A story can be defined as the linear telling of a sequence of events that embeds both the actions and the internal mental life of the actors of the tale. The mindful telling of our tale can be greatly healing of unresolved issues in our life.

The creation of a narrative of our own life involves a "witnessing self" that is also able to observe and comment, paralleling the facets of mindful awareness. Attachment studies reveal that one of the best predictors of a child's attachment to a parent is that parent's life story having what is called "narrative coherence." A coherent narrative is essentially a story that makes sense of our lives in a deep, viscerally full way, beyond merely rationalization and minimization (Siegel & Hartzell, 2003). These restrictive adaptations to ignore what we already implicitly know can create a cohesive narrative frame that is quite different from coherence, restricting us to our self-story themes and blocking true integration that would permit coherence to emerge. Our discussions regarding reflective coherence in Chapter 9 illuminate the nature of this narrative coherence process: With mindfulness we gain access to the full rim of our minds and are able to make sense of whatever elements of memory and ongoing sensation may arise. Interestingly, attachment researchers have also found a "reflective function" (Fonagy & Target, 1997) that correlates with both attuned relationships between child and caregiver and with narrative coherence in the parent. In these ways, narrative integration likely is a fundamental part of the reflective coherence that emerges with mindful awareness.

The experience in therapy of transitioning to a state more receptive to one's own inner nature helps move an individual toward "earned security" of attachment in which the narrative becomes coherent. This process often involves the fluid state of being open to what is, not constrained by what one's adaptation wants the individual to believe occurred. Clearly the parallel between mindful awareness and narrative coherence offers a rich illumination of the potential role of reflection and neural integration at the heart of both. Mindful traits in parents would likely predict both a coherent parental narrative and secure attachment in children. Future research could examine the corresponding hypothesis that secure attachment for children would actually lead to more mindful traits as they grow. Certainly our approach in therapy has this notion at its core: That as we promote interpersonal attunement in secure attachment we are simultaneously encouraging the internal attunement of mindful awareness.

Though some interpretations of mindful awareness practices as "being only in the moment" often de-emphasize focusing on narratives in our lives as they pull us away from direct sensations in the now, I have found that combining these two ways of knowing to be quite powerful. Our personal identities are often revealed in our narrative themes and seeing these for what they are seems to assist the movement within mindfulness toward dissolving these top-down influences. Likewise, being able to develop discernment is a vital component of gaining the mental space to be able to note thematic elements and not get drawn into their seductive allure. Just remembering, especially traumatic events, can be unhelpful at best, and even retraumatizing. Remembering with the focus of deepening an understanding of past events and embracing a fuller way in which the painful sensations of the memories can be more fully tolerated and then resolved is how narrative integration can help. Healing in therapy involves sensing memory in a way in which we experience the textures of affect and somatic sensations in an integrated process as we move from the raw and intrusive nature of unresolved states to the open and mindful presence of resolution. Such a "making-sense" process is fully embodied, not just an intellectual exercise in using words to "explain away" things, but rather to create new insights that bring fresh meaning to old elements of memory. "Making sense" combined with discernment enables us to fully integrate memory into our life story so we can move more freely into the present.

Our life story is not the whole story of who we are. As we work through our own attachment histories, we sense the feeling of the story, observe it as our narrative and not the totality of who we are, conceive of the attachment stance that the narrative reflects, and on a deep ipseitious knowing level we have a bare understanding of a primary self beneath all the adaptation and struggle. Beyond the story of our lives is the essence of who we are.

From that mindful place of discernment, all four streams of awareness fill our self-knowing consciousness and we can now coherently link past, present, and future. The liberation of energy, often accompanied by laughter that seems to emerge with integration of all sorts, is contagious. Anne and Bill could finally laugh with each other as Bill indeed "learned the ropes" of relationships and Anne could develop her own widened hub that enabled her to appreciate the qualities in Bill that she had cherished for so long. No longer alone, each of them could finally discover the fuller sense of attunement, with each other and within themselves, that they had longed for since the beginning of their journeys. This is narrative integration and the emergence of a coherent mind, of presence, of fullness, of receptivity to whatever arises in ourselves and in others. The great news for Anne and Bill was that they had the courage to go to those painful places of the past that allowed them to enter the present more fully, more mindfully.

State Integration

Sandy is a 13-year-old girl who came to me with fears of the edges of desks and sharks in her neighbor's pool. She was doing well in school, had many friends, and got along well with her parents. But over the last six weeks she had become plagued by these fears. I was concerned that she might be developing the irrational thoughts of obsessive compulsive disorder and ruled out exposure to streptococcus bacteria which can be associated with the onset of that condition. There were no recent events that had changed in her life.

I taught her the basic skills of reflective awareness and she learned quickly to enter a state in which she could sense her breath and become aware ("like I'm watching myself from outside myself") of her bombardment of thoughts and worries. After a few sessions and practice at home, she could sense these irrational thoughts as activities of her mind, not all that she was. But this discernment by itself did not change the presence of these worries, it only lessened their intensity. She felt terrified even though she knew it was irrational.

Combining a number of different approaches to obsessive compulsive disorder and anxiety treatment, I offered her the view of a "checker," which is a set of circuits in her brain that scan for danger. This checker system has kept us safe, we discussed, as it scans for danger, alerts us to fear, and motivates us to do something. Scan, alert, motivate: SAM. We discussed how Sandy's checker system seemed to have too much enthusiasm for its job. This is what I told her: "Much like a friend who might share your interest in, say, bike riding, but who wants to ride for 36 hours, you need to negotiate with her to perhaps ride for just three hours. The checker shares a common interest in keeping you safe."

We began a program that utilizes mindful awareness to develop discernment and then first involves having the checker's activities noted, but not changed. This vision of a part of the brain, as we've mentioned before, being involved in one's mind seems, by itself, to help promote a mental distance akin to discernment. This, plus the mindfulness exercises, furthers this capacity to see the checker's activities as not the totality of who the person is. Next, Sandy was to engage the checker in an internal dialogue, similar to labeling the internal events and then carrying out an active interaction with them. "I know you love me and want to keep me safe, but this is over the top." In a third phase, her ritual behavior of knocking an even number of times was gradually reduced. Her automatic motivation behind this ritual was to "be sure nothing bad happened" that she was convinced would if she didn't do them. You might imagine that knocking had become a ritual throughout Sandy's day. Naturally, when nothing happens when she knocks 12 or 14 times dozens of times an hour, her mind becomes convinced that this is what saved her. It's also pretty hard to concentrate in school or to engage with friends and family when you are feeling terrified and compelled to knock or enact other compulsions.

A related mindfulness-based approach for obsessive compulsive disorder (OCD) was utilized in a study, carried out by Jeffrey Schwartz and colleagues (Baxter et al., 1992; Schwartz, 1998), to demonstrate that a "talking therapy" could be shown to alter the way the brain functioned in parallel to the reduction of symptoms. Once people learn this mindfulness-based skill, relapse is less common compared to those on medications who have a return of symptoms once the pharmacological intervention is stopped.

OCD is an example of impaired state integration in that individuals can have a non-worried everyday state of mind with all its variants and then this checker, fear-driven state. One of my teenage patients actually used the abbreviation to coin a perhaps more useful term: "Overactive Checker Deployment." To make sense of this conflict among states, it has been helpful to teach people about the brain's capacity to have excessively active circuits that create states of fear and dread. Knowing about the checker and learning mindfulness techniques of discernment can transform oppression from internal voices and a sense of despair into victory and emancipation from such a prison.

As we come to be more deeply aware of our lives, the need for *state integration* may emerge as we sense that we have very different and often conflictual states of mind. A state of mind involves a cluster of neural firing patterns that have a transient but potent quality to them in the moment. A state organizes our widely distributed processing as an adhesive that interconnects present moment firing onto itself. A state stabilizes the macroassemblies of large-scale neural clusters into a functional unit. We also have self-states in which enduring patterns of firing clusters exist, such as a "me" that plays tennis, reads a book, makes love, or goes for a hike. Each of these repeated patterns of being contains within it an emerging history, often with rules and more readily accessible memory (explicit and implicit) for that state of mind.

Normal adolescence is at first filled with a tension among states that remains out of awareness, but then becomes filled with a sense of these conflicts, and finally a movement toward resolution of the tension across self-states (Harter, 1999). Healthy development is not about becoming homogenous, but involves acknowledging and accepting our various need states and biological drives that are realized within these disparate states of mind. Healthy development from this framework involves coming to accept and integrate one's various self-states of being. Integration of states in this way seems to parallel the COAL mindset fundamental to mindful awareness. As we come to accept these different states of being, we learn to love ourselves for the many ways that we are, not for some idealized sense of how we should be.

Temporal Integration

Tommy was turning 12 when he became obsessed with death. I had seen him years earlier for issues related to worries about the recent death of his uncle with whom he was close. Now he was convinced that he would die from some natural disaster. But even when not worried about calamity, he said that he was thinking "all the time" about what it would be like when he might grow old and then just face death. Whatever it was, he said, he couldn't get death out of his mind. We spoke about his concerns and he asked how he could "be sure that everything would be okay?" That was a great question, one of the basic issues we have to face as a human being.

"Why are we even aware that we die?" he asked, his eyes peeled on mine.

I knew this was the prefrontal existential issue for all of us. Why *do* we have to know that? I felt his anguish, and after a few sessions talking about his uncle and his life without relief from his worries, I thought it was time to introduce him to mindfulness skills. He responded well to the meditation exercise (see Chapter 13). He said that he'd "never felt so peaceful, this is incredible!" We spoke about the ocean and the sense of being beneath the surface. He could just see his worries as brainwaves on the surface, watch them float in, and float out of his awareness.

We practiced mindful meditation during the next few sessions, with him practicing at home for short periods, about 10 minutes each morning. Tommy eventually came to see his worries as the activities at the surface of his mind, not the totality of who he is. He could watch, from the tranquility of the depths of his mind, and notice those worries just come in and out of his conscious awareness. They didn't have to take him over. He could just notice them and not judge them, just let them float off as he rested in the peacefulness of the depths of his mind.

Soon Tommy came to a discovery: "I realize that if I am known by someone, like my family or my friends, then when I die I won't be gone. Being known makes me feel relaxed. I don't worry."

We sat quietly, reflecting together on that profound insight. His eyes widened and he said, "If I'm known I can disappear. And when I die I just become a part of everything."

I nodded my head.

"I'll meditate on that," Tommy said, and we ended our session.

I'll meditate on that, too, I thought.

Patients teach us so much. As we join with each other, patient and therapist, student and teacher, we become fellow travelers along this path of life. There is no end to questions, there are just continual moments of being open to whatever may arise, pain and pleasure, confusion and clarity.

As the prefrontal cortex develops in the first five years of life, it gives us the opportunity and the burden to sense the future. Learning to live with our awareness of the transience of time is the focus of *temporal integration*. Three major aspects of time emerge in this integration: uncertainty, impermanence, and death. We can be immersed fully in the moment, yet our prefrontal cortex can remind us that "this is temporary," as it did during my silent retreat walk in the woods, being sure I did not forget that death would change all. Such a prefrontal preoccupation can put a crimp on enjoying life and make temporal integration come to the foreground in that person's focus, on his or her growth edge. As we realize how things constantly change, we also become acutely aware that nothing can be certain, nothing controlled.

For a left hemisphere, especially, this can feel terrifying in that nothing can be held in sequence or fully predicted. Perhaps the right hemisphere's mode of being is needed as we come to rest in the comfort of acceptance within mindful awareness that helps us deal directly with the uncertainty and impermanence issues of temporal integration. Perhaps this is Tommy's right mode's solution that being known gives us a sense of wholeness in the universe with which we can face death with more equanimity. Even the reality of death becomes a component on the rim of our mind's wheel of awareness that can be noted and welcomed. Temporal integration directly evokes a mindful presence to approach, not withdraw, from these profound existential realities of our prefrontal preoccupations.

Interpersonal Integration

Before we worry about dying, we begin life with just the experience of being. We come to feel our first sense of wholeness, an inseparable part of an undivided world in the womb. This can be called a "ground of being." All of our bodily needs are met and "just being" is a natural way. But once we're born, we must "work for a living" and we find life different, and hard. We are now little doings, not just beings. No matter how attentive our caregivers are, we find our body betrays that sense of wholeness: we need, we want, we ache in the belly. When we are frustrated we wait what feels an eternity to have our needs met by those we now depend on to soothe our distress. We need others, we rely on them for comfort, for our very survival. Attunement with others is a glimmer of hope that emerges from the universal conflict between what was our "ground of being" to now "being a human in the world." We hold on to others for dear life.

Here we see that *interpersonal integration* becomes a vital way in which our brains' hardwiring to connect enables us to feel grounded in the world. Attunement is not a luxury; it is a requirement of the individual to survive and to thrive. As we align our being with the being of another, as we transfer energy and information between each other to resonate, we create an attuned state at the heart of interpersonal integration. Such secure interpersonal attunements likely create states of integration that promote internal attunement and mindfulness as a trait. The neural correlations of secure attachment, mindfulness, and middle prefrontal function overlap with these relational, mind, and neural dimensions of well-being.

In mindful awareness we enter a more receptive state to engage with others in that life-affirming resonance. Mindfulness, as we've seen, also involves an attunement to the self, enabling what was once a total dependence on others for connection to be now bolstered, not replaced, by a deep form of intrapersonal resonance. We become our own best friend and, in turn, become available for such full and receptive relationships with others.

In all of our clinical relationships we build on the centrality of attunement. As with Tommy's realization in the previous segment, our minds resonate, a dance of the deepest aspects of our universal concerns. Even Tommy's insight, his shift in perspective, is exactly the essence of mindfulness as a relational form of internal attunement: we become known to ourselves.

Anne and Bill had found that their cohesive states of adaptations had restricted their capacity to be openly attuned to each other. The work for each of them was to enter a reflective process of integration across the many domains of horizontal, vertical, memory, and narrative that could enable each of them to get to the ipseitious self beyond just narrative cohesion. From that receptive space, they could then regain an internal attunement to the longings to belong that had been distorted during their childhood adaptations. Opening the hub of their individual minds permitted a new way for them to join in this ground of being. Their receptive hubs opened their hearts to connect in ways that only their dreams could have imagined.

Mary's experience with early forms of abuse left her also with a sense of isolation from others that kept her stuck in a state of disconnection, socially and internally. The hub of her mind had become fractured. By finding her way to the basic process of integration of consciousness, by healing the hub of her mind, she could sense the feelings of betrayal and shame that so often fill the hearts of those who have been recipients of familial trauma. Moving toward the belief that the self is defective, a view embedded in the shame that emerges from such profound misattunements and maltreatments, healing is facilitated by seeing that toxic sense of self as an element of the rim, not the totality of one's identity. For Mary, an expanded hub enabled the many layers of integration to be welcomed in her life as she came to make sense of her experiences and move into the present with more clarity and a sense of freedom and open possibility.

It is from this open space in our minds, this reflective spacious hub, that we can engage fully with others. The beauty of mindful awareness is that it clears the path for direct connection within and with each other. As we move into states of coherence within our own minds, as we loosen the cohesive strangles of restrictive narratives and enter the flow of a FACES river of well-being, we become free to be present. This presence brings us to that ground of being, the ipseity of our earliest existence, where we give and receive in a flow that is as natural as breathing.

Transpirational Integration

As I became more immersed in the experience of being with my patients with this framework of the domains of integration in mind, I came to find that a common new form of integration seemed to emerge. This dimension of integration felt like it breathed life across all the other domains, hence the term *transpirational integration*, to denote this sense of "across-breathing." Transpiration seemed to involve the feeling that the person was a part of a much larger whole, beyond the bodily-defined self. People feel a sense of connection to not only other people, as within interpersonal integration, but they sense a deep desire to participate in causes that help others. This feeling of being a part of something in time and space beyond this body-self seems akin to dissolving Einstein's notion, discussed in Chapter 7, of the optical delusion of our separateness.

As we have explored, mindful awareness seems to involve not only a jettisoning of judgments, but an access to ipseity that enables people to feel the bare self beneath adaptation. From this new sense of one's deeper primary self, a feeling of belonging to a larger whole can emerge. Without reflection, we can remain stuck in an optical delusion not only of our separateness, but of the particular rules and mental models with which we've come to have a personal identity that shapes our journey in life. With the reflection of mindful awareness, we can gain a glimpse of a deeper reality—not replacing our identity but expanding it.

In a similar way, with transpirational integration our sense of ourselves is transformed. Transpiration opens our minds to another dimension of perception. The sacred suffuses each breath, our essence, each step through this journey of life. As we breathe life across the many domains of integration, we come to see ourselves as extending beyond the temporal-spatial dimensions that limit our view of the horizon. Transpiration gives us the vision to see beyond what is in front of our eyes, that we are a part of what has gone before, and what will come after these bodies are long gone from this dimension of our lives. Transpiration allows us to see that we leave an eternal imprint on the lives of others and on the world we leave behind.

Seeing transpiration as a part of the spectrum of integration can help us to understand the convergence of its appearance within contemplative and religious practice, and its presence in the non-sectarian studies of happiness and mental health.

Mindful awareness promotes neural integration. Today, more than ever, we desperately need a scientifically grounded view that supports our societal encouragement of reflection to promote compassion and care for each other. The integrative role of the mindful brain offered here may be one approach that can help us find common ground for promoting reflection in our lives now, and for generations to come.

Afterword

REFLECTIONS ON
REFLECTION

W e've come to the last chapter of our present travels together. We've journeyed deeply into ideas, direct experience, science, and some brief reflections on practical implications of the mindful brain. Here we'll touch lightly on some reflections on reflection itself, as we examine the relationship between reflection and morality and the way in which we can cultivate compassion for each other.

REFLECTION AND MORALITY

As the mindful brain develops, discernment is elaborated and we come to realize that the bare, primary self that is revealed with mindful awareness has within it a deep revelation: We share a core humanity beneath all of the chatter of the mind. Underneath our thoughts and feelings, prejudices and beliefs, there rests a grounded self that is a part of a larger whole.

We do not need to evoke a sense of something beyond the mind, but just a reality that we are a part of one species, one set of living beings, a part of nature. This bare awareness—this ipseity— is universal. We share our "ipseitious self" with each other, that grounded core essence beneath our adaptations, beliefs, and memories. From this natural awareness of mindful living, from this discernment, there is a flow of active analysis, perhaps of a non-language sort, that respecting the individual sovereignty of all people, in fact all living beings if not the whole of our planet, is "right."

Of related "neural" note is the finding of an active role of the middle prefrontal cortex in morality. This same region is active as we imagine ethical dilemmas and as we initiate moral action. We come to a sense of ourselves and of others, and a sense of right action and morality, through integrative circuitry in our neural core.

Just as attuning to oneself and approaching experience with COAL is a natural flow of being mindfully aware, so is attuning to the larger world of living beings with a loving stance inherent in this reflective immersion in our deeper selves. This journey is a part of the path to dissolving the delusion of our separateness.

If mindfulness promotes the development of the resonance circuits, then we can imagine that we will become more attuned to the internal lives of others as well as to ourselves. Soon this social circuitry will naturally create states of compassionate concern and empathic imagination. We'll feel others' pain and want to take action. We'll take in others' signals, and create images of their minds in our own. Compassion and empathy can be seen as natural outcomes of mindfulness when it is envisioned as a relational process based on internal attunement. When we become our own best friend, we become open to connecting deeply with others.

The concept of discernment also embraces an analysis of right action not as judgment, but as a moral direction that has a deep universal structure. We could debate the philosophy of that, of course, but let me present to you one perspective. Mindful awareness enables us to sense deeply the underlying adaptations of a social and analytic mind that form our personal and group "identity." These secondary flows of information form the top-down scaffolding of an autobiographical self that often shape us without awareness. This identity creates the baseline perspective governing how we approach the world and relate to each other.

Discernment in its simple, bare vision of a core grounded self gives rise to this sense that, in fact, we *can* have a compassionate way: being kind and caring toward others and ourselves. And we can have a destructive way: being cruel and uncaring. It is here where we can sense the broad moral compass emerging from the clarifying practice of mindful awareness.

This is the teaching of all the spiritual leaders, from Christ to Buddha, Moses to Mohammed. In modern life, these teachings may be invisible. This journey into the facets of the mindful brain also reveals that compassion for each other is a biological imperative beyond the teachings of one group or another. This is a universal lesson so desperately needed in our interactions with each other on local and global levels.

This issue also raises the fundamental question that Matthieu Ricard, a former research microbiologist and now a long-time Buddhist monk, addresses in his book on happiness (2006): "Does being happy make you kind, or does being kind make you happy?" Indeed modern research on "happiness" and leading a meaningful life reveals that being considerate and caring for others is a robust predictor of a deeply rewarding way of life (Seligman, 2003). Kindness creates a profoundly meaningful sense of well-being in yourself and in those around you.

But what gets in the way of such mindful living? Why isn't the world just filled with human beings discerning all over the place, reflecting on life, sharing kindness with each other, day by day?

The secondary influences of memory and identity can lead to automatic ways of living in which beliefs are seen as ultimate realities and create motivational drives to enact those worldviews on others. People can be impulsive and destructive. There is no awareness that those beliefs are activities of the mind, no discernment of a deeper, primary self beneath fear and projection, hostility and hatred. The destruction that can emerge from such mindless top-down enslavements continues to shape our planet as it has for millennia. When we feel our lives are threatened, as research on "mortality salience" reveals (McGregor, Lieberman, Greenberg, Solomon, Arndt, Simon, et al., 1998), we intensify our innate top-down classifier of whom we deem as members of the in-group and therefore cherished, and whom we see as a part of the out-group and worthy of suspicion and attack. In the intensely activated neural structures of threat, our limbic regions influence cortical reasoning and we come to believe, without a doubt, that we are right in our assessments. And "they" are wrong.

When the stakes are high in these intense times of tyranny and technological advance, a mindful awareness of these neural mechanisms and the reflection necessary to disengage from their automatic reactions are desperately needed. Reflection is no longer a luxury, it may be a necessity for our survival.

A REFLECTIVE INTEGRATION

Awareness is a skill that we can learn to develop. How we shape awareness in ourselves and with each other has the potential to shape our brains, for good or for bad.

Mindfulness is an intentional experience that helps harness what we've called the "hub" of our metaphoric wheel of awareness. That reflective center of our minds has many dimensions. Three of these include receptivity, self-observation, and reflexivity. Being receptive, opening our awareness to whatever arises from the rim of our wheel, creates a spacious mental center of gravity that enables body, mind, and relationships to achieve a state of dynamic equilibrium. A second dimension is that of self-observation, in which we can actively note and assess the contents of our own mind as mental events, not the totality of who we are. This discernment is a crucial component of mindful awareness that frees our path. Equally pivotal is the third dimension of being reflective: reflexivity. This is the automatic way in which a reflective mind has awareness of awareness itself.

In combination, all three dimensions of reflection permit us to attain equanimity and to decouple automatic processing as we create the discernment that together yields the many facets of mind-

fulness. Research has included non-reactivity, acting with awareness, non-grasping onto judgments, the ability to describe and label the contents of our inner experience and, in meditators at
least, the role of observation of one's inner life. These many facets
of mindfulness have correlations with specific dimensions of brain
function that we have explored.

By viewing mindfulness as a form of relationship with the self,
we can unravel the strands that connect the three fields of parent-
child attachment, prefrontal neural function, and mindful awareness. The nine functions that emerge from the activity of the middle aspect of the prefrontal region are both the process and the
outcome of mindful awareness practices. Seven of these nine are
also outcomes of secure parent-child relationships. These intimate
connections are filled with interpersonal attunement that enables
the child to feel felt. It is our central proposal that mindfulness is a
form of intrapersonal attunement in which you begin to resonate
with your own internal state.

The various views of mindfulness from researchers in mental
health and education, and the perspectives of historical and modern contemplative practices, can find some common ground in
this relational view of the mindful brain.

Prior learning, established from repeated experiences and reinforced with emotional value, pushes down on perception to dull
the details of incoming bottom-up processes. In this manner, these
top-down neural net assemblies enslave the primary streams and
create, in our subjective experience, a sense of confinement. We
feel distant from sensation, far from direct experience, imprisoned
by our previous history.

In small ways, we walk past the garden and don't stop to smell
the flowers. In larger ways, engrained emotional reactions and descriptive packets of information keep us far from sensory experience. In even more restrictive ways, our personal identity creates a
fixed mindset defining who we "are," and life becomes constrained
by hidden beliefs and patterns we call "personality" or "identity."

Becoming reflective enables us to move beneath the walls of these top-down prisons. Reflective thinking engages imagery as the fluid language of the mind that disrupts the automatic ways in which as adults we tend to become limited by inflexible descriptive summaries of experience. This view suggests the practical point that personal growth within our selves and within our relationships at a minimum should honor the role of imagery to create more flexibility in our lives.

Mindful learning embraces a flexible state of mind as well, creating a respect for uncertainty and the importance of context and perspective. The power of this approach to mindfulness is that it can readily inspire students to become engaged participants in the learning process. Awareness that one's own state of mind matters is central in this approach and helps dissolve old, rigid mindsets that either imprison the self, or leave the self out of the learning altogether.

With attunement between parent and child, we see these same facets at the heart of secure attachment. Viewing mindfulness as a form of internal attunement enables us to propose how this reflective form of awareness creates such flexibility. When our lives are dominated by word-based capsules serving as summations of experience, it is difficult to attune to the inner layer of direct sensory reality. When descriptions and previously created mental models rapidly shape our perception of the world, and our selves, we cannot attain flexibility because we are living a life defined by the past, not in tune with the present.

Attunement internally requires that we shed these top-down constraints and get as close to the "actual" lived self as possible. But as the brain is continually filtering neural activations and translating these into complex layers of firing patterns distant from "actual reality," when and where do we say we've reached "now and here?" What is the actual here and now that let's us know we've arrived?

There is an exhilarating feeling that emerges when the focus of our attention rides the waves of our own intentional flow and grounds us in the present moment and we know that here we've arrived at now. The beauty of being mindful is not that you've arrived anywhere in particular, but that the reality of reflection becomes a home of your heart. Reflection opens the passageway beneath secondary walls, underneath words and worlds of identity, so that we come to rest in an open presence of mind.

Presence is not simple sensation, though it can feel simple and sensuous. Being present feels reflective in the ways we've described: receptive, self-observant, reflexive. We are open to what is, not just summaries of our memory's notion of what ought to be. We observe our selves and attain equanimity through active awareness: feeling flexibly, naming, balancing left and right, approaching rather than withdrawing. These are active reflective engagements with the wild flows of our own unpredictable mind in an uncertain world. Embedded within these active reflections is our meta-awareness, the automatic awareness of awareness that creates a deep knowing of the ebbs and flows of our own mind's activities as habits of mind, not the totality of who we are.

Attunement internally emerges as we sense the primary "who" beneath the secondary chatter of our busy top-down minds. It is this internal attunement with our primary self that yields the powerful feeling of coming home. As poets have so often urged us to consider, we live so far from this person who has loved us for so long but has been so blindly ignored: our primary self. Welcoming that self is the celebration of life that mindfulness invites us to join.

As we reflect on our own internal states, the resonance circuitry that evolved to connect with others' minds is primed to sense the deep nature of our own intentional world. Linking perception and action we create the neural maps of our own intentions and sensory experience, moment-by-moment, as we create an internal resonance, the essence of attunement.

Reflecting inwardly invites us to honor the wordless world of sensation and image. In our busy lives, that is often easier said than done. But "doing" is not the mode that is called for here: being—being human—is the state of mind that we are asked to consider. As a "sideways" form of learning, emphasizing process over content, or an "orthogonal" way of seeing reality, a letting go instead of grasping, mindfulness offers us a new way to be.

The challenge for us all is to see life as a verb, not a noun. We cannot hold on to the fluid river of life, guarantee the certainty of facts, the universality of rules. We need to not only tolerate ambiguity, but learn to treasure its secrets. Being is a moving entity that never ceases to lead us down its winding path. Embracing this dynamic nature of our transient lives liberates us from the prison of our efforts to run from this reality. In mindful awareness, within the reflective hub of our minds, we can welcome this truth into our hearts, and into our collective lives.

It's hard to describe, but perhaps the feeling is best expressed like this: Being is just this. Whatever is here, we—you, me, our patients, students, relatives, friends, strangers, adversaries—can contain the fullness of experience and ride the waves of our streams of awareness within the reflective space of the hub of our minds. That spaciousness can be shared, the wheel of our awareness can become a collective, group experience, filled with awe, and the illusion of our separateness revealed for what it is: a creation of our minds, a neural invention.

Kindness is to our relationships, on this precious and precarious planet, what breath is to life. With reflection we can nurture in each other an access to a self deeper than personal identity, that ipseity of being that we all share. From this mindful place, there may be a path toward healing our global community one mind, one relationship, one moment at a time.

REFLECTION AND
MINDFULNESS RESOURCES

The following is a brief list of organizations mentioned in the text with which I have had direct contact, or serve on their advisory boards, participate as teaching faculty, or actually help administer. This is only a partial listing of the many important organizations in existence that help promote the development of a mindful brain in education, psychotherapy, and everyday life. The name of the organization is followed by a web site address, and in those organizations where I work I've provided direct quotations derived from their mission statements and digital home pages. This list offers a sense of how various elements of our society, from academia to contemplation, are moving in the direction of awareness and reflection as an essential part of our cultural evolution.

Mindsight Institute   *MindsightInstitute.com*

The Mindsight Institute is an educational organization that focuses on how the development of insight and empathy in individuals, families, and communities can be enhanced by exploring the interface of human relationships and basic biological processes. Our institute offers ongoing seminars, immersion training programs, and advanced workshops that explore the application of interpersonal neurobiology to various educational, clinical, and community activities to promote mindsight and the cultivation of well-being.

Mind and Moment

This three-day seminar was subtitled "Mindfulness, Neuroscience, and the Poetry of Transformation in Everday Life." The teachers on this interactive panel were Diane Ackerman, the poet, essayist, and naturalist (author of *An Alchemy of Mind, Origami Bridges,* and *A Natural History of the Senses*); Jon Kabat-Zinn, a pioneering researcher and educator in mindfulness and the founder of Mindfulness-Based Stress Reduction (MBSR) programs (author of *Full Catastrophe Living, Wherever You Go, There You Are,* and *Coming to Our Senses*); John O'-Donohue, the Irish philosopher, poet, and theologian (author of *Anam Cara, Eternal Echoes,* and *Beauty: The Invisible Embrace*); and Dan Siegel, psychiatrist and educator (author of *The Mindful Brain* and *The Developing Mind,* co-author of *Parenting from the Inside Out*). The program covered a wide range of topics focusing on the intersection of mindful awareness practices, science, and the arts, with a special emphasis on the cultivation of well-being, experiential immersion in reflection and poetry, and the interaction among the presenters and the participants. The event was taped in high-definition format and these recordings are available through the Mindsight Institute and are appropriate for a range of educational goals and settings.

Mindful Awareness Research Center (MARC)   *MARC.ucla.edu*

Part of the Semel Institute for Neuroscience and Human Behavior at UCLA, the Mindful Awareness Research Center is dedicated to investigating, evaluating, and disseminating *mindful awareness*—the moment-by-moment process of actively observing and drawing inferences from one's physical, mental, and emotional experiences. Mindful awareness (also known as *mindfulness*) is an ancient concept with over 2,500 years of history and development that is currently making a huge impact on contemporary society.

MARC focuses its efforts on identifying, evaluating, and disseminating the most appropriate and effective Mindful Awareness Practices (MAPs) to foster well-being across the lifespan in clinical and non-clinical settings, cope with the mounting stresses of daily urban life, and assist people to be more self-aware and compassionate individuals.

InnerKids   *InnerKids.org*

Founded in 2001, InnerKids is a national leader in teaching mindful awareness to children in pre-K through middle school. Mindful awareness is a state of present attention in which one observes thoughts, feelings, emotions, and events at the moment they occur without reacting to them in an automatic or habitual way. InnerKids' mindful awareness activities take into account children's developmental differences, train focused attention and awareness, and acknowledge clarity and compassion as part of the process of becoming more attentive and aware. As world events become increasingly complicated, it is critical that children learn to view them from a nuanced perspective; something that can only arise from a calm and focused mind. We know from a millennium of experience in all contemplative traditions that to develop such a mind one needs training and practice.

Center for Culture, Brain, and Development (CBD)   *CBD.ucla.edu*

The Foundation for Psychocultural Research, University of California Los Angeles (FPR-UCLA) Center for Culture, Brain, and Development (CBD) fosters training and research at UCLA to explore how culture and social relations inform brain development, how the brain organizes cultural and social development, and how development gives rise to a cultural brain. At the same time, we aim to understand how the brain makes it natural to acquire, use, and create culture; how development builds on neurally mediated socio-cultural practices; how social relations are culturally informed; how culture is acquired in social interaction; and how culture and social relations are constructed through neurally potentiated developmental processes.

Other Organizations Mentioned in the Text

Garrison Institute   *GarrisonInstitute.org*
Insight Meditation Society (IMS)   *Dharma.org*
Mind and Life Institute   *MindandLife.org*
Mindfulness Based Stress Reduction (MBSR)   *umassmed.edu/cfm/*
Spirit Rock Meditation Center   *SpiritRock.org*

Educational Programs Related to Aspects of Reflection

The Collaborative for Academic, Social, and Emotional Learning (CASEL)   *CASEL.org*
PATHS (Providing Alternative Thinking Strategies)
prevention.psu.edu/projects/PATHS.html

Appendix II

GLOSSARY AND TERMS

The following is a listing of the acronyms, abbreviations, and other terms from the text.

Acronyms

COAL Curiosity, openness, acceptance, and love. The state of mindfulness that is open and receptive to whatever arises in the field of awareness.

COHERENCE Connection, openness, harmony, engagement, receptivity, emergence, noesis, compassion, and empathy. These are the qualities that describe the coherent state of an integrated system.

FACES Flexible, adaptive, coherent, energized, and stable. When a system becomes integrated, it travels down a path with these qualities.

Fourth "R" The term denoting the idea that we can create a basic education in which reflection is added to the basic list of reading, (w)riting, and (a)rithmetic. A fifth "R" could be *resilience*, and a sixth might be *relationships*.

ISO Internal state of the other. The simulated affective, intentional, and physiological states perceived in another that become embedded in oneself. An ISO can be perceived in the signals of another person, giving the sense of "feeling felt" in the moment, of seeing one's mind in that of the other.

MAPs Mindful awareness practices, a term coined by Sue Smalley of the UCLA Mindful Awareness Research Center, describes the broad spectrum of activities that can cultivate mindfulness in our lives.

NOTO Narrative of the other. The way in which we have stories of each other that enable us to keep the other in mind, even when we are not with that person in the present. We sense ourselves in the mind of another by the NOTOs we hear in the stories that others tell that especially reveal how they have seen us, from the inside out.

SAM Scan, alert, and motivate. These processes function to ensure safety and are overly active in those with obsessive compulsive disorder (OCD) and other conditions.

SIFT Sensation, images, feelings, and thoughts. These are some basic elements that we can place in the front of our mind as we "sift" through experience to encourage a broad range of awareness beyond just the often dominant word-based thoughts.

SNAG Stimulate neuronal activation and growth. Within daily life, education, or psychotherapy, the ways we focus our attention and engage our minds will directly snag the brain so that neural plasticity is promoted in those activated regions.

SOCK Sensation, observation, concept, and knowing. These are four streams of awareness that may be seen to each flow into a river of consciousness in the valley of the present moment. Integrating all four streams may be fundamental to the experience of mindfulness.

Some Brain Abbreviations (see figures and discussion in Chapter 2)

ACC anterior cingulate cortex

DLPFC dorsal lateral prefrontal cortex.

IC insula cortex, also known as "insula."

MPFC medial prefrontal cortex. This has divisions, including the ventral (VMPFC) and the dorsal (DMPFC).

OFC orbitofrontal cortex

OMPFC This is the term for the orbitomedial prefrontal cortex, the combined grouping of the OFC and the MPFC.

STG superior temporal gyrus

STS superior temporal sulcus

VPFC ventral prefrontal cortex, including the ventral lateral (VLPFC) and ventral medial (VMPFC) prefrontal cortex

Some Terms

Integration   The linkage of differentiated elements. *Neural integration* involves the synaptic linkage of physically and functionally distinct regions into a working whole.

Invariant representations   Hawkins and Blakeslee's (2004) term for the cortical top-down biasing of incoming bottom-up information through the lens of prior experience, as these neural imprints from memory push down from the top-layers of the cortical columns.

Ipseity   The term used to describe a core sense of self beneath usual personal identity by Lutz, Dunne, and Davidson (in press). The *ipseitious self* is a term we have fashioned to indicate the bare sense of being that can be accessed via mindful awareness practices, residing in a spacious hub of the mind.

Middle prefrontal regions   This is the term used to refer to the major cortical brain regions that include the anterior cingulate cortex (ACC), the orbitofrontal cortex (OFC) and the medial and ventral prefrontal cortex (MPFC and VPFC). These regions often work in conjunction with the insula cortex (IC).

Neuroception   Steven Porges' (1998) term for how the brain perceives ("neuronal + perception" = neuroception) whether the individual is in a state of danger or safety. When safety is assessed, the social engagement system is activated by way of the myelinated "smart" ventral vagus nerve and the facial muscles relax and the mind becomes receptive. This is the state that Porges refers to as "love without fear."

Nine middle prefrontal functions   Review of the literature (see Appendix III) reveals nine functions that involve the collective activity of the middle prefrontal cortex as part of a larger distributed circuit. These complex functions are dependent on these regions but involve a widely distributed set of circuitry beyond only prefrontal neurons which serve to integrate the larger neural system. This list includes bodily regulation, attuned communication, emotional balance, response flexibility, empathy, insight, fear modulation, intuition, and morality.

Reflection   In this text, a process defined as consisting of at least three essential elements: receptivity, self-observation, and reflexivity (awareness of awareness).

Reflective coherence   The integrated state that is created with reflection. The notion here is that reflection can move less integrated states that may be cohesive and rigidly defined or random and filled with chaos into a coherent state, as defined above, that is more flexible and adaptive.

Reflective thinking Stephen Kosslyn's (2005) term for the imagery-based information processing that is more flexible than the descriptive thinking that marks how long-term memory constrains ongoing perception. Descriptive thinking is based on conceptual constructs that may involve words and is less flexible than the fluid nature of imagery that characterizes reflective thinking.

Resonance circuits The neural regions active during interactions that involve attunement, the mutual influence of one entity with another. Included are the mirror neuron system, superior temporal cortex, insula (or insula cortex), and middle prefrontal cortex (see Appendix III).

Self-engagement system A mechanism we have proposed by which mindful awareness creates a parallel state to Porges' interpersonal "love without fear" (see neuroception, above) in attuning to the self with a COAL sense of one's own direct experience of the moment.

Streams of awareness The flow of information that contributes to consciousness and may be seen to filter the nature of the data being received by the hub of the mind. At least four streams can be described, as outlined in the acronym SOCK: sensation, observation, concept, and (non-conceptual) knowing.

Wheel of awareness A visual metaphor of the mind in which one can envision a wheel with the hub, spokes, and rim representing different aspects of attentional experience as described below (see figures in Chapters 4 and 6).

Hub The central aspect of awareness that serves as a source of *executive attention*. Various aspects of becoming aware exist and include the ways the hub can take in elements from the rim in a single-pointed way, driven by the pull of the stimuli (*exogenous attention*) or directed by the mind itself (*endogenous attention*). The mind can also enter a receptive state, in which the hub can be seen as having a spacious quality that is intentionally open to whatever arises on the rim, but—in mindful awareness—maintains a reflective state of awareness. The discernment that emerges from this reflection permits patterns of personality and other activities of the mind to be identified as transient processes, not the totality of who the person is.

Spokes   The directing of attention from rim to hub (exogenous) or from hub to rim (endogenous). Many qualitatively different spokes may be sent through the filter of the streams of awareness (see above) as they link even the same rim point to the awareness of the hub and directly shape how we experience awareness.

Rim   The infinite points of possible elements that can become a part of the focus of attention. The rim can be divided into at least four sectors including the first five senses (data from the outside world), sixth sense (information from the body), seventh sense (elements of the mind itself—thoughts, feelings, images, memories, beliefs, intentions), and the eighth sense (relationships—of oneself with others, something larger than the day-to-day self, or the feeling of attunement with oneself).

Triangle of well-being   Coherent mind, empathic relationships, neural integration. These three elements are not reducible to each other and form three interactive components of well-being.

Appendix III

NEURAL NOTES

THE MIDDLE PREFRONTAL FUNCTIONS

We are using a synthetic approach to examine many ideas, one in particular being the fascinating overlap among secure parent-child attachment, mindful awareness, and prefrontal brain function. In my own clinical work, a patient with a severe head trauma following an automobile accident presented with impairments to certain functions that spanned a wide spectrum, from regulating her body to her moral behavior. The brain scans after her accident unfortunately revealed damage to midline structures, including the orbitofrontal region, the ventral and medial prefrontal areas, and the frontal aspects of the anterior cingulate cortex.

Turning to the research literature I found that these midline areas were often described separately from each other and studied for their unique contributions to mental function and behavior. But in this patient's case, it seemed that the clinical findings revealed ways in which, from her experience and from the research literature taken as a synthetic whole, we could see a set of functions that emerged from the teaming of these areas into a "unit" of neurally integrative circuits. Because of their midline anatomical location along the vertical and horizontal planes, I have used the common language wording of "middle prefrontal" to emphasize the location of these linked regions as a group. Formally, the anterior cingulate is often considered a "limbic structure," and not a part of the prefrontal region. But these prefrontal areas themselves can be considered the "feeling part of the thinking brain" and can be viewed as either the topmost part of the limbic areas or the limbic most part of the prefrontal areas. With either perspective, we can see from the literature that terms we use such as "limbic" or "prefrontal," if taken too literally, may actually limit our understanding when we come to see how integrative these regions in fact are.

When clustered together, the research reveals that each of the regions (orbitofrontal, medial and ventral prefrontal, and anterior cingulate; see Figure 2.2) have unique contributions to the list of nine functions described on pp. 42–44, but that they are also reported to function together in various combinations. It is crucial to realize that the "middle prefrontal functions" rely on these integrative areas in that these varied processes, from body regulation to morality, involve a wide array of neural processes beyond these regions. These functions are created in a distributed circuit of which these middle regions are only a part. Perhaps the part they play is in creating the coordination and balance of integration that are essential for such complex processes to be established. Because of their integrative role, and for the benefit of teaching the idea of executive function as being mediated by all of these middle areas in collaboration with the side (dorsolateral) prefrontal region and the insula cortex, I've found using the term "middle" to be useful, even if not a part of formal scientific terminology.

These middle areas do not seem, in the research data, to be as directly involved as the side region is in the working memory aspect of consciousness, of having something in "the front of our minds." In this way, too, making this grouping of middle versus side prefrontal areas has been helpful in exploring issues such as the automatic aspect of mindfulness as a trait—how we can come to live mindfully without conscious effort—versus the more effortful quality of mindful awareness practices that, in that moment, consciously and intentionally create a mindful state that may preferentially involve more side activation than in the long-term trait condition, as discussed in the text (see pp. 118–121).

For those who are interested in gaining a sense of the more in-depth discussions of data, I am providing in this part of the appendix a gathering of the research publications or reviews that support the "nine middle prefrontal functions" that we've discussed throughout the text. These are the functions that emerge from the activity of these integrative midline regions in conjunction with activity in other areas of the brain. These functions seem to be shared by mindful awareness and, for the first seven at least, from research to date, have also been found as an outcome of secure parent-child attachment (the last two not, to my knowledge, having yet been formally studied). The functions themselves are defined in practical terms in the text in Chapter 2. Here I will provide only the references to illustrate some of the scientific support for this listing and the clustering of these regions under the umbrella term "middle prefrontal" regions.

This wide spectrum of functions is derived from asking the question, "What processes are correlated with the activity of the orbitofrontal, medial and ventral prefrontal, and anterior cingulate cortices?" (the areas damaged after my patient's accident.) The integration of these three regions, combined with the input of the related insula cortex, reveals an executive circuit whose functions span from bodily regulation to social understanding. Critchley (2005) offered a concise overview of this wide range of functions:

> Influential theoretical models propose a central role for afferent information from the body in the expression of emotional feeling states. Feedback representations of changing states of bodily arousal influence learning and facilitate concurrent and prospective decision-making. Functional neuroimaging studies have increased understanding of brain mechanisms that generate changes in autonomic arousal during behavior and those which respond to

internal feedback signals to influence subjective feeling states. In particular, the anterior cingulate cortex is implicated in generating autonomic changes, while insula and orbitofrontal cortices may be specialized in mapping visceral responses. Independently, ventromedial prefrontal cortex is recognized to support processes of internal (self-) reference that predominate in states of rest and disengagement and which putatively serve as a benchmark for dynamic interactions with the environment. Lesion data further highlight the integrated role of these cortical regions in autonomic and motivational control. In computational models of control, forward (efference copies) and inverse models are proposed to enable prediction and correction of action and, by extension, the interpretation of the behavior of others. It is hypothesized that the neural substrate for these processes during motivational and affective behavior lies within the interactions of the anterior cingulate, insula, and orbitofrontal cortices. Generation of visceral autonomic correlates of control reinforce experiential engagement in simulatory models and underpin concepts such as somatic markers to bridge the dualistic divide. (p. 493)

Here we see that the "middle prefrontal" regions function alongside the insula to create a complex set of processes. When these functions are placed together, as in the following list of nine dimensions of interrelated activities, we can see that a larger process is at work to create them: These midline areas are profoundly *integrative,* linking widely spread areas to each other as we've been extensively discussing in the text. Literally, this means that these neural circuits by themselves are not "special," but rather function in the larger neural system to create a wide spectrum of mental and physiological outcomes because they are able to bring the extended nervous system, even those firing patterns of the neural systems of other individuals, into a functional whole. This is the definition of neural integration, the specialty of these regions. Recall that neural integration creates the possibility of coordination and balance. Here we see that the interaction among these important regions creates a highly complex state that enables us to have such potential for everything from bodily regulation and emotional balance to empathy and moral behavior.

In our overall proposal, then, we are illuminating the overlap of secure attachment and mindful awareness practices as facilitating neural activations that "snag" the brain in the direction of neural integration. Prime candidates for this neural integration are the middle prefrontal areas. As secure attachment is promoted by experiences of interpersonal attunement, we are proposing that mindfulness involves the experience of what we are calling internal attunement. As we've discussed, attunement of either sort, according to this line of reasoning, will promote the growth of the integrative fibers of the middle prefrontal areas that are a part of a larger "resonance circuitry," as discussed on pages 347–355. With this stimulation of neural plasticity to activate and grow integrative fibers, the neural correlates of these functions become created and their contribution to well-being is made possible. This view is expressed in the notion of the triangle of well-being that entails neural integration, empathic relationships, and a coherent mind. As we can see from this list, the neural integration from internal or interpersonal attunement sets the stage for coherence and empathy to be established in a person's life.

The following is a list of the nine middle prefrontal functions and a sample of the research and reviews that directly or indirectly support the suggestion that these functions correlate with the integrative activity of these areas.

The list of Nine Middle Prefrontal Functions and selected references:

1. Bodily Regulation

Critchley, H. D., Mathias, C. J., Josephs, O., O'Doherty J., Zanini, S., Dewar, B.-K., Cipolotti, L., Shallice, T., & Dolan R. J. (2003). Human cingulate cortex and autonomic control: Converging neuroimaging and clinical evidence. *Brain, 126*: 2139–2152.

Lane R. D., Reiman, E. M., Ahern, G. L., & Thayer J. F. (2001). Activity in medial prefrontal cortex correlates with vagal component of heart rate variability during emotion. *Brain Cogn, 47*: 97–100.

Nauta, W. J. H. (1971). The problem of the frontal lobe: A reinterpretation. *J Psychiat Res, 8*: 167–187.

Öngür, D., & Price, J. L. (2000). The organization of networks within the orbital and medial prefrontal cortex of rats, monkeys, and humans. *Cerebral Cortex, 10*(3): 206–219.

Porrino L. J., & Goldman-Rakic, P. S. (1982). Brainstem innervation of prefrontal and anterior cingulate cortex in the rhesus monkey revealed by retrograde transport of HRP. *J Comp Neurol, 205*: 63–76.

2. Attuned Communication

Bar-On, R., Tranel, D., Denburg, N. L., & Bechara, A. (2003). Exploring the neurological substrate of emotional and social intelligence. *Brain, 126*: 1790–1800.

Beer, J. S., Heerey, E. A., Keltner, D., Scabini, D., & Knight, R. T. (2003). The regulatory function of self-conscious emotion: Insights from patients with orbitofrontal damage. *Journal of Personality and Social Psychology, 85*(4): 594–604.

Mah, L. W. Y., Arnold, M. C., & Grafman, J. (2005). Deficits in social knowledge following damage to ventromedial prefrontal cortex. *J Neuropsychiatry Clin Neurosci, 17*: 66–74.

Nitschke, J. B., Nelson, E. E., Rusch, B. D., Fox, A. S., Oakes, T. R., & Davidson, R. J. (2004). Orbitofrontal cortex tracks positive mood in mothers viewing pictures of their newborn infants. *Neuroimage, 21*: 583–592.

Schore, A. N. (2003). *Affect dysregulation and disorders of the self.* New York: W. W. Norton.

Trevarthen, C. (2001). Intrinsic motives for companionship in understanding: Their origin, development and significance for infant mental health. *Journal of Infant Mental Health, 2*(1–2): 95–131.

3. Emotional Balance

Blumberg, H. P., Leung, H-C, Skuklarski, P., Lacadie, B. S., Fredericks, C. A., Harris, B. C., Charney, D. S., et al. (2003). A functional magnetic resonance imaging study of bipolar disorder: State- and trait-related dysfunction in ventral prefrontal cortices. *Archives of General Psychiatry, 60*: 601–609.

Bush, G., Luu, P., & Posner, M. I. (2000). Cognitive and emotional influences in anterior cingulate cortex. *Trends Cogn Sci, 4*: 215–22.

Davidson, R. J., Jackson, D. C., & Kalin, N. H. (2000). Emotion, plasticity, context, and regulation: Perspectives from affective neuroscience. *Psychological Bulletin, 126*(6): 890–909.

Happaney, K., Zelazo, P.D., Stuss, D.T. (2004). Development of orbitofrontal function: Current themes and future directions. *Brain and Cognition, 55*:1–10.

Phan K. L., Wager, T., Taylor S. F., & Liberzon, I. (2002). Functional neuroanatomy of emotion: A meta-analysis of emotion activation studies in PET and fMRI. *Neuroimage, 2*: 331–48.

Tucker, D. M., Luu, P., & Pribram, K. H. (1995). Social and emotional self-regulation. *Annals of the New York Academy of Sciences, 769*(1): 213–239.

4. Response Flexibility

Carter C. S., Botvinick, M., & Cohen J. D. (1999). The contribution of the anterior cingulate cortex to executive processes in cognition. *Rev Neurosci, 10*: 49–57.

Chambers, C. D., Bellgrove M. A., Stokes, M. G., Henderson, T. R., Garavan, H., Robertson, I. H., Morris, A. P., & Mattingley, J. B. (2006). Executive "brake failure" following deactivation of human frontal lobe. *J Cogn Neurosci, 18*: 444–455.

Fellows, L. K. (2004). The cognitive neuroscience of human decision making: A review and conceptual framework. *Cogn Neurosci Rev, 3*(3): 159–172.

Gehring, W. J., & Fencsik, D. E. (2001). Functions of the medial frontal cortex in the processing of conflict and errors. *J Neurosci, 21*: 9430–7.

Gottfried, J. A., O'Doherty, J., & Dolan, R. J. (2003). Encoding predictive reward value in human amygdala and orbitofrontal cortex. *Science, 301*(5636): 1104–1107.

Schoenbaum, G., & Setlow, B. (2001). Integrating orbitofrontal cortex into prefrontal theory: Common processing themes across species and subdivisions. *Learning and Memory 8*(3): 134–147.

Turken, A. U., & Swick, D. (1999). Response selection in the human anterior cingulate cortex. *Nat Neurosci, 2*: 920–4.

5. Empathy

Carr, L., Iacoboni, M., Dubeau, M. C., Maziotta, J. C., & Lenzi, G. L. (2003). Neural mechanisms of empathy in humans: A relay from neural systems for imitation to limbic areas. *PNAS, 100*(9): 5497–5502.

Decety, J., & Jackson, P. L. (2004). The functional architecture of human empathy. *Behavioral and Cognitive Neuroscience Reviews, 3*(2): 71–100.

Heisel, A. D., & Beatty, M. J. (2006). Are cognitive representations of friends' request refusals implemented in the orbitofrontal and dorsolateral prefrontal cortices? A cognitive neuroscience approach to 'theory of mind' in relationships. *Journal of Social and Personal Relationships, 23*: 249–265.

Shamay-Tsoory, S. G., Tomer, R., Berger, B. D., Goldsher, D., & Aharon-Peretz, J. (2005). Impaired "affective theory of mind" is associated with right ventromedial prefrontal damage. *Cog Behav Neurol, 18*: 55–67.

de Waal, F. B. M., & Preston, S. D. (2002). Empathy: Its ultimate and proximate bases. *Behavioral and Brain Sciences, 25*: 1–20.

6. Insight (Self-Knowing Awareness)

Beer, J. S., John, O. P., Donatella, S., & Knight, R. T. (2006). Orbitofrontal cortex and social behavior: Integrating self-monitoring and emotion-cognition interactions. *Journal of Cognitive Neuroscience, 18*: 871–879.

Beitman, B. D., & Nair, J. (Eds.). (2005). *Self-awareness deficits in psychiatric patients: Assessment and treatment.* New York: W. W. Norton.

Frith, C. D., & Frith, U. (1999). Interacting minds—A biological basis. *Science, 286*(5445), 1692–1695.

Wood, J. N., Knutson, K. M., & Grafman, J. (2005). Psychological structure and neural correlates of event knowledge. *Cerebral Cortex, 15*: 1155–1161.

7. Fear Modulation

Hariri, A. R., Mattay, V. S., Tessitore, A., Fera, F., & Weinberger, D. R. (2003). Neocortical modulation of the amygdala response to fearful stimuli. *Biological Psychiatry, 53*(6): 494–501.

Phelps, E. A., Delgado, M. R., Nearing, K. I., & LeDoux, J. E. (2004). Extinction learning in humans: Role of the amygdala and vmPFC. *Neuron, 43*: 897–905.

Morgan M. A., Schulkin, J., & LeDoux, J. E. (2003). Ventral medial prefrontal cortex and emotional perseveration: The memory for prior extinction training. *Behav Brain Res, 146*: 121–130.

Sotres-Bayon, F., Christopher, K., Cain, C. K., & LeDoux, J. E. (2006). Brain mechanisms of fear extinction: Historical perspectives on the contribution of prefrontal cortex. *Biol Psychiatry, 60*: 329–336.

8. Intuition

Critchley, H. D., Mathias, C. J., & Dolan, R. J. (2001). Neuroanatomical correlates of first- and second-order representation of bodily states. *Nat Neurosci, 2*: 207–12.

Damasio, A. R. (1994). *Descartes' error*. New York: Grosset/Putnam.

Damasio, A. R. (1999). *The feeling of what happens: Body and emotion in the making of consciousness*. Orlando, FL: Harcourt Brace.

Lieberman, M. D. (2000). Intuition: A social cognitive neuroscience approach. *Psychological Bulletin C., 126*(1): 109–137.

9. Morality

Anderson, S. W., Bechara, A., Damasio, H., Tranel, D., & Damasio, A. R. (1999). Impairment of social and moral behavior related to early damage in human prefrontal cortex. *Nat Neurosci, 2*: 1032–1037.

Bechara, A., Damasio, H., & Damasio, A. R. (2000). Emotion, decision-making, and the orbitofrontal cortex. *Cerebral Cortex, 10*(3): 295–307.

Greene, J. D., Nystrom, L. E., Engell, A. D., Darley, J. M., & Cohen, J. D. (2004). The neural bases of cognitive conflict and control in moral judgment. *Neuron 44*(2): 389–400.

King, J. A., Blair, J. R., Mitchell, D. G. V., Dolan, R. J., & Burgess, N. (2006). Doing the right thing: A common neural circuit for appropriate violent or compassionate behavior. *Neuroimage 30*(3): 1069–76.

Moll, J., de Oliveira-Souza, R., Eslinger, P. J., Bramati, I. E., Mourão-Miranda, J., Andreiuolo, P. A., & Pessoa, L. (2002). The neural correlates of moral sensitivity: A functional magnetic resonance imaging investigation of basic and moral emotions. *Journal of Neuroscience, 22*(7): 2730–2736.

LATERALITY

In the text we discuss various aspects of brain research that explore the nature of laterality. Here I want to emphasize the importance of appreciating the degree of complexity involved in
carrying out research on the brain in general, and on asymmetry
in particular. One methodological issue is that imaging studies
(functional magnetic resonance imaging [fMRI] and positron
emission tomography [PET]) are very difficult to evaluate. The
technical nature of the assessment of degrees of activation and the
statistical methods used to address these differences can result in
quite differing conclusions. Davidson and colleagues (Davidson
et al., 2003) have addressed these issues and have attempted to clarify the nature of laterality effects using a cautious approach to their
findings. In general, though, we need to remain conservative in
how we interpret findings on laterality.

Another issue to note is that within one hemisphere there are
many important regions with functional distinctions, so that to say
the "left side is active" does not have a specificity that may be as
clear as the words sound. We've used the term "left mode" or
"right mode" to emphasize patterns of information processing
rather than a focus on strict laterality of the structures involved in
a task. For example, one sector of the left prefrontal area may be
active while a different sector of the right may also be active. The
brain functions as a whole system, and many varied regions may
have differential activity not determined by which side of the
brain they reside on. For example, there apparently is not a great
deal of overlap, though there may be some, between left hemisphere regions involved in approach and positive affect with those
involved in verbal speech production (Richard Davidson, personal
communication, August 2006). In this way, we should not assume
that because we are in an "approach state" with a left-sided shift in
electrical activity that we are necessarily priming our verbal cen-

ters to become active. Overall, it is helpful to think of integration, as we've discussed, as an important neural mechanism that enables complex functions to emerge. Within a given hemisphere and between left and right sides, linking separated areas with each other may be a key process to keep in mind as we seek correlations between neural function and mental experience.

RESONANCE CIRCUITS AND MIRROR NEURONS

Throughout the text we discuss the possible role of the social circuits of the brain in the experience of mindfulness. The notion that internal attunement is central to mindful awareness raises the idea that we pay attention in a direct way to our own mental experience: We become aware of awareness and attend to intention. As we examined how we come to focus on our own intention, we turned to research on the neural correlates of intention and came to the important discovery of the mirror neuron system.

Mirror properties in the nervous system are essentially defined as the ways in which our social brain has processes in which it perceives the intentional, goal-directed actions of others and links this perception to the priming of the motor systems to engage in that same action. This is the derivation of the term "mirror neuron" in that what we see we become ready to do, to mirror others' actions in our own behaviors. We've discussed the neural correlates of perceiving intention in others, and how that might translate into self-awareness of one's own intention at the heart of mindfulness.

In making this "mirror neuron-mindfulness hypothesis," we are drawing on the broader proposal that mindfulness is a form of internal attunement that harnesses the social circuits of the brain. Research efforts to explore the validity of this perspective can be carried out, with specific points suggested in the text. In turning to the existing research data, I respectfully was seeking out preliminary evidence (collected *post hoc*, or after the fact, as this pro-posal was not what the researchers had been exploring) that would at least be a small hint that there might be some empirical support for this point of view. My own first-person experience felt com-patible with this attunement hypothesis; now I was seeking third-person findings that might also lend some credence to these ideas. Ultimately, future research needs to create a prospective project that posits possible results and then attempts to disprove them, to see if they are valid or not, in the natural course of research de-sign, implementation, and data analysis.

In looking at existing research as discussed in the text, a num-ber of findings were consistent with areas with known mirror neuron properties becoming activated during meditation. For ex-ample, the supplementary motor area (Urry et al., 2004) in mind-fulness meditation and also the premotor activation in the distinct objectless compassion meditation (Lutz et al., 2004) were both consistent with mirror neuron areas. "Consistent" simply means these findings could be a function of the activation of regions with mirror properties, but naturally they also in the end may prove not to be mirror neuron activations.

The presentations of Brefczynski-Lewis (2006), Lazar (2006), and Short (2006) on mindfulness meditation with breath-aware-ness each revealed activation of the related region of the superior temporal cortex. This posterior area seemed to overlap on the scans with areas designated as superior temporal gyrus (STG) and as su-perior temporal sulcus (STS). The cortex in general consists of many folds, with a protruding area called a *gyrus*, and the invagi-nated region termed the *sulcus*. Existing research (Iacoboni et al., 2001) had revealed that imitation had a possible relationship to areas with mirror properties and the STS, and other studies (Brit-ton et al., 2006) have suggested the role of the STG in responding to facial expressions of emotion. In interpersonal attunement, we respond to facial expressions, raising the possible overlap between this gyrus function in facial perception and the more imitative aspects of attunement of the sulcus. Clearly more investigation is needed to tease apart the roles of this superior temporal involvement, sulcus or gyrus, in mindfulness meditation and its possible correlation with the process of attunement and mirroring.

Decety and Chaminade's (2003) review of the research explorations of the role of the STG reveal that this area is involved in the visual perception of socially meaningful body gestures and in the observation of actions that involve biological agents, such as perception of biological motion, similar to the STS, as well as the perception of speech and human sound movements. They stated that the STG is a part of the temporal cortex that

> is an important component in a circuit involved in social cognition (which through direct and indirect connections receives input from both the ventral and dorsal visual streams, the amygdala, the orbitofrontal cortex, and the prefrontal cortices). This cluster of activity was found in both hemispheres when constrasting the conditions of imitating and of being imitated to the condition of self-action. However, it was only present in the left hemisphere when the condition of being imitated was substracted from the condition of imitating the other. This lateralization in the STG is an intriguing finding, and may participate in the neural basis involved in the distinction between first-and third-person information conveyed through the visual modality. We suggest that the right STG could be involved in genuine visual analysis of the other's actions, while the left region could be concerned wih the analysis of the other's actions in relation to the intention of the self. (p. 587)

Here we see that the STG seems to play an important role in creating representations of self, other, and intentional states themselves. In general, then, the superior temporal cortex appears to play an important role in how we come to have a sense of our internal world and map intentions onto ongoing experience.

An important issue that Marco Iacoboni notes (personal communication, September, 2006) is that the STS and STG are higher-order sensory areas that contain neurons with complex visual, auditory, and multisensory properties, but do not have motor properties. Given this non-motor feature, they cannot be considered "mirror," in that the definition of a mirror neuron begins with the involvement of one's own actions, so a mirror neuron must have some motor properties. In Iacoboni's paper on imitation (2005), he clearly distinguishes the parietal and inferior frontal mirror neuron regions from the imitation contributions of the STS for this very reason. In using the terms *mirror neuron system* or *mirror neurons*, Iacoboni urges us to be clear in our language that these phrases refer to the neurons that specifically contain motor properties. Directly linked to these mirror neuron areas are the superior temporal regions that embed complex perceptual processes, including the maps of the prediction of consequences of motor action, what we have called SIMA in this text (sensory implications of motor action). In this way, the superior temporal contribution of SIMA is part of a functionally complex process in which different circuits link directly to each other. Though other authors may include this linked perceptual circuitry as a part of the mirror neuron system, here we will follow Iacoboni's suggestion to "make a clear distinction between these two systems that talk directly to each other" (personal communication, September 2006).

In reviewing the literature further, it seems that the process of behavioral imitation with the involvement of the superior temporal regions and the emotional/physiological resonance that involves the insula have parallel relationships with the mirror neurons. In imitation, the superior temporal regions seem to encode for the complex SIMA process; in emotional resonance, the insula mediates physiological and affective shifts that simulate those perceived in another person. Because of this parallel function in reciprocal enactments (imitative, physiologic, affective), we can create the term "resonance circuit" which directly involves the mirror neurons, but its components are not all motoric so it should not be labeled as being "mirror" in this formal way. In our discussion, we have honored this distinction and refer to this resonance circuitry either directly using this phrase or as areas that "are related to the mirror neuron system" (see Figures A.1 and A.2).

A.1

A.2

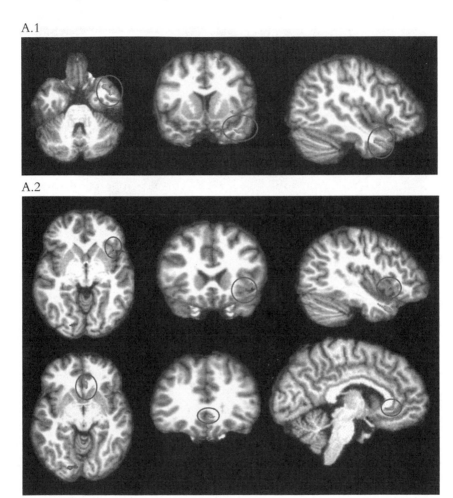

Figures A.1 & A.2 Functional imaging scans taken during breath-awareness meditation revealing activation of the superior temporal gyrus (Figure A.1) and the activation of the insula and the ventral portion of the anterior cingulate (Figure A.2). The superior temporal cortex, insula, and areas of the middle prefrontal cortex (shown here) along with the mirror neuron system are proposed in this text to comprise elements of the "resonance circuits," which may become activated during mindful awareness. Images reprinted with permission of Sara Lazar © 2005.

To explore the science of this a bit further, let me offer you a further view from Carr and colleague's (2003) summary of the interrelationships among imitation, empathy, and the various frontal and parietal mirror neuron areas and their relationship to the multimodal perceptual systems of the superior temporal cortex (please see their original paper for specific references which have been removed from this condensed quotation):

> In the primate brain, neural systems are associated with emotions and action representation. The limbic system is critical for emotional processing and behavior, and the circuit of frontoparietal networks interacting with the superior temporal cortex is critical for action representation. This latter circuit is composed of inferior frontal and posterior parietal neurons that discharge during the execution and also the observation of an action (mirror neurons, and of superior temporal neurons that discharge only during the observation of an action). Anatomical and neurophysiological data in the nonhuman primate brain and imaging human data suggest that this circuit is critical for imitation and that within this circuit, information processing would flow as follows. (i) The superior temporal cortex codes an early visual description of the action and sends this information to posterior parietal mirror neurons (this privileged flow of information from superior temporal to posterior parietal is supported by the robust anatomical connections between superior temporal and posterior parietal cortex). (ii) The posterior parietal cortex codes the precise kinesthetic aspect of the movement and sends this information to inferior frontal mirror neurons (anatomical connections between these two regions are well documented in the monkey. (iii) The inferior frontal cortex codes the goal of the action [both neurophysiological and imaging data support this role for inferior frontal mirror neurons]. (iv) Efferent copies of motor plans are sent from parietal and frontal mirror areas back to the superior temporal cortex, such that a matching mechanism between the visual description of the observed action and the predicted sensory consequences of the planned imitative action can occur. (v) Once the visual description

of the observed action and the predicted sensory consequences of the planned imitative action are matched, imitation can be initiated. (p. 5497)

The planned "imitative action" that is matched is the notion of resonance—for behaviors in imitation, affect in compassion, and, in our proposal, for mental coherence with a form of internal attunement that comes from "resonating" with the self. In essence, these superior temporal regions interact directly with the motor/perceptual processing mirror neurons as a part of the SIMA process, as discussed in detail in Chapter 8 (see Figure 8.1). SIMA may be one aspect of the internal attunement that creates an internally resonant state as we attend to our intentions.

These circuits of becoming aware of other's and one's own processes are discussed further by Decety and Chaminade (2003):

Neuroimaging studies strongly support the view that during the observation of actions produced by other individuals, and during the imagination of one's own actions, there is specific recruitment of the neural structures which would normally be involved in the actual generation of the same actions. The shared representation model may also be applied to the processing of emotions (Adolphs, 2002). In this model, perception of emotion would activate the neural mechanisms that are responsible for the generation of emotions. Such a mechanism would prompt the observer to resonate with the state of another individual, with the observer activating the motor representations that gave rise to the observed stimulus, i.e., a sort of inverse mapping. For example, while watching someone smile, the observer would activate the same facial muscles involved in producing a smile at a subthreshold level and this would create the corresponding feeling of happiness in the observer. There is evidence for this mechanism in the recognition of emotion from facial expression. Altogether, shared representations at the cortical level have been found in action, pain processing, and emotion recognition, which would give us a neurophysiological basis for the operation of social cognition. (p. 594)

In this text we are suggesting that this same social cognitive circuitry is harnessed for the "intrapersonal resonance" of mindfulness as is used when we have compassion and empathy for others. We can propose that this involves a form of self-empathy, one that, like empathy itself, is more complex than imitation or resonance as explored by Decety and Jackson (2004) when they stated

> Empathy is not a simple resonance of affect between the self and other. It involves an explicit representation of the subjectivity of the other. It is a consciously experienced phenomenon. Most importantly, empathy also necessitates emotion regulation for which the ventral prefrontal cortex, with its strong connections with the limbic system, dorsolateral, and medial prefrontal areas, plays an important role. Once again, we do not assume that there is a unitary empathy system (or module) in the brain. Rather, we consider multiple dissociable systems to be involved in the experience of empathy. (p. 93)

In this same manner, when we describe a "resonance circuit" that involves not only mirror neurons plus the insula and superior temporal regions, we are also seeing that this is a distributed system that likely involves aspects of the prefrontal cortex, especially the middle areas. Of note is a study by Creswell, Way, Eisenberger, and Lieberman (submitted), reviewed in the text, that revealed that individuals with mindfulness traits during a task in which they labeled the name of the emotion while viewing an affective facial expression had more activation than controls in two regions: their right ventrolateral PFC and their medial PFC. These activations were associated with a diminishment in the amygdala activation that followed initial viewing of the faces. The authors suggest that the mindfulness skill of labeling internal states may be revealed in the larger prefrontal activation and associated decreased amygdala activation. This study extends the findings of Hariri, Bookheimer, and Maziotta (2000) as mentioned in the text in which labeling was found to lead to a similar profile of prefrontal activation and amygdala deactivation with labeling. Here we see that mindfulness as a trait measure is associated with effective affect regulation.

Taken together, these varied views suggest that empahy for others may require that we be able to modulate our own resonant states such that we do not become the other, but instead feel their subjective experiences. Mindfulness skills may greatly enhance this capacity by simultaneously building our resonance circuitry (for enhanced compassion and empathy) and our prefrontal self-regulatory circuits (for affect regulation). The result would be greater ability to stay open with others, even in the face of their distress.

Mindful awareness itself may harness these resonance (insula, superior temporal, mirror neuron, and middle prefrontal areas) and self-regulatory (especially the orbitomedial and ventrolateral prefrontal) circuits by creating a state of self-empathy that emerges from internal attunement. When we resonate with our own intentional and affective states and combine this with the reflective skills of self-observation and labeling, we create a powerful capacity to enhance our connection to ourselves, and to others.

Overall these ideas raise many researchable questions that can be explored in future projects. If attunement is fundamental to mindfulness, we could explore its correlations in brain function in areas involving social circuitry, including regions related to the mirror neuron system. We also might explore ways in which stimulating neuronal activation and growth with internal attunement might enhance the sensitivity of these social circuits, illuminating some of the neural associations accompanying the reports of enhanced sensitivity to the signals of others and the capacity for mindfulness to promote compassion and empathy.

RELATIONSHIPS AND MINDFULNESS

The discussions regarding mindful awareness explored in this text suggest that the capacity to attune to oneself within a resonant process may reinforce those mental capacities and corresponding neural circuits that support a healthy relationship with other people in personal and professional settings. The anecdotal reports from mindfulness teachers and practitioners suggest that this is the case. What do we know from empirical research? In an excellent review of mindfulness studies, Brown, Ryan and Creswell (in press) offer a succinct and insightful summary of the empirical data in support of these anecdotal reports:

> While the evidence in this area of inquiry is still sparse, preliminary psychometric and intervention research suggests that mindfulness may enhance both the quality of romantic relationships and the communication that happens within those relationships. Barnes, Brown, Krusemark, Campbell, & Rogge (in press) found that higher MAAS-measured trait mindfulness predicted higher relationship satisfaction and greater capacities to respond constructively to relationship stress among non-distressed dating couples. A second study replicated and extended these findings. Using a conflict discussion paradigm, trait MAAS scores predicted lower emotional stress responses to conflict, and this effect was explained by lower emotional stress before the discussion. This corroborates past research, reviewed already, showing that those more dispositionally mindful are less susceptible to negative mood states in general, and suggests that this lower susceptibility is evident in the specific context of romantic couple interactions. The results showed that rather than buffering the effects of stress during conflict, mindfulness helped to inoculate against stress. The capacity of mindfulness to inhibit reactivity to conflict was also evident in the cognitive judgments that each partner made: those higher in trait mindfulness showed a more positive (or less negative) pre-post conflict change in their perception of the partner and the relationship. This study also supported the importance of bringing a mindful state into challenging exchanges, in that state mindfulness was related to better communication quality, as assessed by objective raters.

The trait of mindfulness thus seems to be empirically supported to enhance intimate relationships. What has research revealed regarding interventions to produce mindfulness states that then may generalize in that person's life within a relationship? Brown, Ryan and Cresswell (in press) state that

> Incipient intervention research has also supported the beneficial role of mindfulness in romantic relationships. Adapting the MBSR program to a couples-based program called Mindfulness-Based Relationship Enhancement, Carson, Carson, Gil, and Baucom (2004; see also Carson, Carson, Gil, & Baucom, in press) showed that, relative to wait-list controls, intervention couples (all in nondistressed relationships) had significantly greater relationship satisfaction, autonomy, partner acceptance, and lower personal and relationship distress at post-test and at 3-month follow-up. Evidence also indicated that more day-to-day mindfulness practice was associated with many of these positive individual and couple outcomes.

These authors also suggest that one possible way in which mindfulness helps protect against distress is through an approach state that helps them deal with the negative feelings associated with the possibility of or actual experience of loss and social exclusion. The work of Creswell, Eisenberger, and Lieberman (in preparation) is cited in which those with more mindfulness traits appeared to be less reactive to exclusion. Here is Brown, Ryan, and Creswell's (in press) summary of that fascinating work in progress:

> Undergraduates participated in a virtual ball tossing game with two other "participants" (actually a computer) while undergoing fMRI. In the first task block, the participant was included in the ball tossing game, while in the second block, the participant was excluded during the majority of the throws. After the task, participants reported their perceptions of social rejection during exclusion. Results showed that MAAS-assessed mindfulness predicted lower perceived rejection. Further, this association was partially mediated by reduced activity in the dorsal anterior cingulate cortex (dACC), a region activated during social distress.

In considering ways to improve professional relationships and the impact of mindfulness in clinical training, Brown, Ryan and

Creswell go on to review the work of Shapiro, Schwartz and Bonner (1998), which demonstrates that mindfulness education can improve empathy: "A study with medical students (Shapiro, Schwartz, & Bonner, 1998) found that, relative to wait-list controls, those receiving an MBSR program showed increases in empathy over time, despite the fact that post-course assessments were collected in a high-stress, final exam period. These findings suggest the possibility, to be tested in future research, that mindfulness may enhance professional as well as personal relationship quality."

Of note also are the unpublished findings (Jonas Kaplan, personal communication, October 2006) that self-rated reports of empathy were higher in those individuals with functional brain imaging scans revealing more mirror neuron activation in response to affective cues. Thus, this preliminary data offers the view that enhanced resonance circuit function, at least of the mirror neuron regions, may be associated with empathy and the capacity to attune to others. Perhaps these findings illuminate a possible route by which mindfulness skills enhance interpersonal connection. Overall, it will be helpful to further understand the ways in which mindfulness as a learned skill or an inherent trait of the individual that may be founded on intrapersonal attunement may then create relationship experiences that further reinforce the experience of interpersonal attunement.

Further studies will be needed to explore exactly how mindfulness supports interpersonal well-being. Are sensitivities to the nonverbal signals of others enhanced? Does mindfulness improve the capacity to be compassionate—to feel another's feelings—as well as to be empathic—to understand another's point of view? We are at this point left with preliminary empirical findings supportive of the impression that mindfulness may nurture healthy relationships through a number of mechanisms, including enhanced empathy, emotional balance, response flexibility, and an approach mindset.

DEVELOPMENTAL ISSUES

We have seen that mindfulness can be a teachable skill. Even with patients with known genetic loading with attentional difficulties, a pilot study cited earlier (Zylowska, et al., submitted) associated with our Mindful Awareness Research Center revealed that attention can be improved. Some unpublished findings out of UCLA by Way, Creswell, Eisenberger, and Lieberman (2006) reveal preliminary data to suggest that the predisposition toward the trait of mindfulness may be associated with genetic variation in a certain neurotransmitter system in the brain known to involve individual differences in attentional capacities. The preliminary findings of Way and his colleagues (2006) suggest that the genes responsible for the monoaminergic system that regulates serotonin (especially the regulatory region of the monoamine oxidase A [MAOA] gene), may in part correlate with the occurrence of mindfulness traits in an individual. The fact that this genetic variant may correspond with mindfulness overlaps with research that suggests its role in self-regulation and attention (Caspi, McClay, Moffitt, Mill, Martin, & Craig, et al., 2002; Manor, Tyano, Mel, Eisenberg, Bachner-Melman, Kotler, & Ebstein, 2002; Parasuraman & Greenwood, 2004).

Developmental research also suggests, however, that even in the face of known genetic variants, optimal child rearing and experiences early in life may positively influence the outcome (see Kagan, 1994 for behaviorally inhibited/shy children and Stephen Suomi, 1997, for work in nonhuman primates). Thus, for shy children with a withdrawal tendency (right hemisphere reactivity), parental attunement to their temperament and needs without excessive overprotection or insensitivity led to an approach behavioral trait without anxiety and withdrawal as they matured. Work in primates reveals a similar finding: even with a genetic variant conferring vulnerability, optimal attachment experiences may provide a form of behavioral "inoculation" that enables those individuals to thrive. The general principle is that secure attachment may serve as a source of resilience even in the face of genetic variants that confer risk. Richard Davidson (2006) has suggested that no more than 25% of a person's affective style is genetically determined. With suboptimal or outright traumatic environments that produce neuro-toxic stress, the presence of such genetic risk factors may result in more intense negative developmental outcomes than in those children without such genetic variants. In this regard, we see that genes and experience interact in the creation of developmental pathways of personality. Mindfulness may be one such feature that confers resilience both genetically and experientially.

These findings also imply that some individuals may have constitutional variations that lead to more or less degrees of inherent mindfulness traits, and possibly also to variations in their receptivity to either interpersonal attunement or to interventions that promote intrapersonal attunement. However, temperament research cited above and experience in psychotherapy suggest that attunement of either the inter- or intra-personal form can lead to significant changes in developmental outcome. The important issue is that with genetic factors leading to constitutional challenges to mindfulness, or with experiential factors that produce impediments to mindfulness, reflective skill-building may be important and effective in helping such individuals develop the important capacities for self-regulation and intra-personal attunement. The thesis of this proposal is that the training of such reflective skills will "snag" the brain and promote neural integration, especially mediated by the middle prefrontal areas as a part of the resonance circuitry.

One example of this line of reasoning might be to consider the potentially genetically influenced occurrence of bipolar disorder (BD). Recent work by Hilary Blumberg and colleagues (Blumberg et al., 2004) suggests that part of the middle prefrontal region, the ventral prefrontal cortex, has abnormal inhibitory connections to the lower limbic regions that generate affective states. The abstract of their important work is as follows:

> The deficits of executive control of emotions and impulses of adult BD implicate involvement of a ventral prefrontal cortex (VPFC) neural system that subserves these functions that include the VPFC, as well as its subcortical connection sites of amygdala, striatum, and thalamus. Differences in the timing of major developmental changes in the structures within this neural system suggest that abnormalities in particular components of this neural system may emerge during critical developmental epochs during the course of the illness. Our recent neuroimaging data suggest that abnormalities in the subcortical components of VPFC neural systems may be evident by early adolescence in BD, whereas VPFC deficits progress over the course of adolescence and may be difficult to detect prior to late adolescence or early adulthood. This potential neurodevelopmental model for BD could have important implications for the recognition of early signs of the disorder and for age-specific treatment strategies.

In the single case report described in our discussions in this text (pp. 281–282), it may be that the process of teaching mindfulness skills—even with the potential genetic loading with a familial history of bipolar disorder—may have offered the young adolescent the opportunity to use mental training to develop and strengthen the same "abnormal" middle prefrontal regions that may have been placing him at risk. Interventions can be conceptually imagined and practically carried out that might use these ideas about the mindful brain to offer focused experiential training that could help develop the middle prefrontal areas that support mindfulness skills and more effective self-regulation of emotion and impulses. Careful future studies would need to be carried out to demonstrate that such mental training might be the key to improvement in this young man's and in others' life experiences with the anticipated enhancement in the many prefrontal functions we've been discussing throughout the text. The important message is that the mind can be harnessed to improve the functioning of the brain in a wide array of situations that can help reduce suffering and create the developmental training tools to promote healthy self-regulation in many people's lives.

My hope in offering this theoretical synthesis is that it will help us to further collaborate in many domains of our lives, personal and professional, in the realms of educational, clinical, and academic endeavors, to nurture the mind and contribute to a scientific foundation for the cultivation of well-being.

REFERENCES

REFERENCES

Ackerman, D., Kabat-Zinn, J., & Siegel, D. J. (March 2005). Presented at the panel discussion, 28th Annual Psychotherapy Networker Symposium, Washington DC. [Audio recordings]. Available at http://www.PsychotherpyNetworker.org.

Ackerman, D., Kabat-Zinn, J., O'Donohue, J., & Siegel, D. J. (2006). *Mind and moment: Mindfulness, neuroscience, and the poetry of transformation in everyday life.* Presented at the Mind and Moment Conference, San Francisco, CA. [Audio and video recordings]. Available at http://www.mindsightinstitute.com.

Adele, M. H., & Feldman, G. (2004). Clarifying the construct of mindfulness in the context of emotion regulation and the process of change in therapy. *Clinical Psychology: Science and Practice, 11*(3), 255–262.

Adolphs, R. (2002). Neural systems for recognizing emotion. *Current Opinion in Neurobiology, 12,* 169–177

Aftanas, L. I., & Golocheikine, S. A. (2002). Non-linear dynamic complexity of the human EEG during meditation. *Neuroscience Letters, 330,* 143–146.

American Psychiatric Association. (2000). *Diagnostic and statistical manual of mental disorders—Text revision* (4th ed.). Washington, DC: American Psychiatric Association Press.

Anderson, N. B., & Anderson, P. E. (2003). *Emotional longevity: What really determines how long you live.* New York: Viking.

Armstrong, K. (1993). *History of God.* New York: Ballantine Books.

Austin, J. H. (1998). *Zen and the brain.* Cambridge, MA: The MIT Press.

Austin, J. H. (2006). *Zen-brain reflections.* Cambridge, MA: The MIT Press.

Baer, R. A. (2003). Mindfulness training as a clinical intervention: A conceptual and empirical review. *Clinical Psychology: Science and Practice, 10*(2), 125–143.

Baer, R. A., Smith, G. T., & Allen, K. B. (2004). Assessment of mindfulness by self-report: The Kentucky inventory of mindfulness skills. *Assessment, 11*(3), 191–206.

Baer, R. A., Smith, G. T., Hopkins, J., Krietemeyer, J., & Toney, L. (2006). Using self-report assessment methods to explore facets of mindfulness. *Assessment, 13*(1), 27–45.

Barnes, S., Brown, K. W., Krusemark, E., Campbell, W. K., & Rogge, R. D. (in press). The role of mindfulness in romantic relationship satisfaction and responses to relationship stress. *Journal of Marital and Family Therapy.*

Baxter, L. R., Schwartz, J. M., Bergman, K. S., Szuba, M. P., Guze, B. H., Mazziotta, J. C. et al. (1992). Caudate glucose metabolic rate changes with both drug and behavior therapy for obsessive-compulsive disorder. *Archives of General Psychiatry, 49*(9), 681–689.

Beitman, B. D., Viamontes, G. I., Soth, A. M., & Nitler, J. (2006). Toward a neural circuitry of engagement, self-awareness, and pattern search. *Psychiatric Annals, 36*(4), 272–280.

Benes, F. M. (1994). Development of the corticolimbic system. In G. Dawson & K. W. Fischer (Eds.), *Human behavior and the developing brain* (pp. 176–206). New York: Guilford Press.

Bishop, S. R., Lau, M., Shapiro, S., Carlson, L., Anderson, N. D., & Carmody, J. et al. (2004). Mindfulness: A proposed operational definition. *Clinical Psychology: Science and Practice, 11*(3), 230–241.

Bird, C. M., Castelli, F., Malik, O., Frith, U., & Husain, M. (2004). The impact of extensive medial frontal lobe damage on 'Theory of Mind' and cognition. *Brain, 127*(4), 914–928.

Blakemore, S. J., & Choudhury, S. (2006). Development of the adolescent brain: Implications for executive function and social cognition. *Journal of Child Psychology and Psychiatry, 47*, 296–312.

Blumberg, H. P., Kaufman, J., Marin, A., Charney, D. S., Krystal, J. H., & Peterson, B. S, (2004). Significance of adolescent neurodevelopment for the neural circuitry of bipolar disorder. *Annals of the New York Academy of Sciences, 1021*, 376–83.

Brach, T. (2003). *Radical acceptance: Embracing your life with the heart of a Buddha.* New York: Bantam Books.

Brefczynski-Lewis, J. (2006). *Results of the fMRI study on concentration meditation: "Attentional expertise in long-time Buddhist practitioners."* Poster presentation at the Mind and Life Summer Research Institute, Garrison, New York.

Britton, J. C., Taylor, S. F., Sudheimer, K. D., & Liberzon, I. (2006). Facial expressions and complex IAPS pictures: Common and differential networks. *NeuroImage, 31*, 906–919.

Brown, K. W., & Ryan, R. M. (2003). The benefits of being present: Mindfulness and its role in psychological well-being. *Journal of Personality and Social Psychology, 84*(4), 822–848.

Brown, K. W., Ryan, R. M., & Creswell, J. D. (in press). Mindfulness: Theoretical foundations and evidence for its salutary effects. *Psychological Inquiry.*

Brown, R. P., & Gerbarg, P. L. (2005a). Sudarshan kriya yogic breathing in the treatment of stress, anxiety, and depression: Part I—Neurophysiologic model. *The Journal of Alternative and Complementary Medicine, 11*(1), 189–201.

Brown, R. P., & Gerbarg, P. L. (2005b). Sudarshan kriya yogic breathing in the treatment of stress, anxiety, and depression: Part II—Clinical applications and Guidelines. *The Journal of Alternative and Complementary Medicine, 11*(4), 711–717.

Buchheld, N., Grossman, P., & Walach, H. (2001). Measuring mindfulness and insight meditation (Vipassana) and meditation based psychotherapy: The development of the Freiburg Mindfulness Inventory (FMI). *Journal for Meditation and Meditation Research, 1*, 11–34.

Bush, G., Luu, P., & Posner, M. I. (2000). Cognitive and emotional influences in the anterior cingulate cortex. *Trends in Cognitive Science, 4*, 215–222.

Cacioppo, J. T., Visser, P. S., & Pickett, C. L. (Eds.). (2006). *Social neuroscience: People thinking about thinking people.* Cambridge, MA: The MIT Press.

Cahn, B. R., & Polich, J. (2006). Meditation states and traits: EEG, ERP, and neuroimaging studies. *Psychological Bulletin, 132*(2), 180–211.

Carr, L., Iacoboni, M., Dubeau, M-C., Maziotta, J. C., & Lenzi, G. L. (2003). Neural mechanisms of empathy in humans: A relay from neural systems for imitation to limbic areas. *Proceedings of the National Academy of Sciences, 100*(9), 5497–5502.

Carson, J. W., Carson, K. M., Gil, K. M., & Baucom, D. H. (2004). Mindfulness-based relationship enhancement. *Behavior Therapy, 35*, 471–494.

Carson, J. W., Carson, K. M., Gil, K. M., & Baucom, D. H. (in press). Self-expansion as a mediator of relationship improvements in a mindfulness intervention. *Journal of Marital and Family Therapy.*

Carson, S., & Langer, E. (2004). Mindful practice for clinicians and patients. In L. Haus (Ed.), *Handbook of Primary Care Psychology* (pp. 173–186). London: Oxford University Press.

Casey, B. J., Tottenham, N., Listen, C., & Durston, S. (2005). Imaging the developing brain: What have we learned about cognitive development? *Trends in Cognitive Sciences, 9*(3), 104–110.

Caspi A., McClay J., Moffitt T. E., Mill, J., Martin, J., Craig, I. W., et al. (2002). Role of genotype in the cycle of violence in maltreated children. *Science, 297*, 851–854.

Chadwick, P., Hember, M., Mead, S., Lilley, B., & Dagnan, D. (2005). *Responding mindfully to unpleasant thoughts and images: Reliability and validity of the Mindfulness Questionnaire.* Unpublished manuscript.

Chanowitz, B., & Langer, E. (1981). Premature cognitive commitment. *Journal of Personality and Social Psychology, 41*, 1051–1063.

Chen, K. W. (2004). An analytic review of studies on measuring effects of external Qi in China. *Alternative Therapy in Health Medicine, 10*(4), 38–50.

Cosmelli, D., Lachaux, J. P., & Thompson, E. (in press). Neurodynamics of consciousness. In Zelazo, P. D., Moscovitch, M., & Thompson, E. (Eds.), *The Cambridge handbook of consciousness*. New York: Cambridge University Press.

Cozolino, L. J. (2002). *The neuroscience of psychotherapy: Building and rebuilding the human brain*. New York: Norton.

Cozolino, L. J. (2006). *The neuroscience of human relationships: Attachment and the developing social brain*. New York: W. W. Norton.

Creswell, J. D., Eisenberger, N. I., & Lieberman, M. D. (2006). Neurobehavioral correlates of mindfulness during social exclusion. Manuscript in preparation.

Creswell, J. D., Way, B. M., Eisenberger, N. I., & Lieberman, M. D. (submitted). An fMRI investigation of mindfulness and affect labeling.

Critchley, H. D. (2005). Neural mechanisms of autonomic, affective, and cognitive integration. *J Comp Neurol, 493,* 154–166.

Csikszentmihalyi, M. (1990) *Flow: The psychology of optimal experience*. New York: HarperCollins.

Damasio, A. R. (1999). *The feeling of what happens: Body and emotion in the making of consciousness*. Orlando, FL: Harcourt Brace.

Davidson, R. J. (2000). Affective style, psychopathology, and resilience: Brain mechanisms and plasticity. *American Psychologist,* 1196–1214.

Davidson, R. J. (2004). Well-being and affective style: Neural substrates and biobehavioural correlates. *Philosophical Transactions Royal Society London, B, 359,* 1395–1411.

Davidson, R. J. (2005). Presented at the 13th Annual Investigating the Mind: The Science and Clinical Applications in Meditation Meeting, Washington DC.

Davidson, R. J. (2006). First Annual Mani Bhaumik Award Lecture, University of California, Los Angeles, November 16th.

Davidson, R. J., & Kabat-Zinn, J. (2004). Alterations in brain and immune function produced by mindfulness meditation: Three caveats. Comment. *Psychosomatic Medicine, 66*(1), 149–152.

Davidson, R. J., Kabat-Zinn, J., Schumacher, J., Rosenkranz, M., Muller, D., Santorelli, S. F. et al. (2003). Alterations in brain and immune function produced by mindfulness meditation. *Psychomatic Medicine, 65*(4), 564–570.

Dawson, G., Frey, K., Panagiotides, H., Yamada, E., Hessl, D., & Osterling, J. (1999). Infants of depressed mothers exhibit atypical frontal electrical brain activity during interactions with mother and with a familiar, nondepressed adult. *Child Development, 70*(5), 1058–1066.

Decety, J., & Chaminade, T. (2003). When the self represents the other: A new cognitive neuroscience view on psychological identification. *Consciousness and Cognition, 12,* 577–596.

Decety, J., & Grezes, J. (1999). Neuromechanisms subserving the perception of human action. *Trends in Cognitive Sciences, 3*(5), 172–178

Decety, J., & Jackson, P. L. (2004). The functional architecture of human empathy. *Behavioral and Cognitive Neuroscience Reviews, 3*(2), 71–100.

De Martino, B., Kumaran, D., Seymour, B., & Dolan, R.J. (2006). Frames, biases, and rational decision-making in the human brain. *Science 313*(5787), 684–687.

Devinsky, O. (2000). Right cerebral hemisphere dominance for a sense of corporeal and emotional self. *Epilepsy & Behavior, 1*(1, Part 1), 60–73.

Devinsky, O., Morrell, M. J., & Vogt, B. A.(1995). Contribution of anterior cingulate to behaviour. *Brain, 118,* 279–306.

Dewey, J. (1933). *How we think: A restatement of the relation of reflective thinking to the educative process.* Boston, MA: D.C. Health.

Dimidjian, S., & Linehan, M. M. (2003). Defining an agenda for future research on the clinical application of mindfulness practice. *Clinical Psychology: Science and Practice, 10*(2), 166–171.

Dweck, C. S. (2006). *Mindset: The new psychology of success.* New York: Random House.

Edwards, B. (1979). *Drawing on the right side of the brain.* New York: Jeremy Tarcher.

Einstein, A. (1972). As cited in the *NY Times.* In J. Kabat-Zinn (1990), *Full catastrophe living: Using the wisdom of your body and mind to face stress, pain, and illness* (p. 165). New York: Dell.

Ekman, P. (2003). *Emotions revealed: Recognizing faces and feeling to improve communication and emotional life.* New York: Henry Polk & Co.

Ekman, P. (2005). *What the face reveals: Basic and applied studies of spontaneous expression using the facial action coding system (FACS).* New York: Oxford University Press.

Ekman, P., Davidson, R. J., Ricard, M., & Wallace, B. A. (2005). Buddhist and psychological perspectives on emotions and well-being. *Current Directions in Psychological Science, 14*(2), 59–63.

Engel, A. K., Fries, P., & Singer, W. (2001). Dynamic predictions: Oscillations and synchrony in top-down processing. *Nature Neuroscience, 2,* 704–716.

Epstein, M. (1995). *Thoughts without a thinker: Psychotherapy from a Buddhist perspective.* New York: Basic Books.

Epstein, R. M. (1999). Mindful practice. *Journal of the American Medical Association, 282*(9), 833–839.

Epstein, R. M. (2001). Just being. *The Western Journal of Medicine, 174*(1), 63–65.

Feldman, G. L., Hayes, A. M., Kumar, S. M., & Greeson, J. M. (2004). *Clarifying the construct of mindfulness: Relations with emotional avoidance, over-engagement, and change with mindfulness training.* Paper presented at the Association for the Advancement of Behavioral Therapy, Boston, Massachusetts.

Fellows, L. K., & Farah, M. J. (2005). Is the anterior cingulate cortex necessary for cognitive control? *Brain: A Journal of Neurology, 128*(4), 788–796.

Field, B., Fitzpatrick-Hopler, G., & Spezio, M. (2006). *Initiating research of Christian contemplative practices*. Presented at Mind and Life Summer Research Institute, Garrison, New York.

Fitzpatrick-Hopler, G. (2006, June). *Christian contemplative practice: Centering prayer*. Paper presented at the Mind and Life Summer Research Institute, Garrison, New York.

Fivush, R., & Haden, C. A. (Eds.). (2003). *Autobiographical memory and the construction of the narrative self: Developmental and cultural perspectives*. Mahwah, NJ: Lawrence Erlbaum.

Fletcher, L., & Hayes, S. C. (2006). Relational frame theory, acceptance and commitment therapy, and a functional analytic definition of mindfulness. *Journal of Rational Emotive and Cognitive Behavioral Therapy, 23*(4), 315–336.

Fonagy, P., & Target, M. (1997). Attachment and reflective function: Their role in self-organization. *Development and Psychopathology, 9*(4), 679–700.

Freeman, W. J. (2000). Emotion is essential to all intentional behaviors. In M. D. Lewis, & I. Granic (Eds.), *Emotion, development, and self-organization: Dynamic systems approaches to emotional development* (pp. 209–235). Cambridge, UK: Cambridge University Press.

Frith, C. D., & Frith, U. (1999). Interacting minds—A biological basis. *Science, 286* (5445), 1692–1695.

Frith, C. (2002). Attention to action and awareness of other minds. *Consciousness and Cognition: An International Journal, 11*(4), 481–487.

Frith, U. (2001). Mind blindness and the brain in autism. *Neuron, 32*(6), 969–979.

Frith, U., & Frith, C. D. (2003). Development and neurophysiology of mentalizing. *Philos Trans R Soc Lond B Biol Sci, 358*, 459–73.

Gallese, V. (2003). The roots of empathy: The shared manifold hypothesis and the neural basis of intersubjectivity. *Psychopathology, 36*(4), 171–180.

Gallese, V. (2006). Intentional attunement: NA neurophysiological perspective on social cognition and its disruption in autism. *Brain Research, 1079*(1), 15–24.

Gallese, V., Fadiga, L., Fogassi, L., & Rizzolatti, G. (1996). Action recognition in the premotor cortex. *Brain, 119*, 593–609.

Gallese, V., Keysers, C., & Rizzolatti, G. (2004). A unifying view of the basis of social cognition. *Trends in Cognitive Sciences, 8*(9), 396–403.

Garrison Insitute Report. (2005). Contemplation and education: A survey of programs using contemplative techniques in K-12 educational settings: A mapping report.

Gazzaniga, M. S. (2000). Cerebral specialization and interhemispheric communication: Does the corpus callosum enable the human condition? *Brain, 123*(7), 1293–1326.

Germer, C. K. (2005). Mindfulness: What is it? What does it matter? In C. K. Germer, R. O. Siegel, & P. R. Fulton, (Eds.), *Mindfulness and Psychotherapy*. New York: Guilford Press.

Germer, C. K., Siegel, R. D., & Fulton, P. R. (Eds.). (2005). *Mindfulness and psychotherapy*. New York: Guilford Press.

Giedd, J. N. (2004). Structural magnetic resonance imaging of the adolescent brain. *Ann. N.Y. Acad. Sci., 1021*, 77–85.

Gillath, O., Bunge, S. A., Shaver, P. R., Wendelken, C., & Mikulincer, M. (2005). Attachment-style differences in the ability to suppress negative thoughts: Exploring the neural correlates. *Neuroimage, 28*, 835–847.

Goleman, D. (1988). *The meditative mind: The varieties of meditative experience*. Los Angeles: JP Tarcher.

Goleman, D. (1996). *Emotional intelligence*. New York: Bantam Books.

Goleman, D. (2006). *Social intelligence: The new science of human relationships*. New York: Bantam Books.

Greenberg, M. T. (submitted). Promoting resilience in children and youth: Preventive interventions and their interface and neuroscience.

Greenberg, M. T., Weissberg, R. P., O'Brien, M. U., Zins, J. E., Fredericks, L., Resnick, H. et al. (2003). Enhancing school-based prevention and youth development through coordinated social, emotional, and academic learning. *American Psychologist, 58*(6/7), 466–474.

Greenland, S. K. (2005). *The use of mindfulness practices with trauma victims*. Paper presented at The Children's Institute International Think Tank.

Grossman, P. (in press). Mindfulness practice: A unique clinical intervention for the behavioral sciences. In T. Heidenreich, & J. Michalak (Eds.), *Mindfulness and acceptance in psychotherapy*. Tuebingen: DVTG Press.

Grossman, P., Niemann, L., Schmidt, S., & Walach, H. (2004). Mindfulness-based stress reduction and health benefits: A meta-analysis. *Journal of Psychosomatic Research, 57*(1), 35–43.

Gusnard, D. A., Akbudak, E., Shulman, G. L., & Raichle, M. E. (2001). Medial prefrontal cortex and self referential mental activity: Relation to a default mode of brain function. *Proceedings of the National Academy of Sciences, 98*(2), 676–682.

Gusnard, D. A., & Raichle, M. E. (2001). Searching for a baseline: Functional imaging and the resting human brain. *Nature Neuroscience, 2*, 685–693.

Haken, H., & Stadler, M. (1990). *Synergetics of recognition*. Berlin: Springer.

Halpern, M. E., Güntürkün, O., Hopkins, W. D., & Rogers, L. J. (2005). Lateralization of the vertebrate brain: Taking the side of model systems. *Journal of Neuroscience, 25*(45), 10351–10357.

Hariri, A. R., Bookheimer, S. Y., & Maziotta, J. C. (2000). Modulating emotional responses: Effects of a neocortical network on the limbic system. *Neuroreport: For Rapid Communication of Neuroscience Research, 11*(1), 43–48.

Harter, S. (1999). *The construction of the self: A developmental perspective*. New York: Guilford Press.

Hawkins, J., & Blakeslee, S. (2004). *On intelligence.* New York: Times Books.

Hayes, A. M., & Feldman, G. (2004). Clarifying the construct of mindfulness in the context of emotion regulation and the process of change in therapy. *Clinical Psychology: Science and Practice, 11,* 255–262.

Hayes, S. C. (2004). Acceptance and commitment therapy, relational frame theory, and the third wave of behavioral and cognitive therapies. *Behavior Therapy, 35*(4), 639–665.

Hayes, S. C., Follette, V. M., & Linehan, M. M. (Eds.). (2004). *Mindfulness and acceptance: Expanding the cognitive-behavioral tradition.* New York: The Guilford Press.

Hayes, S. C., Strosahl, K. D., & Wilson, K. G. (1999). *Acceptance and commitment therapy: An experiential approach to behavior change.* New York: Guilford Press.

Hebb, D. O. (1949). *The organization of behavior: A neuropsychological theory.* New York: Bantam Books.

Hesse, E. (1999). The adult attachment interview: Historical and current perspectives. In J. Cassidy & P. R. Shaver (Eds.), *Handbook of attachment* (pp. 395–433). New York: Guilford Press.

Iacoboni, M. (2005). Neural mechanisms of imitation. *Current Opinion in Neurobiology, 15,* 632–637.

Iacoboni, M. (in press). *Mirroring people: Understanding others with mirror neurons.* New York: Farrar, Straus, & Giroux.

Iacoboni, M., & Siegel, D. J. (2004, November). *The implications for mirror neurons in psychotherapy.* Seminar presented at the R. J. Cassidy Seminar, Santa Rosa, CA. [Audio recordings]

Iacoboni, M., & Siegel, D. J. (2006). *Mirror neurons and interpersonal neurobiology in psychotherapy.* Presented at The New York University Biology of Mind Conference, New York.

Iacoboni, M., Koski, L. M., Brass, M., Bekkering, H., Woods, R. P., Dubeau, M. C., Mazziotta, J. C., & Rizzolatti, G. (2001). Reafferent copies of imitated actions in the right superior temporal cortex. *Proceedings of the National Academy of Sciences, 98*(24), 13995–13999.

Iacoboni, M., Woods, R. P., Brass, M., Bekkering, H., Mazziotta, J. C., & Rizzolatti, G. (1999). Cortical mechanisms of human imitation. *Science, 286*(5449), 2526–2528.

Irwin, M. (2005). *Examining the ability of Tai Chi to improve psychological adaptation, health functioning and augmenting baseline and vaccine-stimulated varicella zoster specific immunity in aging.* Paper presented at the Mindful Awareness Research Center, University of California, Los Angeles.

James, W. (1890/1981). *The principles of psychology.* Cambridge, MA: Harvard University Press.

Johanson, G. & Kurtz, R. (1991). *Grace unfolding: Psychotherapy in the spirit of the Tao-te ching.* New York: Bell Tower-Harmony.

Johnson, M. H., Griffin, R., Csibra, G., Halit, H., Farroni, T., & De Haan, M. et al. (2005). The emergence of the social brain network: Evidence from typical and atypical development. Integrating cognitive and affective neuroscience and developmental psychopathology [special issue]. *Development and Psychopathology, 17*(3), 509–619.

Jones, B. (2001). Changes in cytokine production in healthy subjects practicing Guolin Qigong: A pilot study. *BMC Complementary and Alternative Medicine, 1,* 1–8.

Kabat-Zinn, J. (1990). *Full catastrophe living: Using the wisdom of your body and mind to face stress, pain, and illness.* New York: Dell.

Kabat-Zinn, J. (2003a). Mindfulness-based interventions in context: Past, present, and future. *Clinical Psychology: Science and Practice, 10*(2), 144–156.

Kabat-Zinn, J. (2003b). *Coming to our senses: Healing ourselves and the world through mindfulness.* New York: Hyperion Press.

Kabat-Zinn, J., & Kabat-Zinn, M. (1990). *Everyday blessings: The inner work of mindful parenting.* New York: Hyperion Press.

Kagan, J., (1994). *Galen's prophecy: Temperament in human nature.* Boulder, CO: Westview Press.

Kaiser-Greenland, S. (2006a). InnerKids.org

Kaiser-Greenland, S. (2006b). A quantitative program evaluation of courses taught by InnerKids in the winter/spring semester of 2006 for students aged 4 through 12. Paper in preparation.

Keating, T. (2000). *Open mind, open heart.* New York: Continuum Intl. Publishing Group.

Keating, T. (2005). *The orthodoxy of centering prayer.* Presented at the 13th Annual Investigating the Mind: The Science and Clinical Applications in Meditation Meeting, Washington DC.

Keenan, J. P., Wheeler, M. A., Gallup, C. G., & Pascual-Leone, A. (2000). Self-recognition and the right prefrontal cortex. *Trends in Cognitive Science, 4,* 338–344.

Kempermann, G., Gast, D., Gage, F. H. (2002). Neuroplasticity in old age: Sustained fivefold induction of hippocampal neurogenesis by long-term environmental enrichment. *Annals of Neurology, 52*(2), 135–143.

Kornfield, J. (1993). *A path with heart.* New York: Bantam Books.

Kosslyn, S. M. (2005). Reflective thinking and mental imagery: A perspective on the development of posttraumatic stress disorder [special issue]. *Development and Psychopathology, 17*(3), 851–863.

Langer, E. J. (1989). *Mindfulness.* Cambridge, MA: Da Capo Press.

Langer, E. J. (1997). *The power of mindful learning.* Cambridge, MA: Da Capo Press.

Langer, E. J. (2000). Mindful learning. *Current directions in psychological science, 9*(6), 220–223.

Langer, E. J. (2005). *On becoming an artist: Reinventing yourself through mindful creativity*. New York: Ballantine Books.

Lazar, S. (2006). *Mind-body connection: Neural correlates of respiration during meditation.* Presented at Mind and Life Summer Research Institute, Garrison, New York.

Lazar, S. W., Kerr, C. E., Wasserman, R. H., Gray, J. R., Greve, D. N., Treadway, M. T. et al. (2005). Meditation experience is associated with increased cortical thickness. *Neuroreport, 16*(17), 1893–1897.

Legrand, D. (in press). The bodily self: The sensorimotor roots of pre-reflexive self-consciousness. *Phenomenology and the Cognitive Sciences, 5,* 89–118.

Linehan, M. M. (1993). *Cognitive-behavioral treatment of borderline personality disorder.* New York: Guilford Press.

Lutz, A., Dunne, J. D., & Davidson, R. J. (in press). Meditation and the neuroscience of consciousness. In P. D. Zelazo, M. Moscovitch, & E. Thompson, (Eds.) *The Cambridge handbook of consciousness.* Cambridge, UK: Cambridge University Press.

Lutz, A., Greischar, L. L., Rawlings, N. B., Ricard, M., & Davidson, R. J. (2004). Long-term meditators self-induce high-amplitude gamma synchrony during mental practice. *Proceedings of the National Academy of Sciences, 101*(46), 16369–16373.

Main, M. (2000). The Adult Attachment Interview: Fear, attention, safety, and discourse processes. *Journal of the American Psychoanalytic Association, 48,* 1055–1096.

Manor, I., Tyano, S., Mel, E., Eisenberg, J., Bachner-Melman, R., Kotler, M., & Ebstein, R. P. (2002). Family-based and association studies of monoamine oxidase A and attention deficit hyperactivity disorder (ADHD): Preferential transmission of the long promoter region repeat and its association with impaired performance on a continuous performance test (TOVA). *Molecular Psychiatry, 7,* 626–632.

Marlatt, G. A., & Gordon, J. R. (1985). *Relapse prevention: Maintenance strategy in the treatment of addictive behaviors.* New York: Guilford Press.

Mayberg, H. (2005). *Paths to recovery: Neural substrates of cognitive mindfulness-based interventions for the treatment of depression.* Paper presented at the 13th Annual Investigating the Mind: The Science and Clinical Applications in Meditation Meeting, Washington, DC.

Mayberg, H. (2006). Defining neurocircuits of depression. *Psychiatric Annals, 36*(4), 259–271.

McGregor, H. A., Lieberman, J. D., Greenberg, J., Solomon, S., Arndt, J., & Simon, L. et al. (1998). Terror management and aggression: Evidence that mortality salience motivates aggression against worldview-threatening others. *Journal of Personality and Social Psychology, 74*(3), 590–605.

Mead, G. H. (1925). The genesis of the self and social control. *International Journal of Ethics, 35,* 251–277.

Meaney, M. J. (2001). Maternal care, gene expression, and the transmission of individual differences in stress reactivity across generations. *Annual Review of Neuroscience, 24,* 1161–1192.

Meyer-Lindenberg, A., Ziemann, U., Hajak, G., Cohen, L., & Berman, K. F. (2002). Transitions between dynamical states of differing stability in the human brain. *Proceedings of the National Academy of Sciences, 99*(17), 10948–10953.

Mikulincer, M., & Shaver, P. R. (2005). Attachment security, compassion, and altruism. *Current Directions in Psychological Science, 14*, 34–38.

Mind and Life Summer Research Institute, Garrison Institute. (2006). The role of mental training in investigating the mind. [Brochure]. A. Engle.

Napoli, M. (2004). Mindfulness training for teachers: A pilot program. *Complementary Health Practice Review, 9*(1), 31–42.

Natoli, D. (2006). *The POISE approach to education.* Paper presented at the Mind and Moment Conference, Los Angeles, CA. [Audio and video recordings]

Nelson, K. (2003). Self and social functions: Individual autobiographical memory and collective narrative. *Memory, 11*(2), 125–136.

Newberg, A., D'Aquili, E., & Rause, V. (2002). *Why God won't go away: Brain science and the biology of belief.* New York: Ballantine.

Nhat Hahn, T. (1991). *Peace is every step: The path of mindfulness in everyday life.* New York: Bantam Books.

Nimchinsky, E. A., Gilissen, E., Allman, J. M., Perl, D. P., Erwin, J. M., Hof, P. R. (1999). A neuronal morphologic type unique to humans and great apes. *Proc Natl Acad Sci, 96*(9), 5268–73.

O'Donohue, J. (1997). *Anam Cara: A book of Celtic wisdom.* New York: Harper-Collins.

O'Donohue, J., & Siegel, D. J. (2004). *Poetry and the brain.* Psychotherapy Networker Symposium Audio Recordings, October.

O'Donohue, J., & Siegel, D. J. (2005). *Poetry and the brain.* Psychotherapy Networker Symposium Audio Recordings, March.

O'Donohue, J & Siegel, D. J. (2006). *Awakening the mind.* Mindsight Institute Audio Recordings, October. Los Angeles: MindsightInstitute.com.

Obayashi, S., Suhara, T., Kawabe, K., Okauchi, T., Maeda, J., Akine, Y., Onoe, H., & Iriki, A. (2001). Functional brain mapping of monkey tool use. *Neuroimage, 14*(4), 853–861.

Ochsner, K. N. (2004). Current directions in social cognitive neuroscience. *Current Opinion in Neurobiology, 14*(2), 254–258.

Ochsner, K. N., Bunge, S. A., Gross, J. J., & Gabrieli, J. D. E. (2002). Rethinking feelings: An fMRI study of the cognitive regulation of emotion. *Journal of Cognitive Neuroscience, 14*, 1215–1229.

Ogden, P., Minton, K., & Pain, C. (2006). *Trauma and the body: A sensorimotor approach to psychotherapy.* New York: Norton.

Ohnishi, T., Moriguchi, Y., Matsuda, H., Mori, T., Hirakata, M., & Imabayashi, E. et al. (2004). The neural network for the mirror system and mentalizing in normally developed children: An fMRI study. *Neuroreport: For Rapid Communication of Neuroscience Research, 15*(9), 1483–1487.

Parasuraman, R. & Greenwood, P. (2004). Molecular genetics of visuospatial attention and working memory. In M.I. Posner (Ed.), *Cognitive neuroscience of attention* (pp. 245–259). New York: Guilford.

Parks, G. A., Anderson, B. K., & Marlatt, G. A. (2001). Relapse prevention therapy. In N. Heather, T. J. Peters, & T. Stackwell (Eds.), *Interpersonal handbook of alcohol dependence and problems* (pp. 575–592). New York: John Wiley.

Pargament, K. I. (1997). *The psychology of religion and coping: Theory, research, and practice.* New York: Guilford Press.

Pascual-Leone, A., & Hamilton, R. (2001). The metamodal organization of the brain. *Progress in Brain Research, 134,* 1–19.

Phelps, J. L., Belsky, J., & Crnic, K. (1997). Earned security, daily stress, and parenting: A comparison of five alternative models. *Development and Psychopathology, 10,* 21–38.

Porges, S. W. (1998). Love: An emergent property of the mammalian autonomic nervous system. *Psychoneuroendocrinology, 23*(8), 837–861.

Post, R. M., & Weiss, S. R. B. (1997). Emergent properties of neural systems: How focal molecular neurobiological alterations can affect behavior. *Development and Psychopathology, 9,* 907–930.

Prigogine, I. (1996). *The end of certainty: Time, chaos, and the new laws of nature.* New York: Free Press.

Raichle, M. E., MacLeod, A. M., Snyder, A. Z., Powers, W. J., Gusnard, D. A., & Shulman, G. L. (2001). A default mode of brain function. *Proceeding of the National Academy of Sciences, 98*(7), 4259–4264.

Raz, A., & Buhle, J. (2006). Typologies of attentional networks. *Nature Neuroscience, 7,* 367–379.

Ricard, M. (2006). *A guide to developing life's most important skill: Happiness.* New York: Little, Brown.

Ritchart, R., & Perkins, D. (2000). Life in the mindful classroom: Nurturing the disposition of mindfulness. *Journal of Social Issues, 56*(1), 27–47.

Rizzolatti, G., & Craighero, L. (2004). The mirror-neuron system. *Annual Review of Neuroscience, 27,* 169–192.

Rizzolatti, G., Fogassi, L., & Gallese, V. (2001). Neurophysiological mechanisms underlying the understanding and the imitation of action. *National Review of Neuroscience, 2,* 661–670.

Roth, H. D. (1999). *The original Tao: Inward training and the foundations of Taoist mysticism.* New York: Columbia University Press.

Rothbart, M. K., & Rueda, R. M. (2005). The development of effortful control. In U. Mayr, E. Awh, & S. W. Keele (Eds.), *Developing individuality in the human brain: A tribute to Michael I. Posner* (pp. 167–188). Washington, DC: American Psychological Association.

Rueda, M. R., Posner, M. I., & Rothbart, M. K. (2005). The development of executive attention: Contributions to the emergence of self-regulation. *Developmental Neuropsychology, 28*(2), 573–594.

Rutter, M. (1983). School effects on pupil progress: Research findings and policy implications. *Child Development, 54*(1), 1–29.

Santorelli, S. (1999). *Heal thyself: Lessons on mindfulness in medicine*. New York: Crown, Random House.

Salzberg, S. (1995). *Lovingkindness: The revolutionary art of happiness*. Boston: Shambhala Press.

Schacter, D. (1996). *Searching for memory: The brain, the mind, and the past*. New York: Basic Books.

Schore A. N. (2003a). *Affect dysregulation and disorders of the self*. New York: W. W. Norton.

Schore, A. N. (2003b). *Affect regulation and the repair of the self*. New York: W. W. Norton.

Schwartz, J. M. (1998). *Brain lock: Free yourself from obsessive-compulsive behavior*. New York: HarperCollins.

Schwartz, J. M., & Begley, S. (2003). *The mind and the brain: Neuroplasticity and the power of mental force*. New York: Regan Books.

Segal, Z. V., Williams, J. M. G., & Teasdale, J. D. (2002). *Mindfulness-based cognitive therapy for depression: A new approach to preventing relapse*. New York: Guilford Press.

Seligman, M. (2003). *Authentic happiness: Using the new positive psychology to realize your potential for lasting fulfillment*. New York: Free Press.

Semple, R. J., Reid, E. F. G., & Miller, L. (2005). Treating anxiety with mindfulness: An open trial of mindfulness training for anxious children. *Journal of Cognitive Psychotherapy, 19*(4), 379–392.

Shapiro, S. C., Carlson, C. E., Asten, J. A., & Freedman, B. (2006). Mechanisms of mindfulness. *Journal of Clinical Psychology, 62*(3), 373–386.

Shapiro, S. L., Schwartz, G. E., & Bonner, G. (1998). Effects of mindfulness-based stress reduction on medical and premedical students. *Journal of Behavioral Medicine, 21,* 581–599.

Short, B. (2006). *Regional brain activation during meditation slows time and practice effects: A functional MRI study*. Poster presentation at the Mind and Life Summer Research Institute, Garrison, New York.

Siegel, D. J. (1999). *The developing mind*. New York: Guilford Press.

Siegel, D. J. (2001a). Memory: An overview with emphasis on the developmental, interpersonal, and neurobiological aspects. *Journal of American Academy of Child and Adolescent Psychiatry, 40,* 997–1011.

Siegel, D. J. (2001b). Toward an interpersonal neurobiology of the developing mind: Attachment, "mindsight," and neural integration. *Infant Mental Health Journal, 22,* 67–94.

Siegel, D. J. (2003). An interpersonal neurobiology of psychotherapy: The developing mind and the resolution of trauma. In M. Solomon & D. J. Siegel. (Eds.), *Healing trauma* (pp. 1–56). New York: W. W. Norton.

Siegel, D. J. (2006). An interpersonal neurobiology approach to psychotherapy. *Psychiatric Annals, 36*(4), 248–256.

Siegel, D. J. (in press). *Mindsight: Our seventh sense.* New York: Bantam.

Siegel, D. J. & Hartzell, M. (2003). *Parenting from the inside out: How a deeper self-understanding can help you raise children who thrive.* New York: Penguin Putnam.

Sohlberg, M. M., McLaughlin, K. A., Pavese, A., Heidrich, A., & Posner, M. I. (2000). Evaluation of attention process therapy training in persons with acquired brain injury. *Journal of Clinical and Experimental Neuropsychology, 22,* 656–676.

Solomon, M. F., & Siegel, D. J. (Eds.). (2003). *Healing trauma: Attachment, mind, body and brain.* New York: W. W. Norton.

Soltesz, I. (2006). *Diversity in the neuronal machine: Order and variability in interneuronal microcircuits.* New York: Oxford University Press.

Sowell, E. R., Peterson, B. S., Thompson, P. M., Welcome, S. E., Henkenius, A. L., & Toga, A. W. (2003). Mapping cortical change across the life span. *Nature Neuroscience, 6*(3), 309–315.

Sroufe, L. A., Egeland, B., Carlson, E. A. & Collins, W. A. (2005). *The development of the person: The Minnesota study of risk and adaptation from birth to adulthood.* New York: Guilford Press.

Staudinger, U. M. (1996). Wisdom and the social interactive foundation of the mind. In P. B. Baltes & U. M. Staudinger (Eds.), *Interactive minds: Lifespan perspectives on the social foundation of cognition* (pp. 276–315). Cambridge, England: Cambridge University Press.

Staudinger, U. M. (2003). Older and wiser? Integrating results on the relationship between age and wisdom-related performance. *Journal of Research on Adolescence, 13,* 239.

Staudinger, U. M., Singer, J. A., & Bluck, S. (2001). Life reflection: A social-cognitive analysis of life review. *American Psychological Association Review of General Psychology, 5*(2), 148–160.

Staudinger, U. M., & Pasupathi, M. (2003). Correlates of wisdom-related performance in adolescence and adulthood: Age-graded differences in "paths" toward desirable development. *Journal of Research on Adolescence, 13*(3): 239–268.

Stern, D. N. (2003). *The present moment in psychotherapy and everyday life.* New York: W. W. Norton.

Sternberg, R. J. (2000). Images of mindfulness. *Journal of Social Issues, 56*(1), 11–26.

Stoller, R. J. (1985). *Observing the erotic imagination.* New Haven, CT: Yale University Press.

Suomi, S. J. (1997). Early determinants of behaviour: Evidence from primate studies. *British Medical Bulletin, 53,* 170–184.

Svoboda, E., McKinnon, M. C., & Levine, B. (2006). The functional neuroanatomy of autobiographical memory: A meta-analysis. *Neuropsychologia, 44*(12), 2189–2208.

Teicher, M. H. (2002). Scars that won't heal: The neurobiology of child abuse. *Scientific American, 286*(3), 68–75.

Thagard, P. (2002). *Coherence in thought and action.* Cambridge, MA: MIT Press.

Thompson, C. (2006). *Be Known: The call of God in interpersonal neurobiology.* Interpersonal Neurobiology Applications Training, Los Angeles, CA.

Thompson, E., & Varela, F. J. (2001). Radical embodiment: Neural dynamics and consciousness. *Trends Cogn. Sci. 5*(10), 418–425.

Thornton, L. J. II, & McEntee, M. E. (1993). Learner centered schools as a mindset and the connection with mindfulness and multiculturalism. *Theory Into Practice, 34*(4), 250–257.

Tse, P. U. (2005). *Attention and the subjective expansion of time, session 577.4, Minisymposium 577: Time and the brain: How subjective relates to neural time.* Eagleman, D. M. (Chair). Paper presented at the Society for Neuroscience Annual Meeting, Washington, DC.

Tucker, D. M., Luu, P., & Derryberry, D. (2005). Love hurts: The evolution of empathic concern through the encephalization of nociceptive capacity. *Development and Psychopathology, 17,* 699–713.

Tulving, E. (1993). Varieties of consciousness and levels of awareness in memory. In A. Baddeley and L. Weiskrantz (Eds.), *Attention, selection awareness, and control: A tribute to Donald Broadbent* (pp. 283–299). London: Oxford University Press.

Uddin, L. Q., Kaplan, J. T., Molnar-Szakacs, I., Zaidel, E., & Iacoboni, M. (2004). Self-face recognition activates a frontoparietal "mirror" network in the right hemisphere: An event-related fMRI study. *Neuroimage, 25,* 926–935.

Urry, H. L., Nitschke, J. B., Dolski, I., Jackson, D. C., Dalton, K. M., & Mueller, C. J. et al. (2004). Making a life worth living: Neural correlates of well-being. *Psychological Science, 15*(6), 367–372.

Van Praag, H., Kempermann, G., & Gage, F. H. (2000). Neural consequences of environmental enrichment. *Nature Neuroscience, 1,* 191–198.

Varela, F. J., Thompson, E. T., & Rosch, E. (1993). *The embodied mind: Cognitive science and human experience.* Cambridge, MA: MIT Press.

Vygotsky, L. (1986). *Thought and language* (Ed., A. Kozulin). Cambridge, MA: The MIT Press. (Original work published 1934.)

Waldon, W. (June 2006). *Evolving models of mind: From early Buddhism to Yogacara.* Paper presented at the Mind and Life Summer Research Institute, Garrison, New York.

Wall, R. B. (2005). Tai chi and mindfulness-based stress reduction in a Boston public middle school. *Journal of Pediatric Health Care, 194,* 230–237.

Wallace, B. A. (2006). *The attention revolution: Unlocking the power of the focused mind.* Boston: Wisdom.

Walsh, R. (1980). The consciousness disciplines and the behavioral sciences: Questions of comparison and assessment. *American Journal of Psychiatry, 137,* 663–673.

Walsh, R., & Shapiro, S. L. (2006). The meeting of meditative disciplines and Western psychology: A mutually enriching dialogue. *American Psychologist, 61*(3), 227–239.

Waring, N. (in preparation). *Turning toward the bandaged place: A brain tumor odyssey.*

Way, B. M., Creswell, J. D., Eisenberger, N. I., & Lieberman, M. D. (2006). Associations between dispositional mindfulness and genetic variation of MAOA. Unpublished raw data, University of California, Los Angeles.

Weissberg, R. P., Kumpfer, K. L., & Seligman, M. E. P. (2003). Prevention that works for children and youth. *American Psychologist, 58*(6/7), 425–432.

Wilson, E. O. (1998). *Consilience: The unity of knowledge.* New York: Knopf.

Zylowska, L., Ackerman, D. L., Futrell, J., Horton, N. L., Hale, S., Pataki, C., & Smalley, S. L. (submitted). Behavioral and cognitive change in ADHD using mindfulness, meditation.

Zajonc, A. (2006). Love and knowledge: Recovering the heart through contemplation. *Teachers College Record,* 108(9), 1742–1759.

INDEX

INDEX

Note: Page numbers in italic type indicate figures.